Yé Yaille, Chère

Traditional Cajun Dance Music

Yé Yaille, Chère

Traditional Cajun Dance Music

Collected, Transcribed, and Annotated by

Raymond E. François

Swallow Publications, Inc.

ISBN 0-9614245-7-5

Cover design by Benny Graeff.
Cover photo: Carrie Royer Miller, 1939.

Published by

Swallow

Publications, Inc.
Post Office Drawer 10
Ville Platte, Louisiana 70586
ph (337) 363-2177
fx (337) 363-2094

To the memory of
Roy Fusilier, Sady Courville, and Dennis McGee
who passed away while I was working on this book;

and to Alicia,
who made the writing of this book possible.

I' croit qu'il a vu la pierre du tonnerre.

He thinks he has seen the thunderstone.

(This expression describes someone who is very excited about something, real or imaginary. Once people searched in vain for this stone after the thunder "fell.")

Acknowledgements

If I had known how much work this would be, I would never have had the courage to begin.

I would like to acknowledge the help I received from the following people:

Dennis McGee, Sady Courville, Roy Fusilier, Aldus and Bernice Roger, Varise Connor, Allie Young, Preston Manuel, Moïse Robin, and Shelton Manuel, for spending the time to tell me about their music and old times;

Dewey Balfa, for permission to use a quotation;

Carol Rachou, for loaning me recordings to study;

David Rachou, Floyd Soileau, Eddie Shuler, Lee Lavergne, Chris Strachwitz, J.D. Miller, Bee Cormier, Huey P. Meaux, and Dunice P. Theriot, for permission to include material from their recording labels;

Alicia Towster, for helping with computers and editing, and John François, for helping with proofreading;

And, most importantly, all the fine Cajun musicians, living or dead, who contributed to the music I have presented in this book.

Contents

Figures and Tables

Introduction

A musician is just like an insect — play long enough and your woman will come to you.

HOW I CAME TO WRITE THIS BOOK

I was born in Patassa, just southeast of Eunice, Louisiana, in 1931, and reared in L'Anse Chaoui, a little bit further down the road. My father played the accordion. So did our neighbor, Ambrose Thibodeaux. Both my parents loved to dance, and I was often taken to *bals de maison* or *fais dodo*, sometimes even as far away as La Pointe Noire. When I was four or five, my father asked me whether I would prefer to play the violin or the accordion. I thought about it seriously and picked the violin.

First, I tried making my own violin out of a board and some screen wire. It wasn't much good and my parents were cross about having their window screens torn up. I didn't manage to get a real violin until I was thirteen, when I saved up sixteen dollars from picking cotton and ordered one from Montgomery Ward. I experimented a lot with making sounds. My parents couldn't stand listening to that and insisted I practice in my father's school bus. Wade Frugé taught me how to tune my violin, and papa took me to visit my cousin Carrie Royer Miller, who already knew how to play, and she taught me my first song, *La Valse De Grand Bois*. I played my first house dance in Patassa the same year. I remember, when the hat was passed to collect for the musicians, my share was three dollars. It was a lot more fun than picking cotton, and I've been playing Cajun music ever since.

Almost nobody makes a living out of playing Cajun music. I made mine as a school teacher and played music in my spare time. I've played with so many different musicians that I won't even try to list them all. Some bands are very stable, like a good marriage. I always liked to play with a new group, to see what they could do and to hear a new repertoire. I played longest with the bands of "Bee"

Cormier (Church Point Playboys), Terry Cormier and D.L. Menard (Louisiana Aces), Jack Leger, Roy Fusilier, Felton LeJeune, and Aldus Roger.

I guess the idea of this book started when I began to notice that the younger musicians were having trouble playing the music I had grown up with. Very few of them speak French, so it's not surprising that they have trouble with the lyrics. It bothers me even more that they don't know when to change the chords, since I feel this changes the whole structure of the music. Maybe this is natural evolution, but I don't want the music which I have heard and played all my life to be forgotten.

I began by listening to old recordings and writing down the words to songs. I also visited and interviewed some of the older musicians. I realized that what I really needed was some way to get the music transcribed into musical manuscript. I didn't think I could do this myself. Cajun music is learned and played entirely by ear, and my only exposure to musical notation had been a one-semester course in college — where I also learned, for the first time, the correct way to hold a violin; before that I'd taken too much of the weight on my left wrist, which partly cuts off the blood circulation and is very tiring after a few hours. I explored getting grant funds to hire a transcriptionist to help me, but without success.

My solution has been a Macintosh computer. I began with a simple music program that let me enter notes on a staff and play them back to make sure I had written them correctly. Then I used a more elaborate program that would let me add lyrics and produce nicely printed manuscripts. And now I even have a sequencer program which will play the music which I've written down, on a synthesizer. This has been a big help with proofreading my music, and it's fun! One nice day I was working with the window open, and when I looked out I saw I'd gathered a small crowd of students, dancing to my synthesized version of *Pine Grove Blues*.

I've transcribed over 240 songs, and I've been selective. I've left out songs that very closely resemble songs I had already included. I've left out songs that I recognize as simply Cajun versions of popular American songs. And sometimes I've left out songs that showed influence from other styles, such as Country and Western. I know there are many Cajun songs I haven't included, but I think this is a good beginning.

There are some musicians who must be mentioned in any description of traditional Cajun music and they appear in this book too. There are many other fine musicians who deserve more recognition, and I have tried to include many of these as well, but my choices have been influenced by my own experiences — who I've played with or heard play frequently and where I could find examples of the songs I wanted to include. I know there are many very fine Cajun musicians whose names are not mentioned, but this book is intended to be a book of Cajun music manuscript. If I included all the musicians, too, it would turn into an encyclopedia.

WHAT IS CAJUN MUSIC?
People who don't know a lot about the different styles of music that have developed in this part of Louisiana tend to call everything "Cajun music", especially if it's played by local musicians and includes an accordion player. Since this term is used so vaguely, I want to explain what I mean by it and how it is different from Zydeco, another traditional local style.

Traditional Cajun music is played with a diatonic accordion with a single row of buttons, violin(s) usually tuned one step lower than standard pitch, and some instrument to keep the beat; once this was the spoons or the triangle, now the rhythm guitar and drums are more common. Other instruments may be included, too, such as a steel guitar or bass guitar.

Cajun music is the descendent of the music that was brought to this area by the original French settlers and influenced by the contributions of later immigrants, particularly the Germans, who, near the end of the 1800's, introduced the diatonic accordion which has now become an essential instrument in a traditional Cajun band. Because this instrument is limited in its range, Cajun music is now played mostly in the keys of C and G with a C-accordion, or D and A with a D-accordion. In some bands, the accordionist will bring both kinds of accordion and the violin player will carry two violins, one tuned in G and the other in A, so that they can switch keys easily, without changing their fingering positions.

Some of the tunes in the traditional Cajun repertoire can be traced to medieval France, like *The Mardi Gras Song*; others have been developed here or borrowed from other music that we came in contact with. For example, Varise Connor, an outstanding fiddler from Lake Arthur, tells me that his father learned some tunes from Irishmen who worked on the railroad in the early part of the century. And Iry LeJeune was influenced by Hank Williams; *J'ai Fait Une Grosse Erreur* comes from Hank Williams' *I Can't Help It If I'm Still in Love With You*. Songs were borrowed from Cajun music, too; Hank Williams' *Jambalaya* is based on *Grand Texas* by Papa Cairo (Julius Lamperez).

Black musicians have also contributed to Cajun music. Amédé Ardoin, back in the 1930's, contributed greatly to the traditional Cajun music repertoire; the *Eunice Two-Step* is one of his songs. And a few black musicians continue to play in this style, such as Nolton Semien and the St. Landry Playboys from Lawtell, and "Bois Sec" Ardoin and his group from Durald.

An essential element of Cajun music is the rhythm. Traditional Cajun music is dance music; the older styles were derived from Europe and included quadrilles, reels, mazurkas and polkas, some of which can still be heard today from older musicians. Today the waltz, blues and two-step predominate, although the younger generation has not been dancing cheek-to-cheek very much. Since World War II, even two-steps are often jitterbugged. My father describes this kind of dancing by saying, *Ça danse déchaînés; ça s'démanche les bras* (They dance unchained;

they dislocate their arms.). To my father dancing well meant dancing together in unison with little motion of the upper body.

Yes, traditional Cajun music has, itself, changed over the years, and styles vary from band to band. But well-played traditional music has one all-important thing in common: it makes your feet want to jump up and dance the "two-step"!
— a Cajun music fan

Chord changes are another essential feature of Cajun music. Musicians who don't know where to change the chords don't really know the song they're trying to play. A Cajun musician has freedom to improvise, especially when he takes the lead, but he must follow the chord structure and general flow of the melody if he intends to play in the traditional style.

The term "Zydeco" is a phonetic spelling of *les haricots* and comes from a very popular song in this musical style, *Les Haricots Est Pas Salés*. It is a distinctive style of music with insistent, repetitive rhythms which are probably African in origin and, although it does use chord changes, there is a tendency for a single chord to predominate. The principal instruments are either the piano accordion, which became popular in the 1950's, or the double- or triple-row diatonic accordion, and drums, but many zydeco bands also include wind instruments, guitar, and *frottoir* (washboard). This music was played long before the late Clifton Chenier's talent and personal style gained it such widespread recognition.

One reason that Zydeco and traditional Cajun music are so often confused is probably that their repertoires overlap. For example, Clifton Chenier has recorded *Jolie Blonde* in a Zydeco style and Aldus Roger has made a very successful recording of *Les Haricots Est Pas Salés* in a Cajun style.

PLAYING CAJUN MUSIC
For most Cajun musicians, music is something we do in our spare time, after work is done. Few of us have time or opportunity to play more often than a couple of times a week and the idea of a band practicing together is strange to me. We don't rehearse, unless we're planning to make a recording. We just play. Back in the 1930's nobody had TV and lots of people didn't have radios either and it was very easy for any social occasion to turn into a musical event. One of my amusements as a teenager was to get together and play Cajun music with my friends, Eldridge Aguillard, Vinus LeJeune, and Ervin "Dick" Richard. Talk about a different world! I'd go meet them on horseback carrying my violin in a pillow case because I didn't have a case for it yet.

It's still possible to have these informal musical events, if you give some thought to who you invite, but in the 1940's Cajun music moved out of the home and into the dance halls. Some of the customers were soldiers on leave from Camp Polk, who brought money and jitterbug to town; some were people who had attended and hosted house dances previously. I guess it was more convenient to let the dance hall owner arrange things and clean up afterwards, and money was more plentiful. This was the heyday of the Cajun dance band, with some very successful groups like Lawrence Walker, Leo Soileau, J.B. Fusilier, and others. An unfortunate effect, though, was that a dance hall wasn't nearly as suitable a place to take children to as a house dance; too few children fell asleep knowing that Cajun music was part of their parents' lives.

Dance halls aren't so popular any more. There are still some, particularly in the smaller towns, although they may hire Rock or Country and Western bands as well as Cajun musicians. You can also find traditional Cajun music played at some festivals, at the Liberty Theater in Eunice, and at a few restaurants. It's good that parents can take their children to hear Cajun music again, but it bothers me to see people sitting down and chewing food among strangers instead of dancing among friends and neighbors.

For us, dancing was an important social activity. It's not just for dating or married couples. Couples do attend dances together, but they probably don't dance exclusively with each other. Family groups often attend together, and it's not unusual to see a grandson waltzing with his grandmother. And it's all right to ask someone you don't know to dance, although your invitation isn't always accepted.

Playing music is social, too. When there's a musician in the audience—and there often are several—he (or she) may sit in with the band for a while. This gives a regular band member a chance to take a break and visit with his wife or girlfriend who is probably in attendance. No matter how good the guest musician is or how much he plays, when it comes to getting paid, the money is divided evenly between the musicians who were hired to play.

THE STRUCTURE OF CAJUN MUSIC

Cajun musicians can play together without rehearsing beforehand because they all understand the structure of the music. I've already mentioned the rhythm and the chord changes, but there are some other kinds of structure, too.

Usually a song has a tune of eight (or nine) measures and a turn of eight (or nine) measures. I prefer to think of the tune and turn as having nine measures, because the bands I have played with usually put in a rest between the tune and turn to finish out the nine measures; some bands will make a faster transition, and I have usually written the music this way, too. The turn (tourne, in French) is an extended bridge providing a contrast for the tune. Some turns, such as the one for *Fi Fi Poncho*, have double cadence. The turn is rarely sung, but, just like all rules, this one has some exceptions, particularly among the older songs, like those Dennis McGee plays. I'll point these out when we come to them.

When a Cajun band plays a song, usually all instruments, led by the accordion, first play the tune, or possibly the turn, together. Then the vocalist takes the lead, singing the tune. Then the steel guitar, if there is one, takes the lead for two tunes or perhaps two turns, then the violin, for two tunes or two turns. This order of play repeats, beginning with the accordion. This is not a rigid structure; sometimes the vocalist will sing two tunes, instead of just one, when he takes the lead. Sometimes the instrumentalists will play the turn instead of the tune, during their leads. Having a pattern of this sort is important when

musicians haven't played together before. Bands vary on just how they use this pattern. With each song, I've given a suggested order of play; this is something you can change to suit your own preferences and the instruments you are playing.

When a musician takes the lead, he can improvise and embellish according to his taste and talent and the capabilities of his instrument. There are no explicit rules here, so long as you remember the tune, but, to my ear, there are improvisations that sound appropriately Cajun and some that suggest other styles of music, like Country and Western. I think the "right" kind of improvisations are easier when playing with the diatonic accordion and the violin tuned down one step below standard, but this isn't necessary. For example, "Dick" Richard uses standard tuning, but plays in the traditional style. Most good musicians can play both ways.

I might put in grace notes or melodic variations or whatever struck my fancy when it was my turn to take the lead. I haven't included these improvisations or embellishments in my transcriptions. I have just written the basic melody for the tune and turn. You need to learn this before you try to get fancy with the song, anyway.

The vocalist is just as free to improvise as the instrumentalists are. He can change the words of the song to suit himself. Sometimes this results in songs filled with clichés like *malheureuse!, criminelle!,* and *yé yaille!,* but a vocalist has the opportunity to express his own feelings and ideas. Iry LeJeune's songs are a good example. In addition, the vocalist can improvise musically or sing the harmony instead of the tune. You can't assume that the vocal part of a song will be the same as the tune. This is why I've transcribed the tune, turn, and vocal separately.

I won't play a song until I know every note and every word. Yes sir! Like that you can defend yourself, you don't stumble. You don't sing off time, either; you sing right on time. There are still some [who sing whatever comes to mind]. Oh yes, I hear that! I listen to that often. They don't sing the same song alike twice in a row. They mix whatever they want as long as they don't loose the timing, you understand, but if you have to stutter to sing the words, you're behind right there, you see. Therefore, if you know all the words, it's like reading. Like reading, you can hit each word right on the drummer's timing. Each time he'll hit, your word will fall right in line. That's music!

— Roy Fusilier

During the accordion's lead, all the other instruments join in, because the accordion is a relatively loud instrument. During other leads, the remaining instruments will only play to backup or enhance the lead player. The table at the end of this section shows the chords I use to bass when I am not playing the lead.

CAJUN FRENCH
Cajun French is based on the northern French dialects spoken by the original Acadian settlers; this is different from the dialect of the Seine River area that standard French is based on, but I can communicate with French speakers from just about anywhere. Cajun French is not often written down, so figuring out how to do so has been an interesting problem, too. I have tried to use standard French spelling so that anyone who reads French should be able to understand most of the words. If you find errors in my French spelling, you should know that at the time I was growing up, children were punished for speaking French in school and it was not possible for me to learn how to write it until I took a course in standard French in high school. I have nearly worn out a French dictionary, figuring out how to write the words for the songs.

Just like standard French, Cajun French words are usually stressed on the last syllable. (This is why a measure or beat in the vocal sections of a song will usually start on the last syllable of a word.)

If you already know standard French, here are some of the differences you will notice.

•Cajun French is very direct and informal.

•A lot of words in Cajun French are contracted, and sometimes we leave out syllables; for example, we never say the last syllable of words like *table* and *autre* and we usually leave out the first syllable of *petit*. I thought about spelling these words normally anyway, so that they would be easier to read, but that would make too many syllables to be sung properly. If you find some of the contractions puzzling, you can figure out the meaning by looking at the translation.

•Verbs are conjugated a little differently. We don't change verb forms as often as standard French does, and we also have some constructions of our own, such as *être après* ..."to be doing ...." We use only *pas* , not *ne ... pas*, to make a verb negative.

•The vocabulary includes words borrowed from American Indian and African languages, Spanish, and American English.

HOW TO READ AND PLAY THE SONGS
Because I play the violin, I've written the tune and turn with the violin in mind. I assume that if you read music and play the violin, you will probably use standard tuning, so that is how I have written the music, rather than for the violin tuned one step down, the way I normally play. Throughout the book, if a tune is ordinarily played in the key of G, I've usually written the music in the key of A in order to preserve the violin playing position (DGCF) while playing with the C-accordion. Playing a violin in standard tuning with a C-accordion may result in the violin player switching octaves in order to stay in the musical range of the song. (Some musicians deal with this problem very nicely.) The D-accordion poses fewer problems of range.

The bass part is normally so simple that I haven't written it, but each time the chord changes, I show this with the appropriate letter above the musical staff. A rhythm guitar would play one quarter note on every beat. A bass guitar would play one quarter note on the first and third beats for both waltzes and two-steps. I'll point out any exceptions as we come to them.

With each song, I include the following information:

The title. I have sometimes made changes to make it more understandable in standard French. A song can have many titles; I've tried to include most of them in the index.

Key. The key that it would normally be played in by a Cajun band, especially with a C–accordion. As I explained, the transcription may be in another key to accommodate standard tuning on the violin.

Pattern. One way the elements of the song can be arranged; adjust this to suit yourself and your instruments.

Rhythm. Most songs won't need this information, but if there's an unusual feature, I'll describe it here.

Version. The musician or musicians whose versions are the basis for my transcription. When I mention several musicians, it does not necessarily mean they played together; it may mean that I have combined their versions in my transcription. I include abbreviated information about copyright or recording label for each version where I have been able to determine this information. For details, see the section on song credits, at the end of this book.

Sometimes these musicians may also be the originators of the songs, but it can be hard to tell for sure. We don't speak of "writing" a song, since Cajun songs are mostly played and learned by ear. We talk about "making" a song. This can mean various things: creating a variation or arrangement of an existing tune, or new words for a song; recording a song; inventing a new tune.

Related songs. Most Cajun songs have several versions. When these versions were interesting enough or different enough, I may have included more than one of them in this book; these will be the ones whose titles are preceded by "See:". "Also:" means that the songs aren't included, but I thought you'd at least like to know about some of them.

Next comes any additional information I have about the song and, most important of all, the transcription of the the song, usually the tune and turn first, followed by the vocal. Sometimes I include a sample of the bass, too. Each song has a metronome marking to show you about how fast it should be played. You can play a little slower or quite a bit faster, if you prefer. Normally, the stress falls on the first beat of each measure. I have marked exceptions.

I have written English translations of the French vocals almost word for word so that you can understand what the words mean. Sometimes the vocals don't make much sense; they depend on the vocalist's talent for improvisation and also on his memory since it is unusual to write down the words as I have done. The tune is usually more important than the vocals. The voice is used more as another instrument in the band.

Note that I don't intend for you to play through the transcription once and then stop. I expect you to take the parts of the song and play them in a pattern, like a Cajun band does, alternating the tune, turn, and vocal. The exact pattern is up to you; I've suggested a typical pattern, and also supplied a particular one that works well for each song.

Remember that I am only giving you the basics of the song. Cajun musicians love to improvise on the spur of the moment.

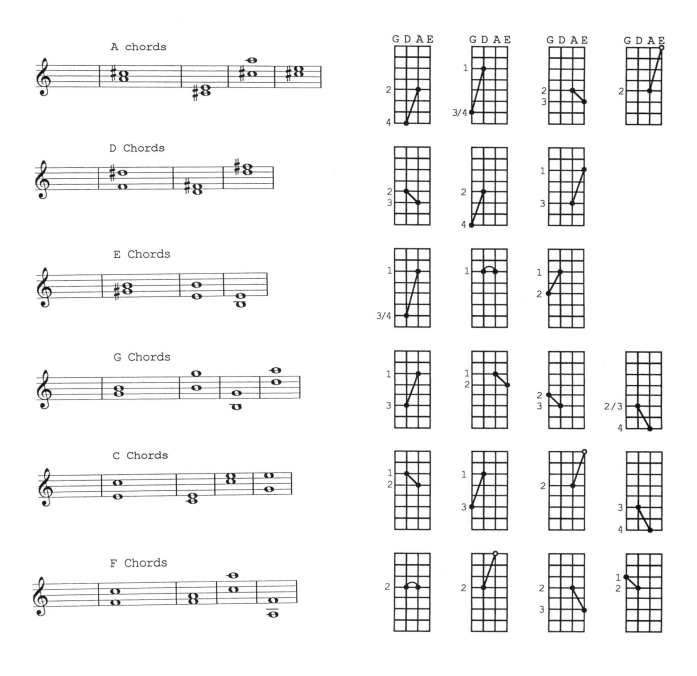

Major violin chords. These bassing chords are shown both in musical notation and as fingering diagrams for a violin tuned standard (A-440). The chords in each row are arranged according to frequency of use; those most commonly used when playing with a D or C diatonic accordion are to the left. With the violin tuned down to G (DGCF), you'd have the advantage of a "better" position for the F-chord with a C-accordion playing in the key of C. Try it! Naturally, with a D-accordion you'd be tuned standard.

Old Songs

The songs and the memories in this section are at least as old as the 1930's, and some, like the Mardi Gras Song are much older. Others, since they were recorded in the 1920's, are at least that old, and very likely even older. I have also included some songs that were recorded later, but which I believe are actually older songs. I am not comfortable with trying to assign precise dates to the songs. Even if I know when the first version of a song was recorded, I also know that many musicians are preserving and reworking traditional materials.

There was someone named Mayuse Courville who was an old time accordion player. I was a young boy when he was playing. When I learned how to play the violin, he learned how to dance to my music. He danced the polka, mazurka, do you know what that is? He and Edna Young, Théophile Young's daughter, Remi Billeaudeaux's wife from Châtaignier, danced mazurkas. They danced any kind of dance. They were some good dancers.

Oh yes! I played polkas and mazurkas and anything else, too, when I was young. They were Cajuns like myself. Mayuse was my wife's uncle. He was a crackerjack number one. Oh, he was a good dancer. Mayuse's brothers were all good dancers, too. Démar Courville could dance a reel. Do you know what a reel is? He could dance a reel. You couldn't hear his feet but you could see them moving. You could hear chit-a-chit-a-chita *on the floor as the others danced. Oh yes! He was fast, fast, and he danced well. My mother danced and her father danced jigs.*

A jig was a foreign dance, no one but they danced that. I've never seen anybody else dance it other than the old Davis couple. His boy, Arville, played that. He was an old violin player. He was one of the best we had back then, he and my father-in-law, my present wife's father. These two played together and the old lady would come up, pull her dress up a bit and call, "Play me Arville's jig!" My friend, she and Dave would start! He was big and about six foot four, a big and tall man,

strong as a Hercules, a German. She would yell, "Play me my jig, Arville!" She'd get on that jig, Jack, and, listen, these two old people would jig. Ha, ha! You should've seen how that was pretty! These two old people would jig and they danced very well. They were very good. They were named Dave and Lucia. They were my wife's grandfather and grandmother.

Arville was a good violin player. Then he started playing with old Fabus Fontenot from La Pointe Sacquette. When you leave Châtaignier, you'd go through Choupique. You'd travel a piece, then you'd enter a neck of the woods, a point called La Pointe Sacquette. Yes, I played for Mayuse and Edna. I was the one who played all the young people's dances. Then, I was eighteen, nineteen years old. I played the violin as well as I play now, better, in fact, because now the dances have changed a bit. I changed the tunes that I used to play. I played reels, breakdowns and square dances. These are all different tunes. The reel is different, the contredanse is a different case. I don't know what the difference is, but there is a difference some kind of way. The reel, the women and men didn't hold each other. Each danced their own way. For the breakdown, they would hold their fingertips and they'd dance while watching who would make better steps.

Yes, oh yes! In that time, people were good dancers. Poof! Oh yaille! Yes, there were some good dancers. There was Démar Courville, my wife's uncle, who was a good dancer in those times. In a contredanse they would form eight couples and they would call, "Family all around!" They would make a round on the floor and when they'd get back to the starting point, they'd reverse direction and come back to the starting point again. The couple dancing together would hold each other, with the girl holding the man's arm and they would go all around the house. They would do the "back-up" at the same place. The couple faced each other across the room and would do two advancing steps toward each other while dancing. The girl would go get a man and take him to the other side, then she would turn to her partner and station herself with him while the others repeated the same maneuvers. They would advance and meet different partners. They knew what to do. They danced like that in all the places where I played — at Châtaignier, L'Anse Bourbeuse and Choupique. These were all places where I lived.

— *Dennis McGee*

In those days, the dances were private and held in private homes. You had to be invited in order to attend the dance. The square dance and other types of dances would require a certain number of people. The good dancers would usually be invited, maybe eight, ten, or twelve people to form couples.

My mother didn't care too much for dancing but she liked to listen to the music. She was interested in my father's music. My father decided to make a tune of his own and gave it a name. He called it Eraste and Devien *after himself and my mother. He called another* Ball et Charlot, *for the two horses that he'd hitch on the wagon to go play his dances, and he named another for me and my sister,* Sady and Sedia.

Of course, they always brought us to the dance and there would be a room provided for us when we arrived. My mother would be in charge of us in this particular room and she'd stand near the door and watch the activities. She noticed the couples carefully and could tell if they were in love, breaking up, or making up.

— *Sady Courville*

Aimer et Perdre

Key. C
Pattern. Accordion: one Tune; Vocal #1; Accordion: one Tune; Vocal #2; Accordion: one Tune; Vocal #3; Accordion: two Tunes (No Turn).

Version. Joseph Falcon, vocal and accordion (OT).
Related songs. See: *Ma Chère 'Tite Fille* (Leo Soileau). Also: *La Valse de la Rosa* (Leo Soileau-1937); *Cher 'Tit Monde* (Nathan Abshire).

When I was small, there weren't many accordion players. I started playing at about the age of eight. There were many violin players, though. I remember an old uncle who played the violin and I'd go to listen to the music. When I'd arrive, I'd ask him to play the violin. He'd play for me and I learned some old songs from him that maybe I've now forgotten. I was more interested in playing the accordion. I'd take a piece of cardboard and fold it to look like an accordion bellows and I'd sit down and pretend to play. Seeing this, my father and mother decided to buy an accordion for me. I paid three dollars and fifty cents for my first accordion.

— Allie Young

gnonne, oui pour   moi, oui, pour   moi mais t'ou- bli-
rer de ta mam-   an...(__   __   **instrument**
voir pour toi-   même (__   __   **instrument**
par- ti chez   moi! Si c'est   moi qu'est mal- chan-

er   mais   comme   j'ai   fait.
___   ___   ___   ___   )
ceux   dans   la   Ville   Platte!)

Love and Lose

(1)
Oh, dear little one, I loved you! I lost you by rambling on the highways.
Look what I've done to myself, dear! I miss you, pretty girl!
Yes, you're cute for me to forget you as I did.
Look, dear, you're beautiful to me, pretty heart!
I love your beautiful eyes and your pretty face, dear.
Instead of seeing you leave and separate from your mother!
(2)
Oh, dear little one, hey, it hurts! Think of me, unhappy one!
Hey, you'll cry soon and see for yourself!
(3)
Oh, you'd like the girls from Ville Platte!
They're so cute, but I don't know what's the matter with them.
They seem so nice and so adorable, but not one of them wants me.
I'm going home! I'm so unlucky in Ville Platte!

Allons à Lafayette

Key. G
Pattern. Accordion: one Tune and one Turn; Vocal #1; Accordion: one Turn and one Tune; Vocal #2; Accordion: one Turn and one Tune; Vocal #3; one Turn.

Version. Joseph Falcon, vocal and accordion (OT).
Related songs. See: *Lafayette Two-Step* (Aldus Roger); *Jeunes Gens de la Campagne* (Dennis McGee).

This was the first Cajun recording, made in 1928. Then, Lafayette, Louisiana, was just another of the small towns in southwestern Louisiana; the oil industry changed it a lot and today it is known as the Hub City.

The original meaning of the word *nèg'* is a black person, but it is also very commonly used among whites as a term of endearment. Here I have translated it as lover; it could also mean husband. *'Tit Nèg'* is a fairly common nickname in Cajun families; a possible translation would be Sonny.

1-   Al-   lons   à   La-   fay-   ette   mais
             Pe-   tite,   t'es   trop mi-   gnonne pour
             Mais   toi,   mais   jo-   li   coeur, 'garde
2-   (Repeat   first   two   verses.)
             Mais   oui,   mais   t'es de   moi   si
3-   (Repeat   first   verse.)
             Pe-   tite,   t'es   trop mi-   gnonne pour
             que   moi   mais   j'   mé-   rite   pas   tous

pour   chan- ger   ton   nom.   On   va   t'ap- pller   ma-
faire ta   cri- mi-   nelle! Com-   ment tu   crois   mais
donc   mais   quoi t'as   fait! Si   loin comme moi   j'su'd'

loin   de   moi, mi-   gnonne! Tu   peux me   cre-   ver 'l

faire ta   cri- mi-   nelle! Ob-   serve moi   bien, mi-
ça   mais   t'a- près   faire! T'a-   près quit- ter   ton

dam,   ma-   dam   Ca-   naille   Co-   meaux!
moi   j'peux   faire mais moi   tout   seul?
toi,   mais   ça,   ça m' fait   pi-   tier!

coeur, jo-   lie   et   jo-   lie   fille!

gonne, tu vas   voir   mais pour   toi-   même
nég'   mais   pour   mais t'en   al-   ler!

Let's Go to Lafayette

(1)
Let's go to Lafayette to change your name! We'll call you Madam, Madam Rascal Comeaux!
Little one, you're too cute to do me wrong! How come you believe that I can make it all alone?
But you, pretty heart, look what you've done! So far as I am from you, why it's pitiful!
(2)
Let's go to Lafayette to change your name! We'll call you Madam, Madam Rascal Comeaux!
Little one, you're too cute to do me wrong! How come you believe that I can make it all alone?
Why yes, you're so far away from me, cute one! You can break my heart, pretty, pretty girl!
(3)
Let's go to Lafayette to change your name! We'll call you Madam, Madam Rascal Comeaux!
Little one, you're too cute to do me wrong! Look me over, my beauty, you'll see for yourself
that I don't deserve all the things you're doing! You're leaving your lover to go away!

Albert Broussard, Doug Kershaw's maternal grandfather, played the violin and I'd listen, which encouraged me to learn. Then the Aguillards, Oscar and Valsan, were very good players from whom I learned some songs. I observed how they played. Also, my father played. And there was Sidney Broussard who was a good player, too. There were many good players a long time ago and they played a lot of violin music. When I started to play dances, it was mostly violin music, not many accordions until Joe Falcon made some recordings. Then it started being just accordions after that. ... My old dad played square dances, reels and polkas but these went out of style when I started playing. I played only the waltzes and two-steps. I could play a few square dances, but I wasn't as good as my father and the Aguillards had been. The Aguillards couldn't be beat! If some of these men had gone to Nashville, many people over there would've fallen on their backs when they heard these men. They were that good.

During the years when only the violin was used to play dances, I had a string band consisting of my two brothers and one of my first cousins. There were many small string bands everywhere. In Gueydan, there were the Clarks; in Lacassine, the DeRouens; in Elton, Leo Soileau, but it's as I say, when the accordions took over, the string bands faded out. When I started playing, it was at the Red Hall. That was a beautiful dance hall, the best floor I've ever seen anywhere. This was around 1925.

During my father's time, I played house dances. My father told me that when the railroad was being built, there were many Irishmen who were working on it. These people had been away from their country for a long time and they were lonesome. When they'd find out that there was a Cajun dance, they'd come. There were some good musicians among them and my father learned some songs from them. Oh yes! They didn't understand themselves very well but they got along.
— Varise Connor

Amédé Breaux's Two-Step

Key. G   *Version.* Varise Connor.
Pattern. Violin: two Tunes and one Turn, etc.

Instrumental. Varise Connor told me that he
had "unburied" this song by Amédé Breaux.
All the songs Varise played for me were ones
he had taped in standard tuning; they included
many old American and English tunes which
he loves too.

Valse d'Amour I

Key. C
Pattern. Violin: two Tunes, one Turn and one Tune;
Vocal #1; Violin: two Tunes, one Turn and one Tune;
Vocal #2; Violin: two Tunes, one Turn and one Tune.

Version. Austin Pitre (©Flat Town).
Related songs. See: *Gabriel* (Leroy "Happy Fats"
LeBlanc; Oren "Doc" Guidry). Also: *Valse d'Amour*
(Leo Soileau).

Don't confuse this song with Dennis McGee's *Valse d'Amour*, which is quite different. I've transposed this song to A because of a better violin position. Although Austin Pitre recorded this song in the 60's, it is an old song.

1-   Mam'   et   pap'   m'a   tou'l'   temps
     "C'est pas   la   peine   de   faire   l'a-
2-   "C'est pas   la   peine   d'mand-   er   les

dit,   "Es-   père l'   vent d'   nord   quand   t'es   plus
mour,   t'as   pas d'   du-   vet   su' l'   île   d'la
filles,   t'as   pas d'   i-   dée   de   te   ma-

grand",   parce   que   moi   j'au-   rais   vo-   lu,   oui,   al-
main. C'est pas   la   peine   les   ai-   mer,   t'as   pas d'   du-
rier. C'est pas   la   peine   de t'   ma-   rier,   t'as   pas d'   du-

ler   pour   faire   l'a-   mour.
vet   su' l'   coin d'   les   lèvres."
vet   su' l'   coin d'   les   lèvres."

The Waltz Of Love

(1)
Mom and Dad always told me,
"Wait for the north wind when you're older," because I wanted to go make love.
"It's no use to make love, you don't have any fuzz on the back of your hand.
It's no use to love them, you don't have any fuzz on the corner of your lips."
(2)
"It's no use to ask the girls, you don't intend to get married.
It's no use to get married, you don't have any fuzz on the corner of your lips."

Yes, we played some music, me and Amédé [Ardoin] and me and Angélas [LeJeune]. And I played with someone else. Henry LaFleur! He was from Ville Platte. We had rented Ernest Soileau's dance hall. Henry played the accordion pretty good, but I was the one who made all the music. I played the violin well. We had some dances every Saturday night. You had to climb up some big stairs to enter the hall on the second floor. We only had an accordion and violin. I had to play loud for the people to hear, but they'd hear because we had some good instruments. He had a good accordion; besides, he was a big strong man who played loudly ... In those days, they had some low C-accordions and you couldn't rig them to sound louder than the violin. The violins sounded as loud as the accordions in that time. Oh yes. LaFleur had a little weak accordion; it didn't sound loud like today's accordions. It would sound loud enough for people to hear, but my violin sounded loud enough to cover the accordion. I've always played my violin loudly. Oh yes. I guarantee you that when I'd play my violin, they'd hear me. Oh yes!

— Dennis McGee

Valse d'Amour II

Key. F
Pattern. Violin: one Tune and one Turn; Vocal #1;
Violin: one Turn, one Tune and one Turn; Vocal #2;
Violin: one Turn and three Tunes.
Rhythm. This song is a *valse à deux temps* as it has two
dotted quarter notes per measure for rhythm guitar. The
bass pattern for all four of Dennis McGee's *valse à deux
temps* is: 1st measure, one dotted quarter rest and one
dotted quarter note; 2nd measure, one dotted quarter
note and one dotted quarter rest; 3rd measure, two
dotted quarter notes. Repeat over until the end of each
song. See the sample of the bass.

Version. Dennis McGee (©Flat Town).
Related song. See: *'Tit Maurice* (Oren "Doc"
Guidry; Leroy "Happy Fats" LeBlanc).

Don't confuse this song with Leo Soileau's or
Austin Pitre's *Valse d'Amour* which are both
different tunes. The vocal tune is similar to
'Tit Morris.

*Dennis McGee and I had started playing the
violin together in the early 20's at the age of
thirteen or fourteen ... There was a man called
Preacher Martin who was interested in young
people and he knew that Dennis and I played
music together. So one day, maybe in 1925 or
26, he approached me and asked, "Would you
like to play music on the radio?" There
weren't too many radio stations at that time. I
said, "Well, where?" He answered, "In
Shreveport." I asked, "Well, how will we get
up there?" "That's no problem." he said,
"We'll ride the train. We'll go broadcast at a
radio station called KWKH." I said, "Go
ahead and make the arrangement; we'll be
glad to go." He added, "There's no pay!" I
said, "That's alright, we'll just go for the fun
of it, because I love to go and do something
for people." He assured me that he'd pay all
the expenses and make the proper
arrangements.*

*We left here early that morning on the Rock
Island and then in Alexandria we got on the
S.P. and went to Shreveport. I thought that the
broadcasting station was in town, but it was*

*way out in the country. So they put us in a car
that looked like one hundred feet long. There
were seats between the front and back seats.
There were other people riding, the officials
and the workers. We drove out in the country;
I don't know how far we went, but we finally
got to the radio station to make our broadcast.
I used to sing and Preacher Martin knew that.
He asked, "What would you like to sing?" Al
Jolson had just come out with Sonny Boy, so I
sang that. Then Dennis McGee and I played
Cajun folk music. We played about six or
seven numbers. It was the first time Cajun
music had ever been put on radio. I know that,
because old man Preacher Martin told me so.*

*A few years afterwards, in 1928 , I think,
I saw Preacher Martin and Matt Frugé at the
store and they called me in the office to ask me
if Dennis and I would go to New Orleans to
make some records. I told them to go ahead
and make arrangements; we'd be glad to go.
He said, "Somebody heard y'all on the radio
and they'd like for y'all to make some records." That was another job done without
pay. We went to New Orleans and recorded.
Joseph Falcon had just recorded the accordion, in about 1926 or 27. We were the first
twin fiddlers to be put on records.*
— Sady Courville

La Valse d'Amour

(1)
Tu coursies trop les hommes, ma 'tite fille qu' a autant, ma chère chérie.
Not' amitié nous tient ensemb'. T'es la seule dans la Louisiane moi j' peux aimer.
(2)
Allons essayer de s' comprend' et r'venir ensemb', chérie.
Tu connais j' t'aime toujours et not' amitié autant dans les chagrins.

The Waltz of Love

(1)
You chase men too much, my little girl who has so many, my dear darling.
Our friendship holds us together. You're the only one in Louisiana I can love.
(2)
Let's try to understand one another and get back together, darling.
You know I still love you and our friendship is in so much sorrow.

L'Anse de Belair

Key. C
Pattern. Violin: two Tunes; Vocal #1; etc. There is no turn in this song.

Version. Dennis McGee (MS).
Related song. See: *La Branche du Mûrier* (Iry LeJeune). Also: Mulberry Waltz (Ambrose Thibodeaux; Aldus Roger).

This was the first recording of *La Branche du Mûrier*. L'Anse de Belair is southeast of Ville Platte, Louisiana.

Southwestern Louisiana, the area where I grew up, is mostly prairie and woodland. The most interesting natural features of the landscape are the small streams, which we call bayous, surrounded by woodland. Sometimes a spur of the woods sticks out into the surrounding prairie and we call this a *pointe*. We also use *anse* to mean a place where the wood curves around the prairie, like the handle of a bucket or a cooking pot, which is what *anse* really means. I translate this as cove, but remember that it is a cove of land, not of water.

Many of the early French place names in the prairie contain the words *pointe* or *anse*. The game in the woods and the fish in the bayous were important sources of food, even when I was growing up. My father was very skillful at hunting and fishing and kept us well supplied with squirrel, rabbit, duck, turtle, and fish. Now, the bayous are too polluted with agricultural runoff and oilfield waste and we're losing the woods to make more fields for soybeans, rice, and crawfish.

Musicians often name a song after a place. Maybe this is where they first heard the song, or where they were frequently asked to play it. These titles may be the only place where these French place names will be preserved. We still use them in conversation, but the phone book and the Post Office and the mapmakers all want to substitute English names. Patassa, where I was born, is officially called Perchville, which is at least a kind of translation, and L'Anse Chaoui has been renamed Hundley Community, after a lady that taught school there a long time ago.

Belair Cove

(1)
Bye-bye, dear little one, forever of my days. I'll go home all alone, my pretty heart.
(2)
Just look how you've treated me, pretty heart. Unfortunate one, remember how you've treated me, dear.
(3)
Remember, my darling, I'd sit in my kitchen window to see you so well when you passed.
(4)
I cut the limb off of my mulberry tree, dear, to see you pass, dear, when you're going somewhere.
(5)
Unfortunate one, each time, dear, you made me dream of you. Already, I take it hard to see you, pretty heart.
(6)
You know the good Lord will punish you for all that you've made me do, darling. Unfortunate one, dear little Black!
(7)
Unfortunate one, you shouldn't do all that, pretty little Blacko. You've turned your back on me!

♩ = 133

D

```
1-        "Bye-      bye,"      cher     'tit     monde,      pour
2-        'Gardez    donc mais  ça       t'as     fait        avec
3-        Rappelle-  toi,       ma       ché-     rie, j'm'assisais
4-        J'ai       coupé      de       la       branche     de
5-        Malheu-    reuse,     chaque   fois,    chère,      tu m'as
6-        Tu con-    nais       le       bon      Dieu        va t'pu-
7         Malheu-    reuse      tu       de-      vrais       pas
```

A

```
toujours   de      mes       jours.  J'm'en    irai     à       la
moi,       jo-     li        coeur.  Malheu-   reuse,   rap-    pelle-
mais       dans    la        fenêtre d'ma      cuisine  pour    te
mon        mû-     rier,      chère,  pour te   voir     pas-    ser,
fait       rê-     ver        à toi.  Dé-       jà,      j'le    prends
nir        pour    tout       ça      tu m'as   fait     faire,  ché-
faire      mais    tout       ça.     Jo-       lie      'tit    "Black-
```

D

```
maison     mon            tout seul,  mon      joli       coeur.
toi        ça t'as        fait        avec     moi        chère.
voir       pas-           ser         aus-     si         bien.
chère,     quand          toi         t'es     par-       ti.
dur        de t'          voir,       jo-      li         coeur.
rie.       Malheu-        reuse,      chère    'tite      "Black!"
o,"        tu             m'as        tour-    né l'      dos!
```

Two-Step de l'Anse aux Pailles

Key. C
Pattern. Accordion: two Tunes; Vocal #1; Violin: two Tunes; Accordion: two Turns and two Tunes; Vocal #2; Violin: two Tunes; Accordion: Two Turns and two Tunes; Vocal #3; Violin: two tunes; Accordion: two turns.

Version. Dewey Balfa (©Flat Town).
Related song. Also: *Lake Charles Two-Step.*

L'Anse aux Pailles is an area near Prairie Ronde, northwest of Opelousas, Louisiana, where a lot of wild prairie grass grew.

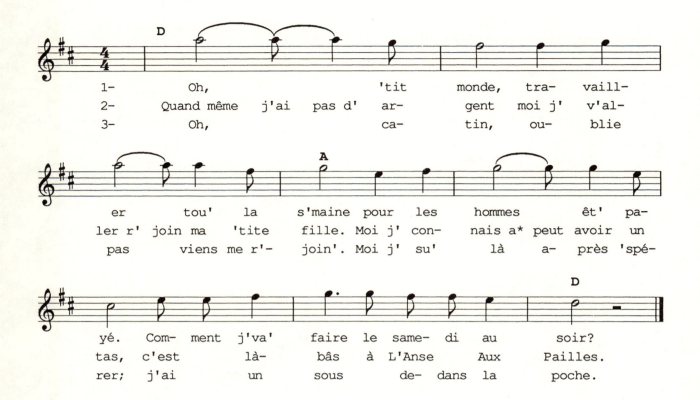

1- Oh, 'tit monde, tra- vaill-
2- Quand même j'ai pas d' ar- gent moi j' v'al-
3- Oh, ca- tin, ou- blie

er tou' la s'maine pour les hommes êt' pa-
ler r' join ma 'tite fille. Moi j' con- nais a* peut avoir un
pas viens me r'- join'. Moi j' su' là a- près 'spé-

yé. Com- ment j'va' faire le same- di au soir?
tas, c'est là- bâs à L'Anse Aux Pailles.
rer; j'ai un sous de- dans la poche.

Straw Cove Two-Step

(1)
Oh, little one, I worked all week long for the men to be paid. What will I do Saturday night?
(2)
Even though I have no money, I'll go meet my dear little girl. I know she has a lot, over there in Straw Cove.
(3)
Oh, doll, don't forget, come meet me. I'm here waiting, without a cent in my pocket.

Baieonne

Key. F
Pattern. Violin: Parts 1, 2 and 3; Vocal #1; Violin: Parts 2, 3 and 1; Vocal #2; Violin: Parts 1, 2 and 3; Vocal #3; Violin: Parts 3, 1 and 2.

Version. Blind Uncle Gaspard, vocal and Dela Lachney, violin (OT).

As is common in so many Cajun song titles, the spelling of French leaves much to be desired. For example, the song title *Baoille* meant nothing to me. I had to determine what was meant by listening to the vocal. *Baie* in French means "bay" in English, as "a bay horse." Locally, *baie* with the suffix *-onne* is used as a nickname for a women with chestnut or auburn-blonde hair.

Notice how the instrumental and vocal parts are arranged. It is difficult to standardize this song under one tune or vocal part.

♩ = 155

G

1- Oh chère, ma chère baie- onne, viens donc en-

core ma chère l'a- mie. Ma vie est rui- né!

C'est la cause de toi, ma chère baie- onne

2- Si j'a- vais dé- jà é- cou- té ma chère veille ma-

man, j'se- rais pas dans la mi- sère. Oh

chère, ma chère ma- man, tu m'as lais- sé i- ci

comme un pauv' or- phe- lin du pa- ys. Oh,

chère, viens donc me r' join' un cher grand jour a-

v'nir, ma chère baie- onne, ma chère l'a- mie.

3- Oh chère chère baie- onnne, au jour de ma mort, c'est toi je vou- drais donc qui s'rait au ras d' moi a- vec ton mou- choir. Oh, chère, si ja- mais je viens à mou- rir, viens donc pas- ser ta chère grosse main blanche au- tour d'ma tête.

Auburn-blond

(1)
Oh, dear, my dear Auburn-blond, come back again, my dear friend.
My life is ruined! It's because of you, my dear Auburn-blond.
(2)
If I had already listened to my dear old mother, I wouldn't be in misery.
Oh, dear, my dear mama, you left me here like a poor country orphan.
Oh, dear, come meet me some grand day to come, my dear Auburn-blond, my dear friend.
(3)
Oh, dear Auburn-blond, on the day of my death,
it's you I'd want close to me with your handkerchief.
Oh, dear, whenever I die, come wipe your dear large white hand about my head.

La Banane à Nonc' Adam

Key. G
Pattern. Accordion: two Tunes; Vocal #1; Steel Guitar: two Tunes; Violin: two Tunes; Accordion: two Tunes; Vocal #2; Steel Guitar: two Tunes; Violin: two Tunes; Accordion: two Tunes ("Bee" Cormier and the Church Point Playboys).

Versions. Elton "Bee" Cormier, vocal; Rodney LeJeune, vocal (*Seventy-three Special*, Cr-Cj); Nathan Abshire, instrumental (©Flat Town).
Related songs. Also: *L'Acadien Two-Step* (Nathan Abshire); *Seventy-three Special* (The Rambling Aces).

Nathan puts the turn in his instrumental; he plays two tunes and two turns; then the violin plays two tunes, etc. I have used Nathan's turn in the transcription. Bee's vocal is an old version. Rodney LeJeune and the Rambling Aces improvise by naming the song for a nightclub in Texas which is located on Highway 73. I've included both sets of vocals; the first two vocals are Rodney's and the last two are Bee's.

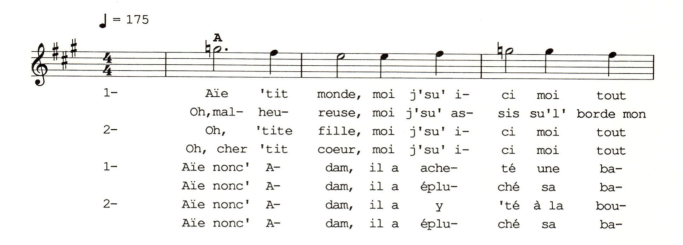

♩ = 175

```
1-      Aïe    'tit    monde, moi  j'su' i-  ci  moi     tout
        Oh,mal- heu-   reuse, moi  j'su' as- sis su'l' borde mon
2-      Oh,    'tite   fille, moi  j'su' i-  ci  moi     tout
        Oh, cher 'tit   coeur, moi  j'su' i-  ci  moi     tout
1-      Aïe nonc' A-    dam,   il a  ache- té  une     ba-
        Aïe nonc' A-    dam,   il a  éplu- ché sa      ba-
2-      Aïe nonc' A-    dam,   il a  y     'té à la bou-
        Aïe nonc' A-    dam,   il a  éplu- ché sa      ba-
```

```
seul;  mais  per-    sonne  pour  m'ai-  mer mais  moi  tout
lit    mon   cha-    plet   dans  la     main 'près pri-
seul;  moi   j'aime- rais   tu    t'en r' viens  une  aut'
seul;  moi   j'aime- rais   tu    t'en r' viens... 'nir me r'
nane;  une   ba-     nane   as-   sez    grande, une  ba-
nane;  sa    ba-     nane   alle a tom-  ber   en   mor-
tique; il a  ache-   té     une   ba-    nane,  une  ba-
nane;  sa    ba-     nane   all a tomb-  er    en   mor-
```

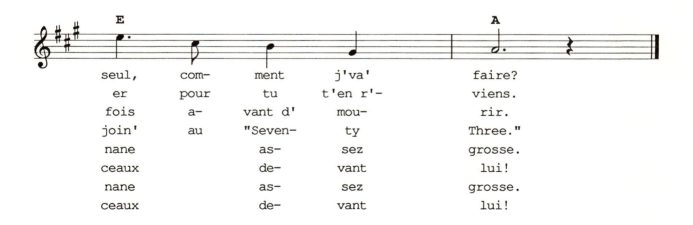

```
seul,  com-   ment    j'va'         faire?
er     pour   tu      t'en r'-      viens.
fois   a-     vant d' mou-          rir.
join'  au     "Seven- ty            Three."
nane          as-     sez           grosse.
ceaux         de-     vant          lui!
nane          as-     sez           grosse.
ceaux         de-     vant          lui!
```

Seventy-three Special

(1)
Oh, little one, I'm over here by myself with no one to love me. I'm all alone, what will I do?
Oh, unfortunate one, I'm sitting on the edge of my bed with prayer beads in my hand praying for you to come back.
(2)
Oh, little girl, I'm here by myself; I'd like for you to come back one more time before death.
Oh, dear little heart, over here by myself; I'd like for you to come back and meet me at the Seventy-three.

Uncle Adam's Banana

(1)
Oh, Uncle Adam, he bought a banana; a big enough banana.
Oh, Uncle Adam, he peeled his banana; his banana fell down in pieces at his feet.
(2)
Oh, Uncle Adam, he went to the store; he bought a banana, a big enough banana.
Oh, Uncle Adam, he peeled his banana; his banana fell to pieces in front of him.

My father was a musician. He played accordion and had a band. He played dances at different places, in dance halls and homes. I continued going to school but didn't like it. I was more interested in the accordion. I started learning how to play the accordion and watched for my chances. Dad didn't like for me to play the accordion because of my school, but I was watching my chances. When he wasn't around, I'd take the accordion and play on it. It took time but I gradually learned to play. Then when I learned, sometimes my father would take me to the dances, but I wasn't in love yet. I still was too young, so instead of going inside the dance hall with the adults, I'd stay outside with my little friends who had come too.

Instead of staying in the dance hall, we'd stay outside, especially when the moonlight was shining and we waited for our chance. Back then, the people brought their bottles of moonshine to the dances and hid their bottles everywhere. In those days people went to the dance in buggies, horseback, on foot, in wagons and in cars. They'd hide their bottles in buggies, in wagons, in cars and under the corners of the dance hall. And, also behind fence posts, anywhere they could hide their bottles. When they danced, they wanted a drink and came outside to drink then return into the dance hall. We were watching all that. When the bottle was empty, it was thrown on the ground and we would go and pick up the bottle. The next day, we'd sell the bottle for a nickle. That was amusing for us!

— Moïse Robin

Les Barres d' la Prison

Key. G
Pattern. Play theme between vocals.

Version. Canray Fontenot (©Tradition Music). An earlier version of this song is attributed to Douglas Bellard.

This is a blues song from the black community between Eunice and Basile, Louisiana.

"Mmm– mmm– mmm– mmm, cher 'tit gar- çon moi j' va'

jam- ais te r'- voir. Toi t'as é- tais con- dam- né pour la ba-

lance de ta vie dans les barres d'la pri- son.

4- J'dit, "Chère vieille ma- man, pleure pas pour

moi; i' faut tu prie pour ton en- fant pour es- say-

er d' sau- ver son âme de les flammes de l'en- fer.

Theme Played between verses

Prison Bars

(1)
Good-bye, dear old mother! Good-bye, poor old dad! Good-bye to my brothers and my dear little sisters!
I've been sentenced for the rest of my life behind prison bars.
(2)
I began rambling. I began doing wrong. I was hard-headed, I got into trouble.
Now I'm sentenced for the rest of my life behind prison bars.
(3)
My dear old mother! She got on her knees holding her head with both hands. Crying, she said, "Mmmmmmm!
Dear little boy, I'll never see you again. You've been sentenced for the rest of your life behind prison bars."
(4)
I said, "Dear old mother, don't cry for me. You must pray to try and save your son's soul from the flames of hell."

Valse de Bayou Chêne

Key. G
Pattern. Accordion: two Tunes; Vocal #1; Accordion: two Turns and one Tune; Vocal #2; Accordion: two Turns and one Tune; Vocal #3; Accordion: one Turn.

Version. Iry LeJeune (©Tek).
Related songs. Also: *Big Boy Waltz* (Iry LeJeune).

Bayou Chêne is an upper tributary of Bayou Lacassine, located south of Welsh, Louisiana.

Bayou Chêne Waltz

(1)
Oh, doll, what will you do all alone? Oh, my lover, it's useless to go meet you.
Oh, baby, I started rambling. Why, little one, are you like that in my home?
(2)
Oh, doll, you said you couldn't marry me. Oh, someone else — I'll complain to your parents.
Oh, doll, you passed by Sunday afternoon, you passed and gave me your hand; you left crying.
(3)
Oh, doll, these are my last words I can tell you except just the part I have to say to your family who don't want to see me anymore.
Oh, cute one, it's no use for me to leave you like this, always suffering in misery, unable to have you.

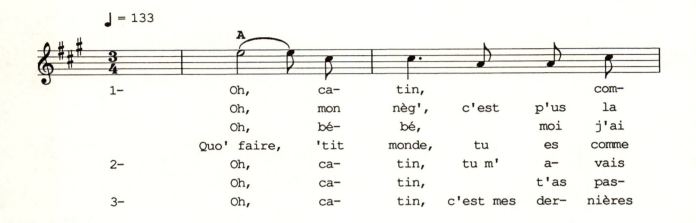

toi-- moi j' va' m' plai-   ner   à   tes   pa-   rents!
ner   ta   main; t'as   par-   ti   en   pleu-   rant.
part   à   ta   fa-   mille qui veux p'us m' voir.

Oh,   mi-   gnonne, c'est pas la   peine moi j' te laisse comme

ça;   tout l'   temps dans les mi-   sères a- près sou-

ffert,   ni   ca-   pab' t'a-   voir.

Bayou Pompon

Key. D
Pattern. Accordion: two Tunes and one Turn; Vocal #1; Accordion: one Tune and two Turns; Vocal #2; Accordion: two Tunes and one Turn; Vocal #3; Accordion: one Tune; Vocal #4; Accordion: one Tune and two Turns; Vocal #5; Accordion: two Tunes.

Version. Angélas LeJeune (OT).

There are many versions of this old tune. I don't know where this particular bayou is, but a bayou named Pompon should be a fantastic place. I like to imagine the bridge on Bayou Pompon is the one that inspired Iry LeJeune's Love Bridge Waltz.

Angélas LeJeune was Iry's uncle. I played with Angélas once, at Port Barré. I remember he had very long fingers.

My dad and his friends used to talk about him, that he was the best musician, the best singer they had ever heard. I thought he really played and sang well. He always had a large towel over his shoulder. It was hot, and after each dance he'd wipe his face, poor thing, and holler, Yuppi! Lâche pas! *("Don't let go!") They'd throw him a quarter and ask him to play a certain tune. "Like what?," he'd ask. Then they would whistle the tune for him. "Oh, yes! I remember it!" he'd say. There was no name for the tune yet but they would make him play the tunes he had made. He's the one who made* Bayou Pompon, *and what we call the* Kaplan Waltz *today. He called it* La Valse de Pointe Noire. *Yes! The words that Angélas put in that recording are better than the ones they sing today. That's what I think. The words matched the song better.*

He played well, and he was an old time player. He played until he was eighty. He played in Texas and other musicians went there to dislodge him but they never could. It was the old man they wanted, because he played so well still, at his age.

— Roy Fusilier

I played with Angélas LeJeune for years! He was one of the best accordion players I played with, and more exciting ... Listen, he'd rise and let out a big yell. You talk about a big yell, you'd notice! He'd play Donnez-moi Mon Chapeau, *a two-step. I still play that two-step. It's a pretty one ... Ai yé yaille! He and I could sing that! Poor old Angélas! Then, poor Ernest Frugé was right there bassing me with the violin. That was a good violin player! Oh yes, very good. Angélas was a very good accordion player.*

— Dennis McGee

Joe Falcon, Amédé Breaux, Leo Soileau, and I had made some records. There was a contest in Opelousas, but they didn't want us to play because we had made records. They chose the best besides us and the one who won was Angélas LeJeune. He was asked to go to the Roosevelt Hotel in New Orleans to make recordings. Angélas and I arrived at about the same time and I was there when he made Bayou Pompon. *"Bois Sec" Ardoin and his band was there, too, and they made* Les Flammes d'Enfer. *Right after they were finished, Leo and I made our record. This was in 1929.*

— Moïse Robin

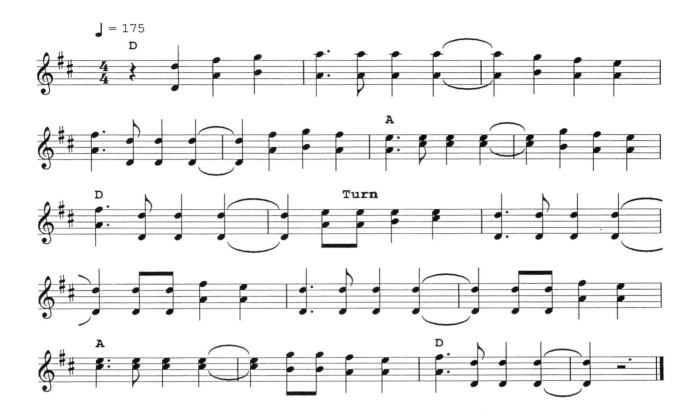

Bayou Pompon

(1)
Oh, it's sad, dear! It's sad to see you leaving me.
(2)
Oh, remember well the time I was with you on the bridge of Bayou Pompon, dear.
(3)
Oh, it's sad to see myself today always in misery.
(4)
Oh, everywhere I can go, it seems that I'd have to see you with your lover.
(5)
Oh, I know that soon you'll regret the lies you are trying to make me believe.

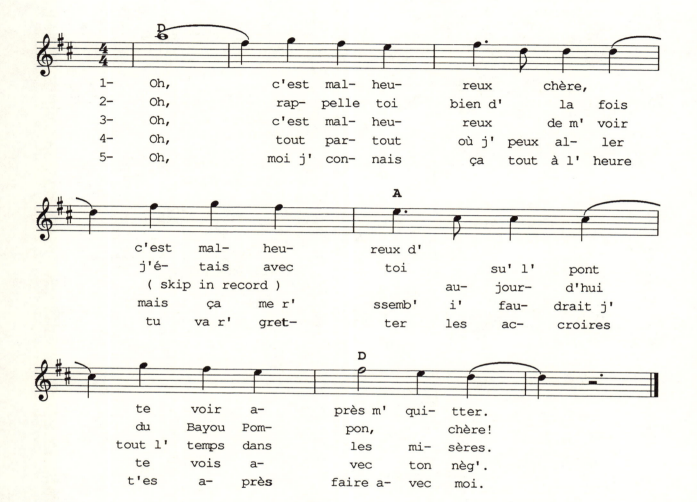

1- Oh,   c'est mal- heu-   reux   chère,
2- Oh,   rap- pelle toi   bien d'   la fois
3- Oh,   c'est mal- heu-   reux   de m' voir
4- Oh,   tout par- tout   où j' peux al- ler
5- Oh,   moi j' con- nais   ça tout à l' heure

c'est   mal-   heu-   reux d'
j'é-   tais   avec   toi   su' l'   pont
(skip in record)   au-   jour-   d'hui
mais   ça   me r'   ssemb'   i'   fau-   drait j'
tu   va r'   gret-   ter   les   ac-   croires

te   voir   a-   près m'   qui- tter.
du   Bayou   Pom-   pon,   chère!
tout l' temps dans   les   mi- sères.
te   vois   a-   vec   ton   nèg'.
t'es   a-   près   faire a- vec moi.

Valse de Bayou Teche I

Key. G played on a D accordion.
Pattern. Accordion: one Tune, one Filler and one Tune; Vocal #1; Accordion: two Fillers and one Tune; Vocal #2; Accordion: one Tune; Vocal #3; Accordion: one Filler and one Tune; Vocal #4; Accordion: one Filler and one Tune.

Version. Columbus Frugé (OT).

I am reluctant to define a turn in this song, instead I used the term Filler. This pattern is more or less my own.

Don't confuse this song with Nathan Abshire's *Valse de Bayou Teche.*

Bayou Teche is a long, sluggish, meandering stream. Its name comes from a Choctaw Indian word which means "big snake". It is along this bayou that the first Acadians settled. They used the bayou for a natural highway almost all the way to Opelousas. Pirogues, which are very light boats, almost capable of navigating on the morning's dew, are still used on this bayou.

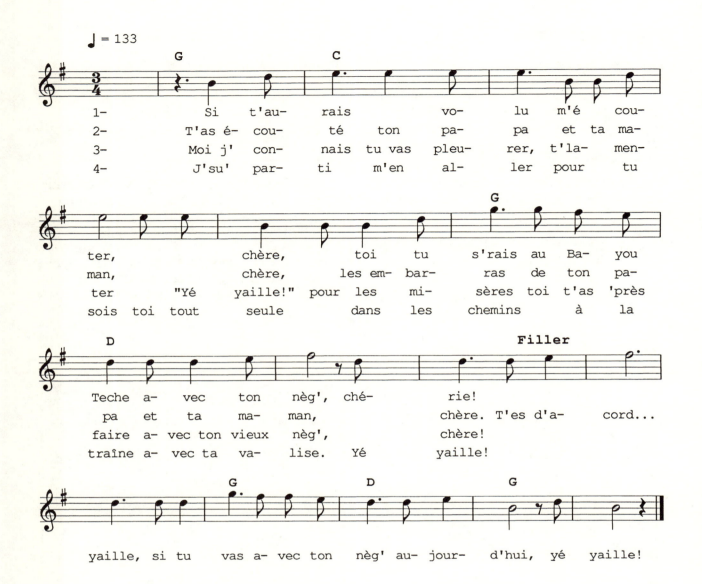

Bayou Teche Waltz

(1)
If you would've listened to me, dear, you would be over there on Bayou Teche with your lover, darling.
(2)
You listened to your father and mother, dear, the obstructions of your father and mother!
Dear, you agree! It hurts! If you go with your lover today— It hurts!
(3)
I know you'll cry and lament, "Oh, it hurts!" for all the miseries you're causing your old lover, dear!
(4)
I'm leaving so that you can go wandering alone in the roads with your suitcase. It hurts!

Valse de Bayou Teche II

Key. G

Pattern. Accordion: two Tunes; Vocal #1; Violin: two Tunes; Accordion: two Tunes; Vocal #2; Violin: one Tune.

Version. Nathan Abshire (©Flat Town).

"Under the broom" is slang for whatever domestic risk you are taking. The mention of the brother-in-law in the last line may be a fragment of a missing verse.

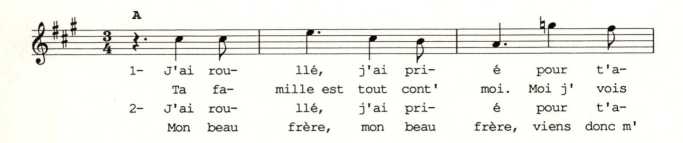

The Bayou Teche Waltz

(1)
I traveled, I prayed to have you, dear, to have you with me at home.
Your family is against me, dear, I don't understand. I must pass under the broom to meet you.
(2)
I traveled, I prayed to have you, dear, to have you with me in my room.
My brother-in-law, my brother-in-law, come see me, dear, please come see me dying at Bayou Teche.

Bébé Créole

Key. C
Pattern. Violin: one Tune; Vocal #1(Tune); Violin: one Tune; Vocal #2 (Turn); Violin: one Turn; Vocal #3 (Tune); Violin: one Tune; Vocal #4 (Turn); Violin: one Turn; Vocal #5 (Tune); Violin: one Tune.
Rhythm. See the sample of the bass part at the end.

Version. Dennis McGee (OT).
Related song. See: *C'est Pas la Peine Tu Brailles.*

Creole means something that's native to the French part of Louisiana. When my mother was a young girl, she preferred to be called Creole; she says it made her very angry to be called a Cajun. Now, whites prefer to be called Cajun, but French-speaking blacks still use Creole.

Creole Baby

(1)
Now look, unhappy one!
You abandon me forever, unhappy one!
Oh, it hurts! I'm going away to die.
(2)
Say good-bye, dear mama! Don't do that to your lover!
But you'll make me die forever one of these days, unhappy one.
Say bye-bye, dear old mama!
(3)
Just look at my rosaries you've bought me, dear unhappy one.
But just look; for always, unhappy one!
Unhappy one, say bye-bye to your dad and your mom!
(4)
Just look! Don't do that with me, dear little one.
Oh yes, unhappy one, don't, do it just for you;
but do that less, dear little girl!
(5)
Just look, unhappy one! Just look at the little rosary!
To travel the roads every day and every night!
It's for you, unhappy one! You're pretty!

reuse, dit 'bye- bye' à ton pap' et ta mam'!
nuits! C'est pour toi, mal- heu- reuse! T'es jo- lie!

Turn

4- 'Gar- dez donc! Fais pas ça a- vec moi, chère 'tite. Oh

oui, mal- heu- reuse, fais pas, fais les juste pour

toi; mais faire ça mais moins, chère 'tite fille!

Ma Blonde Est Parti

Key. G
Pattern. Accordion: two Tunes and one Turn; Vocal #1; Accordion: two Turns; Vocal #2; Accordion: two Turns; Vocal #3; Accordion: one Turn and one Tune.

Version. Amédé, Ophy, and Cleoma Breaux (OT).
Related songs. See: *Jolie Blonde* (Varise Connor, tune; Preston Manuel, vocal). Also: *La Fille d' la Veuve* (Iry LeJeune); *La Reine de Mon Coeur* (Elton "Bee" Cormier).

This version is from the first recording of *Jolie Blonde*, as sung by Amédé Breaux.

My Blonde is Gone

(1)
Pretty blonde, look what you've done!
You've left me to go away, to go away, yes, with someone else.
What hope and what future can I have?
(2)
Pretty blonde, you left me all alone to go to your family.
If you wouldn't have listened to the advice of others, you'd be here with me today.
(3)
Pretty blonde, you thought there was only you.
There isn't just you in the world for me to love.
I can find more than another, pretty blonde. God knows, I have a lot!

Blues de Texas

Key. D
Pattern. Violin: All instrumental parts are played
before first vocal; then play the part designated between
vocals.

Version. Dennis McGee (MS).

Cajuns like to sing about Texas. It was our
western frontier and many Cajuns migrated
there.

I've written the first three vocals with the
music, although there are five. Each vocal is
different! Here are the last two French vocals.

(4)
J'ai passé porte en porte. J'ai demandé la charité,
quan'même un 'tit morceau d' pain.
Comment tu veux moi, j' le fais moi tout seul
dans les chemins tous les jours et tous les nuits?
(5)
J' su' après guetter pour qu' un me ramasser.
Ça me donne de l'assistance et d' l'aide
pour un pauv' orphelin comme moi.

(1) J'su' par- ti pour al- ler dans l' Tex- as. J'ai pas- sé à Eu- nice m'ache- ter un pain d' cin' sous. J'ai man- gé la moi- tié pour mon dé- jeu- ner. J'ai 'gar- dé l'aut' moi- tié pour mon dî- ner. (2) J'ai mar- ché moi tout seul, ché- rie. J'ai mar- ché tous les jours et tous les nuits comme un pauv' mal- heu- reux. (3) De- puis à l' age de quinze ans j'su' or- phe- lin de père et d' mère. J'ai trai- né les ch'mins jus- qu'à l' age de trente- huit ans.

Texas Blues

(1)
I'm leaving to go to Texas. I stopped in Eunice to buy myself a five cent loaf of bread.
I ate half of it for breakfast. I kept the other half for my dinner.
(2)
I walked all alone, darling.
I walked every day and every night like a poor unfortunate.
(3)
Since the age of fifteen I've been an orphan, without a mother and father.
I rambled on the roads till the age of thirty-eight.
(4)
I passed from door to door. I asked for charity, for even a little piece of bread.
How do you want me to manage all alone in the roads every day and every night?
(5)
I'm waiting for someone to pick me up.
They give assistance and help to a poor orphan like me.

Blues Français

Key. G
Pattern. Accordion: one and 1/2 Tunes; Vocal #1 (last half of tune); Violin: two Tunes; Accordion: two Tunes, one Turn and 1/2 tune; Vocal #2 (last half of tune); Violin: two Tunes; Accordion: one Tune.

Version. Nathan Abshire (OT).
Related song. Also: *Tante Dalli* (Ambrose Thibodeaux).

I transposed this song to D because of a better violin position. Other lyrics to this tune are about Aunt Dalli's little boy who drowned among water lilies in the Coulée Rosa or Rozas.

A *coulée* is a stream or, as we say, a gulley, and is a tributary of a bayou.

French Blues

(1)
Oh, you hurt me, little one!
(2)
It's sad to see me, I could cry with both hands!

La Branche du Mûrier

Key. C
Pattern. Accordion: two Tunes; Vocal #1; Accordion: two Turns and two Tunes; Vocal #2; Accordion: two Turns and two Tunes.

Version. Iry LeJeune (©Tek).
Related songs. See: *L'Anse de Belair* (Dennis McGee). Also: *Mulberry Waltz* (Aldus Roger; Ambrose Thibodeaux).

Ann Savoy's book tells the history of this song. Although Iry LeJeune's musical career belongs to the late 1940's and early 1950's, he was preserving and reworking some earlier songs, which I've included in this section of the book.

Mulberry Tree Waltz

(1)
Look, dear little girl, every Sunday afternoon, I am there in my house suffering and lonesome.
Went through a lot of grief, I still grieve over you. See for yourself that I could pass in front of your home.
(2)
Look what you've done! Cut off the limb from my mulberry tree to see you pass in front of your papa's home.
See, dear little girl, how I and these small children miss you; we're grieving, and you don't want to come back!

Breakdown la Louisiane

Key. D
Pattern. Violin: two Tunes and two Turns; Vocal #1; Violin: one Tune and one Turn; Vocal #2; one Tune and two Turns; Vocal #3; Violin: one Tune and one Turn.

Version. Walker Brothers (OT).
Related songs. See: *Valse à Kathleen* (Dennis McGee and Sady Courville), *Valse des Grands Bois* (Carrie "Mignonne" Royer Miller). Also: *Valse de la Belle* (Shirley Bergeron); *Valse de l'Anse Maigre* (Dennis McGee and Sady Courville); *Valse à Will Kegley* (Will Kegley); *Pochéville* (Joseph Falcon-a mixture of *Tolan Waltz* in the Turn and *Valse des Grands Bois* in the Tune); *Valse de Crowley.*

I've included two Tunes and two Turns to show double and single variations in the manuscript. This is an easy song to learn and is one of the first songs I played.

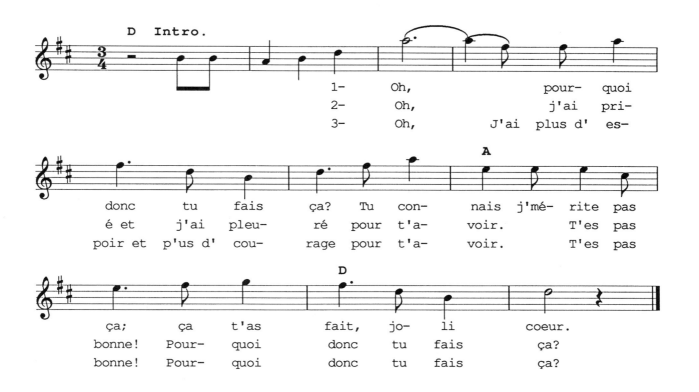

Louisiana Breakdown

(1)
Oh, why do you do that? You know that I don't deserve what you're doing, pretty heart.
(2)
Oh, I prayed and I cried to have you. You're no good! Why do you do that?
(3)
Oh, I have no hope and no courage to have you anymore. You're no good! Why do you do that?

Valse de ’Cadien

Key. G
Pattern. Accordion: one Tune; Vocal #1; Accordion: two Turns, one Tune; Vocal #2; Accordion: two Turns, one Tune; Vocal #3; Accordion: one Turn.

Version. Iry LeJeune (©Tek).
Related song. Also: *La Vieille Valse de la Louisiane* (Ambrose Thibodeaux).

’*Cadien* is short for *Acadien* (“Acadian” or “Cajun” in English). The Acadians were French settlers in Nova Scotia, also known as Acadia, who were forcibly dispersed by the English in 1755. Many of them made their way to Louisiana, where the Spanish authorities encouraged them to settle in unclaimed territory west of New Orleans. They were joined in this area by settlers from elsewhere. One of my mother’s ancestors came from Montreal by way of the Mississippi valley about 1770; another came from Holland in the early 1800’s He used the name Contini while he was working for Jean LaFitte; later on, he called himself Sittig. The François family came from France, near Nancy, in the 1840’s. Many people of German and British descent also came to southwestern Louisiana. These different groups of settlers intermarried with the original Acadians and their descendants are the Cajuns of today.

I have read various theories about where the name Acadia comes from. The one I like best is that it comes from an Indian word *aquaddie*, the name for the pollok fish found in the waters around Nova Scotia. Many early Louisiana place names, such as Choupique, Patassa, l’Anse Chaoui, Bayou Teche, Pecanier also came from Indian words.

I learned La Vieille Valse de la Louisiane *from Angélas LeJeune. He recorded it and I listened to him play it. I recorded it in my head. In those days, when I sat down and listened to a song, if it was to my taste, I would come pretty darn close to playing it. I heard it several times and I’d replay it till I knew it. When I recorded it, we played it the same way. Angélas was like me, he liked that old waltz a whole lot.*

— *Ambrose Thibodeaux*

Cajun (Acadian) Waltz

(1)
Well, it hurts! Dear little one, why are you like that, in so much misery?
Well, it hurts! I'm not doing anything to you; I want you to be like you were.
(2)
Well, it hurts! All that pain! You should listen to your old lover one time when I tell you something.
Little girl, remember, think when your father already mistreated you so much.
(3)
Ah, I'd want you to come back to me, dear little one, lay your dear little head upon my shoulder;
let your dear little tears fall freely and be forgiven for all you've done.

Valse de Calcasieu

Key. D
Pattern. Accordion: two Tunes; Vocal #1; Accordion: two Tunes; Vocal #2; Accordion: four Tunes; Vocal #3; Accordion: one Tune.

Version. Iry LeJeune (©Tek).
Related songs. Also: *War Widow Waltz* (Lee Sonnier); *La Valse d'Elton* (Ambrose Thibodeaux); *Pine Grove Waltz*; *La Valse de la Veuve* (Ambrose Thibodeaux); *Quoi C'est T'as?* (Moïse Robin); *Poor Man's Waltz.*

Calcasieu is the name of the parish in south-west Louisiana where Lake Charles is located. Calcasieu is an Indian word and the name of a chief who lived there; it means Crying Eagle.

Calcasieu Waltz

(1)
Well, look! I know you'd like to come back home to meet your lover.
Well, doll, I'd like for you to come back, even once before you die.
(2)
Oh, pretty one, what will I do? How can you believe I'm always there for you?
Oh, little girl, always thinking in sorrow about not ever being able to have you!
(3)
Oh, little girl, look! Remember! You will always listen to anyone but me.
Well, it's no use to tell you anything, you look at me without ever being happy.

Valse de Carencro

Key. C

Version. Leopold François (*T'as Volé Mon Idée*); Gerald Broussard (*Valse de Prairie Ronde*, Cr-Cj). *Related songs.* See: *Valse à Alida* (Aldus Roger).

My dad calls this tune *T'as Volé Mon Idée* ("You Stole My Mind"); it has vocals of its own, but he doesn't remember all of them. He told me that his sister used to sing this tune when he was a boy.

I've included the lyrics that go with *Valse de Prairie Ronde*.

Carencro is a town just north of Lafayette, Louisiana. It was named for all the buzzards occupying the region before the town was settled; probably a buzzard rookery was located there. There is a story that a circus elephant died and was hauled outside of Lafayette where the buzzards ate it, but I don't believe this. Carrion crow became Carencro in French and English.

Valse de Prairie Ronde

(1)
Oh, bébé, moi j'm'ennuie un tas de toi. Moi j'aimerais tu t'en r'viens une aut' fois avant trop tard.
Oh, c'est mon coeur moi j' connais qu'est cassé. Aujourd'hui la faute est là mais c'est pas moi.
(2)
Oh, 'tite fille, quo' faire on s'a quitté? Les mentris, la parole que tous l' monde après épailler!
Oh, catin, moi j' connais que tu t'ennuies. Aujourd'hui toi t'es là après pleurer. C'est trop tard!

Prairie Ronde Waltz

(1)
Oh, baby, I'm lonesome a lot for you. I'd like for you to come back once more before too long.
Oh, I know my heart is broken. Today the fault is there but it's not mine.
(2)
Oh, little girl, why did we leave each other? The lies, the word that everybody's spreading!
Oh, doll, I know that you're lonesome. Today you're there crying. It's too late!

Casse Pas ma Tête

Key. G
Pattern. Violin: two Tunes, two Turns; Vocal #1;
Violin: two Tunes, two Turns; Vocal #2; two Tunes,
two Turns.

Version. Dewey Balfa (©Flat Town).

I recorded this song at the Planetarium grounds in Lafayette, Louisiana, during the annual Cajun Music Festival in 1984. Dewey didn't sing it, but he said the title of this song is *Aïe yé yaille, Adéa, Cogne P' us su' ma Tête* ("Oh It Hurts, Adéa, Quit Thumping on My Head"). *Casse pas ma tête* as used locally means to stop nagging or constantly worrying someone about a particular thing.

Dewey also said this was "an old song that I learned from my daddy who learned it from his grandparents."

When I listen to old timers like Mr. Dennis [McGee], Mr. Sady [Courville] and some of the older musicians that have encouraged me in playing and preserving Cajun music, it *makes me realize that we have something worthwhile, even more than I did back twenty or some years ago when I was invited to go play at Newport, for the Jazz and Heritage and Folk Festival. And from that time, I saw it was a necessity to work with the young people who are interested in the culture of this area. When you're cut you bleed; if you bleed, you bleed Cajun blood. And you don't necessarily have to be of Cajun descent to be a Cajun, because my ancestors on my father's side were Scotch-Irish and on my mother's side, they were Acadians. I think it's a well-planted seed when you leave your knowledge to some young people. If we don't do this, this music will die and there is no reason for it to die, because it's so beautiful."*

— Dewey Balfa

1- Oh yé yaille! Yé yaille, A-de- ya! Toi t'as
Oh yé yaille! Yé yaille, A-de- ya! Mon, ma
2- Oh yé yaille! Yé yaille, A-de- ya! Toi t'as
Oh yé yaille! Quand t'es su' ma tête, mon, ma

cas- sé ma tête, mais cogne p'us su' ma tête.
tête i'me fait mal, mais cogne p'us su' ma tête.
cas- sé ma tête, et mon,ma tête me fait mal.
tête me fait mal, et toi t'as cas- sé ma tête.

Don't Nag Me

(1)
Oh it hurts! It hurts, Adéa!
You nagged me, but don't nag anymore.
Oh it hurts! It hurts, Adéa!
My head hurts, but don't nag anymore.
(2)
Oh it hurts! It hurts, Adéa!
You nagged me, and my head hurts.
Oh it hurts! When you're nagging,
my head hurts and you've broken my head.

One-Step des Chameaux

Key. D
Pattern. Accordion: two Tunes; Vocal #1; etc. There is no turn in this song.
Rhythm. The bass has two-half notes per measure.

Version. Amédé Ardoin, vocal and accordion, and Dennis McGee, violin (OT).

I tried to standardize all the lyrics from the first vocal. Chameaux is a family name around Basile, Louisiana. This song was recorded by the famous black accordion player and vocalist, Amédé Ardoin with Dennis McGee.

I had a lot of respect for the black, Amédé Ardoin. I learned more about playing music with an accordion from Amédé than from anybody else I played with. When I started playing the violin in the country, the blacks would have dances in homes and Amédé was always the man they would get to play. You talk about people who would have a good time! They could dance and really enjoy themselves. The dust would fly, you could hardly see the inside of the house! I had just started playing and I learned to play bass with an accordion. I'd listen to the bass and melody on his accordion and I'd make my own bass in there.

To finish telling you about Amédé, he started playing for white people, private dances, and holidays like New Year's Eve and Mardi Gras. I enjoyed and learned a lot of music from Amédé. We played dances in Châtaignier and some house dances to celebrate holidays. I'll never forget, one late afternoon on a New Year's Eve, some people who liked music very much came for me to play music with Amédé Ardoin. Just the two of us, violin and accordion. We started at about four or five o'clock and we played that afternoon a while, then ate supper. Then we started playing early that night and at midnight we had a gumbo. We all stopped and ate all the gumbo. They all wished each other a good New Year; then we started playing again till the next morning.

When I returned home, the sun was coming up. Yes sir! It was a very big night, but you didn't notice the time because the people were amusing themselves. But you know, when you're doing something you like, you don't notice the time and you don't get tired.
— Sady Courville

Amédé Ardoin and I played together too ... He was about only five feet tall. I'm sure he wasn't more than five feet tall, but you talk about strong! Cher, that was a real man! Pooh! I saw him wrestle with a big black called Jim. He weighed about 225-230 pounds and he ran into that little Amédé one day in my presence. I said to myself, "He'll break Amédé's neck!" Listen! When I knew something, he had thrown him down and was on top of him. Jim Ned! That was his name. He worked in the rice warehouses and thought he could beat Amédé, but Amédé threw him down and he stayed down ...

Yes, me and Amédé played some music everywhere. We even played on Bayou le Noire. We went and played there on a Saturday night, then Sunday night we played in Lake Charles proper. We stayed there and spent the day at one of my cousins. Then that night we played for them and went back home. ... We played for the whites or the blacks, it didn't make any difference. They all paid us the same. Oh yes! The little black, Amédé, was a good accordion player for the blacks and he was good for the whites. He was a good accordion player, that little Amédé, and a good singer.
— Dennis McGee

Chameaux's One-Step

(1)
Oh, mother, don't listen to that! What will I do? Anywhere I go my heart hurts, pretty one.
(2)
Oh, that will be so hard! What will I do? Oh yes, that makes me feel sad, baby, look what you're doing!
(3)
Oh, if I had the courage! Yes, I can't ever go visiting, on account of these troubles you cause me.
I don't see that I deserve that, doll!
(4)
Oh, I ignore you, when I go to your place. I never, never, never see you, you dear little girl, baby!
(5)
Just remember doll, darling, when I went to your home Sunday afternoon what happened over there.
It's just for you I must go!

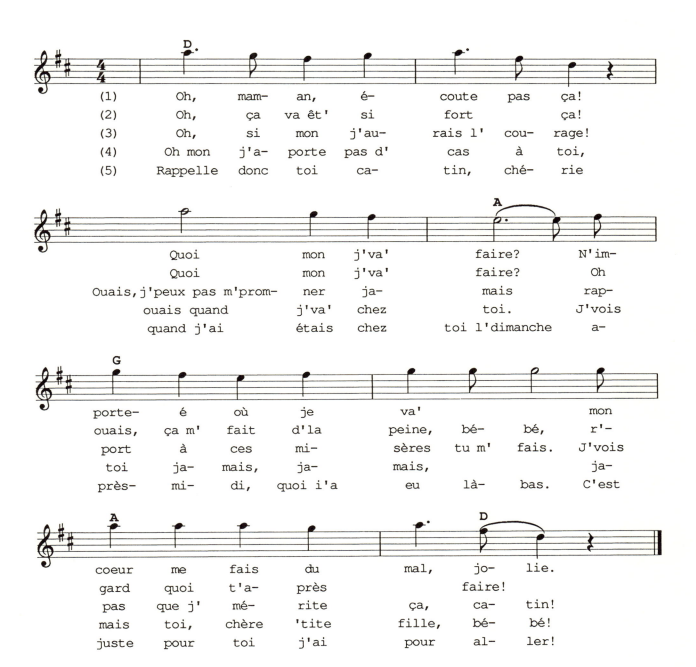

Valse de Châtaignier

Key. C
Pattern. Accordion: two Tunes and one Turn; Vocal #1; Steel Guitar: two Tunes; Violin: two Tunes; Accordion: one Tune; Vocal #2; Accordion: one Tune.

Version. Austin Pitre (©Flat Town).
Related song. Also: *Dodge City Waltz* (Joe Bonsall).

Châtaignier is the French word for chestnut tree and is also the name of a community about five miles northeast of Eunice on the road to Ville Platte, Louisiana.

Austin likes to refer to himself in the third person. Notice how the vocal part differs from the instrumental tune.

Châtaignier Waltz

(1)
Well, my dear baby, you know I take it hard,
not to have you with me at my house to finish your dear days.
(2)
Ah, but dear little heart, see your lover!
He's there in misery to finish his dear days, unfortunate one.

Chère Alice

Key. G
Pattern. Accordion: two Tunes and one Turn; Vocal #1; Violin: two Tunes; Accordion: two Turns; Vocal #2; Violin: two Tunes.

Version. Lawrence Walker (©La Lou).
Related Songs. See: *Rainbow Waltz* (Austin Pitre). Also: *Country Waltz* (Lawrence Walker); *Valse à 'Tit 'Dam Hanks* (Angélas LeJeune).

'Dam is a nickname for Adam, who rides a tall horse named Henry. I've also included the lyrics for the same tune entitled, *Valse à 'Tit 'Dam Hanks*. *'Tit* ("little") is often used as a term of endearment. That's why names may be prefaced with T; even places of business are named, for example, T-Joe's. Many people had no opportunity to learn how to spell in French; that's why you'll see signs in front of restaurants advertising crawfish "A-2-fay" instead of *étoufée*.

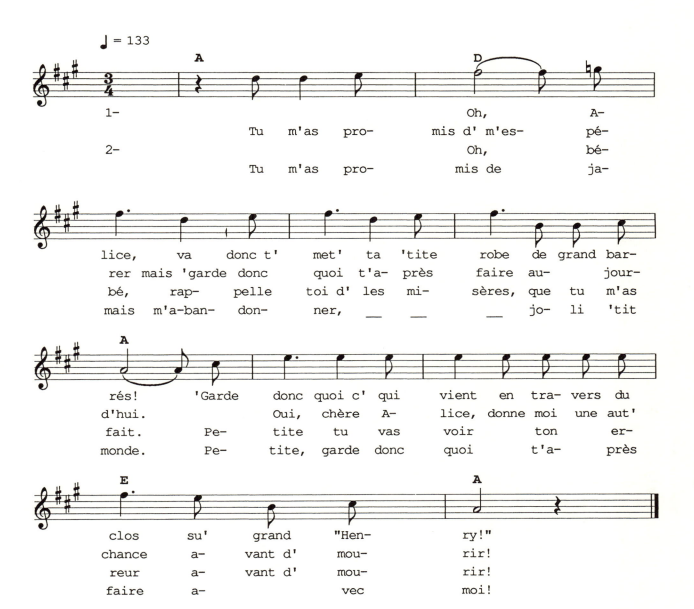

Dear Alice

(1)
"Oh, Alice, go put on your nice dress with the wide stripes.
Just look who's coming across the field on big Henry!"
You promised to wait for me, but look what you're doing to me today.
Yes, dear Alice, give me one more chance before I die.
(2)
Oh, baby, remember all the misery you've caused me.
Little one, you will see your error before you die.
You've promised never to abandon me, pretty little one.
Little one, just look what you're doing to me.

Valse à 'Tit 'Dam Hanks.

(1)
Oh, Alice, 'garde 'tit 'Dam, 'garde 'tit 'Dam qui s'en r'vient!
Moi j' vois la tête à grand "Henry" par dessus tout les aut'.
'Tit 'Dam a 'rrivé; il a droit foncé pour la cour du magasin.
Il a trouvé Alice après dérober du maïs.
(2)
I' a d'mandé à sa mam'; elle dit, "'Tit 'Dam, j'ai pour l'avoir pour mon coeur."
I' a d'mandé à son pap'. I' dit, "'Tit 'Dam, t'es un tas trop chétif."
Il a 'trapé son fusil; il a pointé droit pour son coeur.
J'y ai ôté le fusil et j'y ai bien caché la "jog."

Little Adam Hanks' Waltz

(1)
"Oh, Alice, look at little Adam, look at little Adam who's coming!
I see big Henry's head over all the others."
Little Adam arrived; he rushed straight for the barn yard.
He found Alice shucking some corn.
(2)
He asked her mom (for Alice); she said, "Little Adam, I must have her for my heart."
He asked her dad; he said, "Little Adam, you're a lot too shabby."
He (the father) caught his shotgun; he pointed it straight for his heart.
I took away the shotgun and I hid the jug well.

Chère Mam'

Key. D
Pattern. Accordion: two Tunes; Vocal #1; Violin: two Tunes; Accordion: two Turns; Vocal #2; Violin: two Tunes; Accordion: two Turns; Vocal #3; Violin: two Turns; Accordion: two Tunes.

Version. Gervais Quibodeaux, vocal, with Ambrose Thibodeaux (©La Lou).
Related songs. Also: *Hé, Mom* (Amédé Breaux); *Mama, Where You At?* (Mayuse LaFleur).

Amédé Breaux is credited with making this song, but Mayuse LaFleur recorded it with Leo Soileau in 1928.

Dear Mom

(1)
Oh, mom, where are you? Dear mom, I'd like to see you one time before I die!
Oh, mom, where are you, dear?
(2)
Oh, mom, where are you? Dear mom, I'd like to see you one time before I die!
Oh, mom, I'd like to see you, dear!
(3)
Dear mom, where are you? It hurts! I'd like to see you one time before I die!
Oh, mom, where are you, dear?

1- Oh mam', à où toi t'es? Chère mam', j'vou-
2- Oh mam', à où toi t'es? Chère mam', j'vou-
3- Chère mam', à où toi t'es? Oh yaille! J'vou-

drais te voir une fois a- vant d' mou- rir!
drais te voir une fois a- vant d' mou- rir!
drais te voir une fois a- vant d' mou- rir!

Oh mam', à où toi t'es chère!
Oh mam', j'aime- rais te voir, chère!
Oh mam', à où toi t'es chère!

Ma Chère 'Tite Fille

Key. C
Pattern. Violin: one Tune and one Turn, one Tune and one Turn; Vocal #1; Violin: one Turn; Vocal #2; Violin: one Turn, one Tune and one Turn; Vocal #3; Violin: one Turn; Vocal #4; Violin: one Turn, one Tune and one Turn; Vocal #5; Violin: one Turn.

Version. Leo Soileau (OT).
Related songs. See: *Aimer et Perdre* (Joseph Falcon). Also: *La Valse de la Rosa* (Leo Soileau); *Cher 'Tit Monde* (Nathan Abshire).

Notice that the turn is played at the end of each vocal to resolve the ending. Leo has two different names for the same song. Moïse Robin basses on the accordion. Because of a better violin position, I've transposed the key to G. I've included both sets of words that Leo Soileau used with this tune.

Leo and I played dances and we were paid four dollars each. At that time we played with no amplification, only acoustic. Leo always wanted to take the lead when we played. He kept the lead and I had to follow him. It's bothersome to always follow a violin, you see. It's difficult. I had to play below his violin's volume. We didn't play too long together, about one year.
                                  — Moïse Robin

When my brother got married, he stopped playing completely. I got myself another player, one named Élius Soileau, a good violin player known in the territory, Leo Soileau's cousin. He's an old violin player raised at Durald, near me. Hé, he's a man who gives a good sound to the violin! Prettier than Leo. With an accordion, gentleman, his notes were great, yes! He played lead well, too! He played double stops, some pretty keys! Leo

was just the opposite. He didn't get along too well with an accordion. The accordion had to follow him. Yes, Élius always told me that Leo had never learned to bass the accordion. Élius told me that he wanted to show Leo how, but Leo remarked that bassing was nothing, that one had to play. Élius bassed and when I passed him the song he'd pick it up. He'd pick it up right on time. Pretty, pretty! And play the tune fancy. And he told me Leo never wanted to learn bassing, just to lead. He told me something I didn't know, maybe it's true. Élius told me, "Leo is my cousin but if you listen to him, you can have him play the same tune over again but he won't play it the same way. He's hard to follow, the accordion must follow him." They had to play together a long time to make a record, to get used to him. It would strain him, the other had to follow. That man was hard to follow. It was as though he wasn't playing the song the same way. He put the turn too soon or too late. You know, you can play two tunes, then the turn to your waltz or one-step, then play two tunes again, then climb on the turn again, but you mustn't stay too long on the same thing. It's not pretty, you must change it.
                                  — Roy Fusilier

My Dear Little Girl

(1)
Oh, you, little one, do look, miserable one, what you're doing to me, dear!
(2)
Oh, unhappy one, do look, you, little one, where I am today is for you, dear!
(3)
Oh, do come see! You, little one! You! It hurts, dear! You, little one!
You! In the end, you will make me cry, dear!
(4)
Oh, you, little one, darling — You, little one, you can give thanks to your daddy!
(5)
Oh, you, little one, don't do that with me! You, little one, you will cry! You, little one, darling!

Valse De La Rosa

(1)
Oh, chère, promets moi t'es juste pour moi, ouais, jolie fille, jusqu'à l' jour mais de ta mort, bébé.
(2)
Oh, chère, moi j'connais mais t'as perdu mais plus que moi, t'as perdu mais juste toi que moi j'aime, bébé.
(3)
Oh, chère, promets moi mais bonne 'tite fille, jusqu'à la mort, jolie coeur, pour ton nèg', chère.
(4)
Oh, chère, moi j'connais mais moi j' m'en va' c'est pour te r'join', jolie coeur.
Pourquoi donc, tu fais ça à moi, jolie?

Rosa's Waltz

(1)
Oh, dear, promise me you're mine, pretty girl, until the day of your death, baby.
(2)
Oh, dear, I know that you've lost more than me, you've lost...just that I love you, baby.
(3)
Oh, dear, promise me, good little girl, till death, pretty heart, for your lover, dear.
(4)
Oh, dear, I know I'm leaving to go meet you, pretty heart. Why do you do that to me, pretty one?

Chère Tout-Toute

Key. A
Pattern. Accordion: two Tunes; Vocal #1; Violin: two
Turns; Accordion: two Tunes; Vocal #2; Violin: two
Tunes; Accordion: two Tunes.

Version. Preston Manuel, vocal (©La Lou).
Related songs. Also: *Grand Chênière Waltz* (Blackie
Forestier); *Valse de Marais Bouleur* (Cleoma
Falcon); *Valse de Huit Jours* (Leopold François);
Chère Toutou (Rufus Thibodeaux).

J.B. Fusilier first recorded this song while
Preston Manuel was playing in his band. There
have been many recordings of this song since
then, because it is so popular. As often as not,
the first song played by a Cajun band is this
tune, partly because it's so familiar that it
gives them confidence and partly because it
helps to make sure that all the instruments are
tuned properly. Many of the older violin
players play the first three measures of the turn
an octave higher.

"Tout-Toute" is a nickname meaning "my
everything." J.B. Fusilier named this song for
his daughter.

Dear Everything

(1)
Oh, but dear Everything, look what you're doing to me, unhappy one.
You thought there was only you in the country of Louisiana
who could love and care for me, dear little heart.
(2)
Oh, but dear little heart, don't forget the words you said to me before leaving.
You believed, dear Everything —!
Come see what happened to your old lover!

1- Oh mais chère Tout- Toute chère,
2- Oh mais cher 'tit coeur, malheu- heuse,

'garde donc quoi t'a- près faire a- vec
ou- blie pas les pa- roles que tu m'as

moi, mal heur- euse. Tu croy- ais y a- vais juste
dit avant d' par- tir. Tu croy- ais, mais chère Tout-

toi dans l' pa- ys d'la Loui- saine pour m'ai-
Toute, chère! Viens donc voir quoi c'est y a

mer et m' soi- gner, cher 'tit coeur.
eu à ton vieux nèg'.

Valse des Chérokis

Key. D
Pattern. Accordion: two Tunes; Vocal #1; Violin: two Turns and two Tunes; Vocal #2; Accordion: two Tunes and two Turns.

Version. Gervais Quibodeaux, vocal (modified), Ambrose Thibodeaux, accordion (©La Lou).
Related songs. Also: *Two-Step à Comeaux* (Aldus Roger; Don Guillory).

Yé Yaille! can also be used to express excitement, much as we use the word "Wow!" in English. Here, I use it in the usual fashion. *Chérokis* is the name given to a small tree often used as firewood on the prairie. *Baieonne* is a nickname for a reddish blonde. If you know how to cook Muscovy duck and boil crawfish the way Cajuns do, you're eating well!

Cherokee Waltz

(1)
Oh, it hurts! Come meet me at Baieonne's; we'll cut some firewood and eat some Muscovy duck.
Oh, little girl, look how your old lover searched for you last night anyhow.
(2)
Oh, it hurts! Come meet me at Baieonne's; we'll pick up some chips and boil some crawfish.
Oh, it hurts! Remember how your old lover looked for you last night, little girl.

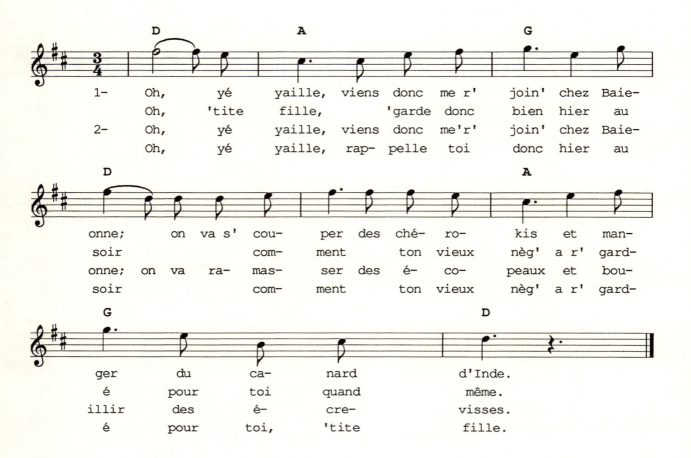

1- Oh, yé yaille, viens donc me r' join' chez Baie-
   Oh, 'tite fille, 'garde donc bien hier au
2- Oh, yé yaille, viens donc me'r' join' chez Baie-
   Oh, yé yaille, rap- pelle toi donc hier au

onne; on va s' cou- per des ché- ro- kis et man-
soir comment ton vieux nèg' a r' gard-
onne; on va ra- mas- ser des é- co- peaux et bou-
soir comment ton vieux nèg' a r' gard-

ger du ca- nard d'Inde.
é pour toi quand même.
illir des é- cre- visses.
é pour toi, 'tite fille.

One-Step de Choupique

Key. G

Pattern. Violin: two Turns; Vocal #1; Violin: one Tune; Vocal #2; Violin: one Tune, one Turn, and one Tune; Vocal #3 (A & B); Violin: two Tunes; Vocal #4; Violin: one Turn and one Tune.

Rhythm. Bass has two strong half-notes per measure.

Version. Dennis McGee (MS).

Choupique is a community located six miles north-northeast of Eunice, Louisiana and is a Choctaw Indian name of the Bowfin fish (Amia calva L.). Its common English names are "cypress trout," "grentle" or "mudfish."

I was raised in Choupique. I lived there from the age of four until I was fourteen years old. ... When you go to Châtaignier, you cross a little stream called La Coulée Choupique. There were many choupiques *in that time. And some big ones! They were three feet long! I* caught many on my line when I was young. I fished with a pole. The water was deep, but it wasn't wide. There were a lot of *choupiques that would come from Bayou Marron, which fell into Bayou des Cannes and it fell into Bayou Nezpiqué. They all joined. The fish would travel upstream when it rained a lot. Once the fish were in Coulée Choupique, they'd stay; they couldn't go back when the water went down. People would sein the fish and set lines.*

— *Dennis McGee*

Choupique One-Step

(1) La la la la, la la la la la la, la la la la la, la la le la la!
Look at my sweetheart! Is she leaving?
(2) Now, now, now! Don't do that with me! Don't leave with anyone else but me!
Unfortunate one! Darling! But look at my sweetheart!
(3) La la la, la la la la la la, la la la la, la la la la la la, la la la la la la la la la la la!
Look at my sweetheart! She's leaving with someone else!
Unfortunate one! Darling! But don't do that, sweetheart. Look! Darling!
(4) Oh, it hurts! What will I do always by myself like a poor unfortunate?!
But dear darling, don't do that to me! Unfortunate one! Darling!

Choupique Two-Step

Key. G
Pattern. Accordion: two Tunes; Vocal #1; Violin: two Tunes; Accordion: two Tunes; Vocal #2; Violin: two Tunes; Accordion: two Tunes.

Version. Nathan Abshire (©Flat Town).
Related song. Also: *Jolie Catin* (Alphonse "Bois Sec" Ardoin) — which is not the same as Iry LeJeune's *Jolie Catin.*

Don't confuse this song with Dennis McGee's *One-Step De Choupique.* Notice that pullet and colt are pet names in our Cajun culture for young girls and boys. Nathan Abshire and Iry LeJeune both use these terms.

1- Hé jo- lie ca- tin,   ouais, mais moi j' m'en
2- Hé jo- lie ca- tin,   jo- lie, tu m' fais du

va',   moi j' m'en va' dans   grand Chou- pique pour
mal,   fais du mal, jo- lie pou- lette!

voir   des   belles   'tites   blondes!
J'va' pleu- rer   pour   toi!

Choupique Two-Step

(1)
Well, pretty doll, I'm going, I'm going to big Choupique to see some beautiful little blonds!
(2)
Well, pretty doll, you're hurting me, hurting me, pretty pullet! I'll cry for you!

Church Point Breakdown

Key. C
Pattern. Accordion: two Tunes; Vocal #1; Accordion: two Turns and one Tune; Vocal #2; Accordion: two Turns and one Tune; Vocal #3; Accordion: two Turns and one Tune.

Version. Iry LeJeune (©Tek).

The introduction is used to introduce the first part of each vocal, and the second measure is actually sung in the second part of the vocals. This song was named for Church Point, Louisiana, and probably originated around there.

```
                                                      Eh      yé
1-                          Eh,    rap- pelle  toi,   ca-
                            Eh,    ça  me r'-  semb', 'tite
2-                                                    Eh      yé
                            Oh,    tu  de-     vrais  ja-
3-                                                    Eh,     bé-
```

```
yaille, mal- heu-  reuse! Tous  les   jours dans ma  mai-
tin,    ton  pa-   pa et ta  ma-    man  t'a tou- jours
yaille, tous les   jours après souf-  frir dans ma  mai-
fille,  tous les   jours tu con-   nais      pour ve-
bé,     tous les   jours moi j' su'   là   su' ma  ga-
mais    m'ou- bli-  er   'tant loin q'  moi      j'peux pas t'
```

```
son        j'a-   près mais t'es- pé-  rer.
dit d' pas faire  ça   a-   vec ton   nèg'.
son,   p'us per-  sonne qui  vient me r'- join'.
nir puis voir quo' faire que  moi j' su'   là.
lerie  après 'pé-  rer   pour toi, vieux nèg'.
dire   comme au-  tant j'm'en- nuie de   toi.
```

Church Point Breakdown

(1)
Oh it hurts, unhappy one! Everyday in my house I'm waiting for you.
Oh remember, doll, your father and mother always told you not to do that to your lover.
(2)
Oh, it hurts, to suffer at home everyday, nobody to come meet me anymore!
Oh, little girl, it seems that everyday you'd know to come see why I am there.
(3)
Oh, baby, everyday I am there on my porch waiting for you.
Oh, you should never forget me. I can't tell you how much I miss you.

Country Gentlemen

Key. G
Pattern. Accordion: two Turns; Vocal #1; Accordion: four Turns; Vocal #2; Accordion: three Turns; Vocal #3; Accordion: two Turns.

Version. Iry LeJeune (©Tek).
Related songs. Also: *Jeunes Gens de la Campagne* (Jimmie Venable); *Don't Get Married* (Iry LeJeune); *Couche-couche Après Brûler.*

Such warnings are usually given to the "young country lads" instead of the "young country girls," as in this song by Iry. This song is also called *Don't Get Married* or *Jeunes Gens de la Campagne*, but don't confuse it with Dennis McGee's song with the second title; the tune is different. This may be why Iry approved of giving this song an English name.

Of course, we change the pattern so that the tune is played, too. Just use the vocal as a guide.

I've also included the lyrics for *Couche-Couche Après Brûler*, which is an old version of the same tune. Couche-couche comes from the Arabic word couscous which is a durum wheat semolina prepared with boiling water and a little salt. It is popular in France, too.

Wheat wasn't grown in Louisiana, so cornmeal was substituted for the main ingredient. Here's a good recipe once used by many Cajuns for supper or breakfast.

2 cups yellow cornmeal
1 and 1/2 cups milk
1 and 1/2 teaspoon salt
1/2 cup cooking oil
1 teaspoon baking powder

Mix cornmeal, salt, baking powder and milk. Add mixture to hot oil in a heavy skillet on high heat. Let a crust form and then stir well once or twice. Lower heat to simmer, cover and let steam for 15 or 20 minutes. Serve with cane syrup and cottage cheese. We also used clabber or milk and sugar.

1- Jeunes filles de la cam- pagne mari-
'Gard donc c'est par rap- port t'es-
2- Jeunes filles de la cam- pagne mari-
La femme est mal- her- reuse mais
3- Jeunes filles de la cam- pagne mari-
C'est pas la peine dire "Non!"; I'vont

ez vous- aut' ja- mais. 'Gar- dez quoi moi j'ai
saies à les aim- er! J'connais donc d'êt' mu- si-
ez vous- aut' ja- mais. 'Gar- dez comme moi j'ai
les en- fants est plus. 'Garde donc comme c'est misé-
ez vous- aut' ja- mais. Jeune fille c'est une amu-
tou- jours te condam- ner, I'vont t'faire les ai- mer,

fait... mis une femme dans l'em- ba- ras.
cien, ça paye- ra pas comme ça!
fait, j'm'ai mis dans les mi- sères.
rab'e d'les voir à la train comme ça!
sette; 'garde donc, com- ment j'va' faire?
chère, I'vont tou- jours t'con- dam- ner.

Country Gentlemen

(1)
Young country girls, don't ever get married. Look what I've done, put a woman in trouble.
Look, it's because you try to love them; I know, being a musician, it won't pay that way.
(2)
Young country girls, don't ever get married. Look what I've done, got myself in trouble.
The wife is unhappy, but the children are even more unhappy.
Look how miserable it is, to see them scattered around like that.
(3)
Young country girls, don't ever get married. A young girl is an amusement; look, what will I do?
It's useless to say "No!"; they will still condemn you.
They'll make you love them, dear, they'll still condemn you.

Couche-couche Après Brûler

(1)
Mon nèg' est pas arrivé, couche-couche après brûler,
Caillette est pas tiré, va voir quelle heure il est.
(2)
Soleil est proche couché, couche-couche après brûler,
Caillette est pas tiré, va voir quelle heure il est.

Couche-couche is Burning

(1)
My lover has not arrived, the couche-couche is burning,
Caillette (spotted cow) is not milked, go see what time it is.
(2)
The sun is almost down, the couche-couche is burning,
Caillette (spotted cow) is not milked, go see what time it is.

Sur le Courtableau

Key. G
Pattern. Accordion: two Turns; Vocal #1; Steel Guitar:
two Turns; Violin: two Turns; Accordion: two Turns;
Vocal #2; Accordion: two Turns. There is no reason
why an instrument could not have played the vocal tune
in this song, too.

Version. Nathan Abshire (©Flat Town).

Nathan spoofs about the boiled frogs (we fry
'em) and fiddler or sand crabs, but boiled
crawfish is standard Cajun fare. Bayou
Courtableau is a bayou in St. Landry Parish
and was an early waterway to Washington,
Louisiana, from the Atchafalaya River. The
bayou was named for Jacques Courtableau
who owned land in this area in the late 1700's.

On the Courtableau

(1)
We're going on the Courtableau, little one, to gather some wood-chips,
wow, to make some fire, baby, to boil some crawfish.
We're going on the Courtableau, little one, to gather some wood-chips,
wow, to make some fire, baby, to boil some fiddler crabs.
(2)
We're going on the Courtableau, little one, to gather some wood-chips,
wow, to make some fire, baby, to boil some bullfrogs.
We're going on the Courtableau, little one, to gather some wood-chips,
wow, to make some fire, baby, to boil some fiddler crabs.

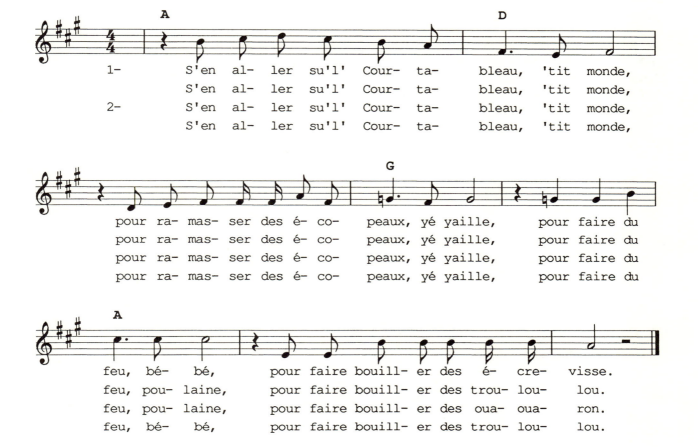

1- S'en al- ler su'l' Cour- ta- bleau, 'tit monde,
   S'en al- ler su'l' Cour- ta- bleau, 'tit monde,
2- S'en al- ler su'l' Cour- ta- bleau, 'tit monde,
   S'en al- ler su'l' Cour- ta- bleau, 'tit monde,

pour ra- mas- ser des é- co- peaux, yé yaille, pour faire du
pour ra- mas- ser des é- co- peaux, yé yaille, pour faire du
pour ra- mas- ser des é- co- peaux, yé yaille, pour faire du
pour ra- mas- ser des é- co- peaux, yé yaille, pour faire du

feu, bé- bé, pour faire bouill- er des é- cre- visse.
feu, pou- laine, pour faire bouill- er des trou- lou- lou.
feu, pou- laine, pour faire bouill- er des oua- oua- ron.
feu, bé- bé, pour faire bouill- er des trou- lou- lou.

Courville Breakdown

Key. F
Pattern. Violin: two Tunes and two Turns, etc.
Rhythm. The bass consists of four quarter notes per measure.

Version. Dennis McGee and Sady Courville (©Flat Town).

This piece has no vocal.

I was successful with my music. It wasn't that it was so good, but it was some old music that no one had heard before. Yes, the breakdowns and the reels and all that, the contredanses. *There's a lot of people who had never heard that. Courville and I can play the breakdowns and the reels like the fellows in Arkansas. [I learned them from] Arville Courville, the one who played jigs for his mother to dance. That's all he would play, the old dances:*

contredanses, *reels, breakdowns, square dances, things like that. The waltzes, polkas, mazurkas, Jim Crows ... These are all dances I've played and can play. A Jim Crow was a dance for old timers. They would jump from one side to the other. The men and the women would jump together, like a toad! Yes, it was a strange dance but it was pretty for those who knew how to dance it. The polka and mazurka were the same, you had to know how to dance for them to be pretty.*

—Dennis McGee

Valse de Courville et McGee

Key. G
Pattern. Violins: three Turns and two Tunes, etc.

Version. Dennis McGee and Sady Courville (MS).

This instrumental is named for Sady Courville and Dennis McGee, violin partners who recorded this song.

My father and his brother Arville were both violin players who learned the music from their mother, my maternal grandmother, who was a Frugé. Her family were all musicians and she knew the tunes her brother played. She'd sing these folk tunes to my father and brother. These folk tunes were brought here by the Cajuns back in the late 1700's. My father and Uncle Arville started playing twin violins when they were young boys. They were very popular because they were good musicians.

I guess it was a gift that I had in music, that I learned that music, nobody showing me anything. All my daddy had showed me was how to hit the strings with a couple of sticks when I

was a child. I guess I play the second fiddle better than I play the melody, because I've practiced bassing all the time. My father was a second fiddler, too; when he and his brother would play, that's what he played all the time...

People used to make fun of me and other Cajuns who played Cajun music. That was the reason that you won't find my name on some of the records Dennis McGee and I made. They asked me why I didn't want my name on those records. I said, "Because people are making fun of me and I want to try and better myself." But, I am for the program of Cajun culture. Then, the last number we made, I let them put on there Courville and McGee Waltz. *That's the only record my name was on.*
— Sady Courville

Crapaud

Key. G
Pattern. Violin: two Tunes and two Turns, etc.

Version. Dennis McGee (thanks to Jeanie McLerie Keppeler and Ken Keppeler).

I want to tell you where I was born and raised, a place called Crapaudville! You talk about a big village! You should've seen that! There was a school house and a store: Crapaudville. My father went to Texas to visit someone he knew and brought back a horned toad. He had put that in a shoebox and then he went on a picnic for a Fourth of July celebration, a big picnic in Elton under the big oak trees. All the family gathered there once a year. So, he had brought his toad in his box and was charging ten cents to those who wanted to see it.

My father's nickname was Nook, so from then on they called him Nook Crapaud. He owned

that little store, that's where I was born, right there at the old place. He had the store right there next to the house ... That's how Crapaudville was born, but there's nothing there now. It was all broken up, the houses and the school are no longer there. The store isn't there, it's just a main highway now. When I was there, it was just an old dirt road. It was boggy, boggy, boggy! You could hardly pass there with a model-T when it rained. It was necessary to put chains on the wheels. Now, today, you can go a hundred miles per hour on that highway. That highway goes straight to Pine Island.
— Preston Manuel

Creole Stomp

Key. G
Pattern. Accordion: two Tunes and one Turn; Steel Guitar: two Turns; Violins: two Turns; Accordion: two Turns and two Tunes.
Rhythm. Bass for the tune is the usual "quarter note-quarter rest method" but for the turn, straight eighth notes are often used.

Version. Aldus Roger (©La Lou).
Related songs. Also: *Lewisburg Two-Step* (Reggie Matte); *Louisiana Ace's Special* (Elias Badeaux); *Church Point Two-Step* (Ambrose Thibodeaux); *Galop Créole* (Merlin Fontenot).

This instrumental has many variations and is frequently used as a theme song by Cajun bands.

At the age of sixteen, when I started playing house dances, the hat was passed around to collect money for the musicians. We usually picked up a dollar and a half, two dollars. That was a lot of money then; cotton sold for one and a half or two cents a pound. It took a large bale of cotton to bring in twenty-five dollars. Now you know it was rough, eh? You had credit for one year at the store for twenty-five or thirty dollars. You could buy half a calf at the butcher shop for fifteen dollars, and a larger calf would sell for almost thirty dollars. You can see how cheap things were ...

Usually groups stayed together for a much longer time. Yes, you stayed a long time with a group and you wouldn't make as much money as today. Now, if a musician is offered three or four dollars more, he will leave and play with another band.
— Aldus Roger

I started playing house dances when I was about sixteen years old, just with the accordion and triangles or spoons. This was before we had electricity in our neighborhood. We had house dances every week. Young people would go around on horseback to invite others. No automobiles! Young and old people would come to the dances which were played at night. Sometimes the weather would be very hot. The old ladies were always watching the young girls. They couldn't go out with a boy, it wasn't like it is today.
— Allie Young

Valse Créole

Key. G
Pattern. Violin: play whole song as written

Version. Varise Connor.

The lyrics have been forgotten if ever there were any. *Créole* originally meant those born in the colony, to distinguish them from those born elsewhere. The term evolved to include vegetable and animals developed here, such as Creole tomatoes and ponies. Eventually Creole took on the connotation of "the best."

Valse de Crève de Faim

Key. D minor
Pattern. Violin: one Tune; Vocals #1 & 2; Violin: one Tune; Vocals #3 & 4; Violin: one Tune.

Version. Hobo Bertrand (©Tek).
Related song. Also: *Working Blues* (Leopold François).

This is one of my favorite songs.

This old song is really a blues, but "Hobo" Bertrand's version, with its faster tempo, can be danced like a waltz. I have seldom played this song at dances, because of the minor chords, but I taught it in a workshop at Ashokan, New York, and musical groups from Massachusetts and Florida have requested the words. With Jimmy Gaspard on guitar, I also recorded it for the theme song of a Canadian film, *La Butte de Coquille*, which was made in Louisiana.

The words my father learned for the Working Blues are:

C'est l' pipe et l' tabac et la sueur d'un maudit nèg';
Mais laissez-moi vous dire mais une chose.
C'est pas ça qui sent l'odeur de ma belle.

After integration *maudit nèg'* was replaced by *vieux mulet.*

It's the pipe and tobacco and sweat of an old mule.
But let me tell you one thing.
That doesn't smell like my sweetheart.

The Starvation Waltz

(1)
You took me to travel, to travel in the big woods to combat misery and cry of starvation.
(2)
I passed in front of the door, in front of your father's door.
Your father was sitting under a tree whittling away misery and crying of starvation.
(3)
I passed in front of the door, in front of your mother's door.
Your mother was sitting on the porch talking idly and crying of starvation.
(4)
I passed in front of the door, in front of the door of your house;
I was in my buggy traveling with my big top-hat.

Valse Criminelle

Key. G
Pattern. Accordion: two Tunes; Vocal #1; Violin: two
Tunes; Accordion: two turns; Vocal #2; Violin: two
Tunes; Accordion: two Turns and two Tunes.

Version. Mayuse LaFleur, vocal, and Leo Soileau
(Vi).

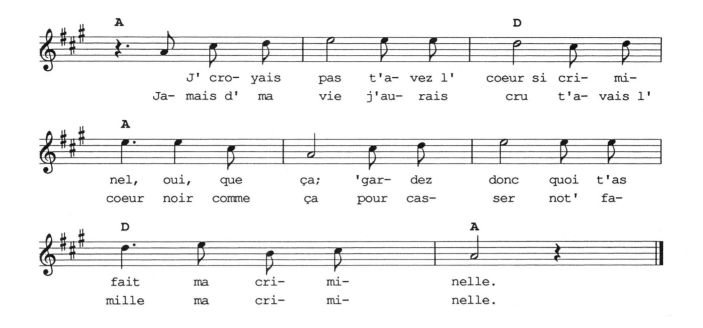

J' cro- yais   pas   t'a- vez l'   coeur si cri- mi-
Ja- mais d' ma   vie   j'au- rais   cru   t'a- vais l'

nel, oui, que   ça; 'gar- dez   donc quoi t'as
coeur noir comme ça   pour cas-   ser   not' fa-

fait ma cri- mi-   nelle.
mille ma cri- mi-   nelle.

Criminal Waltz

(1)
I didn't think you had a criminal heart like that.
Look what you've done, my criminal.

(2)
Never in my life would I have believed you had a heart
as black as that, to break up our family, my criminal.

Two-Step de Criminelle

Key. C
Pattern. Accordion: Part 1 and Part 2; Vocal #1; Steel
Guitar: Part 1 twice; Accordion: Part 1 and Part 2;
Vocal #2; Steel Guitar: Part 1 twice; Accordion: Part 1.

Version. Sidney Brown (©Tek).

Criminal Two-Step

(1)
Oh you, little girl, come meet me alone, doll, me alone in misery.
I don't know how I'll manage, dear rosy cheeks, not knowing where you are. My criminal!
(2)
Oh I'm alone; I'm so lonesome! I don't see how I'll manage in the house, crying.
I don't have any news from you, dear doll. Come meet me in misery.

1- Oh mais toi, 'tite fille, viens me r'-
2- Oh j'su' moi tout seul; comment j'm'en-

join' moi tout seul, ca- tin, moi tout
nuie! Moi j' vois pas comment j'va' faire moi tout

seul dans les mi- sères. Moi j' con- nais pas com- ment
seul dans la mai- son a- près pleu- rer. J'ai p'us d'

j'va' faire, chère joues roses, pas d' con- naît' et où toi
nou- velles ouais de toi, chère ca- tin. Viens me r'-

t'es. Ma crim- in- elle!
join' dans les mi- sères.

Crowley Two-Step

Key. D
Pattern. Accordion: two Tunes and two Turns; Steel
Guitar: two Tunes; Violin: two Turns; Accordion: two
Tunes and two Turns; etc.

Many variations are possible. This song is
often used as a band's theme song.

Dansez, Codinne

Key. D
Pattern. Violin: Tune and Turn twice; Vocal: once;
Guitar or other instrument: One Tune and Turn; Violin:
one Tune and Turn; Vocal: once; Guitar or other in-
strument: one Tune and Turn; Violin: one Tune and
Turn; Vocal: once; Violin: one Tune and Turn.

Version. Raymond François.

Macaque, the name of the violinist in this
song, is still used as a nickname, but I haven't
heard the name Codinne used except in this
song. This song, which I believe is quite old, is
rarely played in the dance halls; it has almost
been forgotten because of the tricky bass
which I've included. This song is compli-
mentary to the Cajun cuisine.

chose qu'est bon c'est qu'que chose qu'est doux. Du pi- ment

en bas l' queue pois- son c'est qu'que

chose qu'est bon c'est qu'que chose qu'est doux.

Dance, Codinne

Dance, Codinne! Dance, Codinne! It's Monkey who's playing the violin.
Dance, Codinne! Dance, Codinne! It's Monkey who's playing the violin.
Some pepper below the fish's tail is something good, something sweet.
Some pepper below the fish's tail is something good, something sweet.

Demain C'est Pas Dimanche

Key. G
Pattern. Violin: two Tunes; Vocal #1; Violin: one Tune; Vocal #2; Violin: play rest of Tune; Vocal #3; play rest of Tune then play two Tunes an octave higher in second position using the E string; Vocal #4; Violin: one Tune; Vocal #5; Violin: one Tune; Vocal #6; Violin: play rest of Tune; Vocal #7; Violin: one Tune then play two Tunes an octave higher in second position using the E string; Vocal #8; one Tune.

Version. Leo Soileau (OT).
Related song. Also: *Rosa, Demain C'est pas Dimanche* (Dennis McGee).

There is no Turn in this song. Create your own version for the instrumental using the vocal as a guide.

My dad told me Leo Soileau was criticized for the poor French used in his songs, which makes it hard to tell what he is singing sometimes. The phrase in the sixth vocal which I hear as *J'aurais l' malheure* has been interpreted in various other ways, such as *Jody, my love* and *Jurez, my Lord.* The last two words of the fourth vocal should be *Adieu, Rosa* instead of *Jo-jo Rosa.*

Moïse Robin played bass on the accordion in Leo Soileau's 1929 recording of this song.

We went to Frank Dietlein, a newspaper columnist in Opelousas, to take us over there to Richmond, Indiana, to make the record. We were in a hotel there at night and they wanted to play a farce *("trick") on me. You see, I had never been on a long trip like that; I had always been raised in the country. When we arrived at the hotel, Leo Soileau and Dietlein arranged a plot. Leo knew a man in Léonville that I'd spoken of, John Spy, who had a store and was a friend of mine. Leo went in another room next door. Dietlein stayed on this side with me to answer the telephone. When Leo called, Dietlein answered the phone and said, "Moïse, it's for you." I said, "Hello! Who's talking?" Leo answered, "This is John Spy from Léonville. How are you doing over there?" I replied, "It's good! It's good!" They started laughing and I found out it was Leo who was calling instead of John Spy.*

When we left Richmond, to come back to Opelousas, it was on an old time coal-burning locomotive. They paid us over there to make the records. In those days they paid us twenty-five dollars and fifty dollars per record, which was a large sum at that time. When they paid us, Leo drank over there and ate all the way back, renting a place to sleep, but I saved my money. It took twenty-four hours to make the trip. I didn't sleep; I just stayed sitting in my seat. I didn't want to spend a nickle! I didn't want to eat either; I kept my money. When I came back, I bought myself a little car with the money. I had fifty dollars to use as a down payment on a model-T Ford.

After this record was made, people looked for trouble with me. I had to say that I didn't sing that song. It was Leo Soileau who had made that record and I was playing with him. I had to follow him, therefore they were looking for trouble with me and they were angry with me. They were disturbed over this a long time before I could make them understand. Then, one day, Father LaChapel, the priest of Léonville heard that particular record. He happened to ask Arthur Stelly, who had a grocery store in Léonville, "Who sang that? Who made that record?" Arthur Stelly said, "It's Moïse Robin." The priest said, Moïse Robin? Non! C'est le bourriquet à Joe Robin. ("Moïse Robin? No! It's Joe Robin's jackass." Joe was Moïse's father.) The priest was angry and said it wasn't something to sing. I was carrying all the blame; everybody thought I had sung in the recording ...[Leo Soileau] was over there in Ville Platte, you see, and I was over here among my own people. When the record was played among my own people, I was blamed for it. They accused me of having made that record.

— Moïse Robin

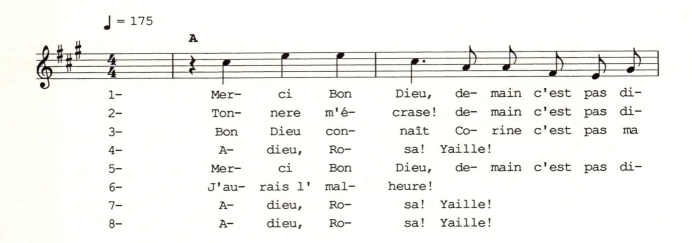

1-   Mer- ci Bon Dieu, de- main c'est pas di-
2-   Ton- nere m'é- crase! de- main c'est pas di-
3-   Bon Dieu con- naît Co- rine c'est pas ma
4-   A- dieu, Ro- sa! Yaille!
5-   Mer- ci Bon Dieu, de- main c'est pas di-
6-   J'au- rais l' mal- heure!
7-   A- dieu, Ro- sa! Yaille!
8-   A- dieu, Ro- sa! Yaille!

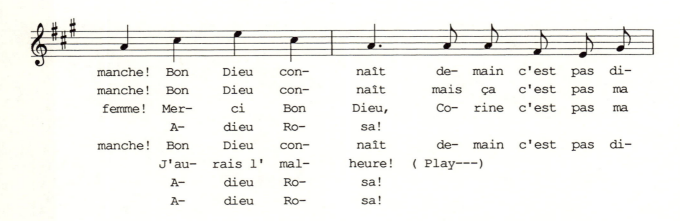

manche! Bon Dieu con- naît de- main c'est pas dimanche! Bon Dieu con- naît mais ça c'est pas ma
femme! Mer- ci Bon Dieu, Co- rine c'est pas ma
    A- dieu Ro- sa!
manche! Bon Dieu con- naît de- main c'est pas di-
    J'au- rais l' mal- heure! (Play---)
    A- dieu Ro- sa!
    A- dieu Ro- sa!

manche! Ton- nerre m'é- crase! De- main c'est pas di-
femme! (Play---)
femme! (Play---)
    J'au- rais l' mal- heure, "lord!"
manche! Ton- nerre m'é- crase!

    Bon Dieu con- naît de- main c'est pas di-
    Ton- nerre m'é- crase! Ro- sa c'est pas ma

manche! Mer- ci   Bon   Dieu!

A- dieu, Ro-   sa!

Co- rine c'est pas ma   femme!

manche! Mer- ci   Bon   Dieu!
femme! Mer- ci   Bon   Dieu, Ro- sa c'est pas ma   femme!

Tomorrow isn't Sunday

(1)
Thank God tomorrow isn't Sunday! The good Lord knows tomorrow isn't Sunday!
May the thunder smash me! Tomorrow isn't Sunday! Thank God!
(2)
May the thunder smash me! Tomorrow isn't Sunday! The good Lord knows that's not my wife!
(3)
The good Lord knows Corine's not my wife! Thank God Corine's not my wife!
(4)
Farewell, Rosa! Ouch! Farewell, Rosa! I would be so unlucky, Lord. Farewell, Rosa!
(5)
Thank God tomorrow isn't Sunday. The good Lord knows tomorrow isn't Sunday!
May the thunder crush me! I know that's not my wife!
(6)
I'd be so unlucky! I'd be so unlucky!
(7)
Farewell, Rosa! Ouch! Farewell, Rosa! The good Lord knows tomorrow isn't Sunday! Thank God!
(8)
Farewell, Rosa! Ouch! Farewell, Rosa! May the thunder smash me!
Rosa's not my wife! Thank God Rosa's not my wife!

Rosa, Demain C'est Pas Dimanche

Key. C
Pattern. Violin: play 1st and 2nd parts. Vocal #1.
Violin: play 1st and 2nd parts. Vocal #2. Violin: play
1st and 2nd parts.

Version: Dennis McGee (©Flat Town).
Related song. See: *Demain C'est Pas Dimanche* (Leo
Soileau and Moïse Robin, 1929). Dennis recorded
this version in the '70's.

The tune and tempo are influenced by early
Zydeco music. Amédé Ardoin, who played
accordion with Dennis, used many of his own
songs in the dances they played. Also see my
notes for the previous song.

Rosa, Tomorrow isn't Sunday

(1 & 2)
Farewell, Rosa! Thank God, Rosa's not my sister! Farewell, Rosa!
Thank God, tomorrow isn't Sunday! I'd be so unfortunate!

(1) & (2) A- dieu Ro-   sa!   Mer- ci, bon

Dieu,   Ro- sa ç'est pas ma   soeur!

A- dieu, Ro-   sa!   Mer- ci, bon

Dieu,   de- main ç'est pas di- manche!

J'au- rais l' mal- heure!

Devillier Two-Step

Key. C
Pattern. Violin: two Turns; Vocal #1; Violin: two
Turns, two tunes and one Turn; Vocal #2; etc.

Version. Dennis McGee (©Flat Town).
Related songs. Also: *Don't Bury Me*; *The Cemetery*;
Enterre-moi Pas; *Enterre-moi Pas dans l'Cimetière*.

Devillier is a family name.

Devillier Two-Step

(1)
Little girl, when I die, bury me under the bed. Cry for someone, someone who will love you!
Oh, pretty girl! Dear pretty one! Oh, don't do that! Little girl, that hurts me!
(2)
Hey, little girl! Dear, don't forget me! Hey, bad-mannered girl, that hurts me!
Oh, pretty girl, why are you like that? Dear, you're leaving me, little girl, in misery!

1-   'Tite   fille,   quand va' mou-   rir,   enterre
            Oh,   jo-   lie   fille!
2-   Hé,   pe-   tite   fille!
            Oh,   jo-   lie   fille, quo'-

moi   en   bâs   du   lit.   Pleure   pour   que'
Cher   jo-   li   monde!   Oh,   fais   pas
Chère, ou- blie   moi   pas!   Hé,   vilaines ma-
faire mais t'es   comme   ça?   Chère, t'es a- près m' quit-

un,   que'   un   qui   va t'ai-   mer!
ça!   'Tite   fille, ça m' fait   du   mal!
nières,   ça m'   fais   du   mal   à   moi!
ter,   'tite   fille, dans les   mi-   sères!

Donnez-moi Mon Chapeau

Key. G
Pattern. Accordion: two Tunes; Vocal #1; Violin: two
Tunes; Accordion: one Turn; Vocal #2; Violin: two
Tunes; Accordion: one Turn and two Tunes.

Version. Gervais Quibodeaux, first vocal (©La Lou);
Iry LeJeune, second vocal (©Tek).
Related songs. Also: *Attrape-moi, Je Tombe* (Leo
Soileau-1935); *La Valse de la Rosa* (Leo Soileau);
Attrapez-moi Mon Chapeau.

In this version, the lover is ready to go when
he hears his sweetheart's parents fussing.

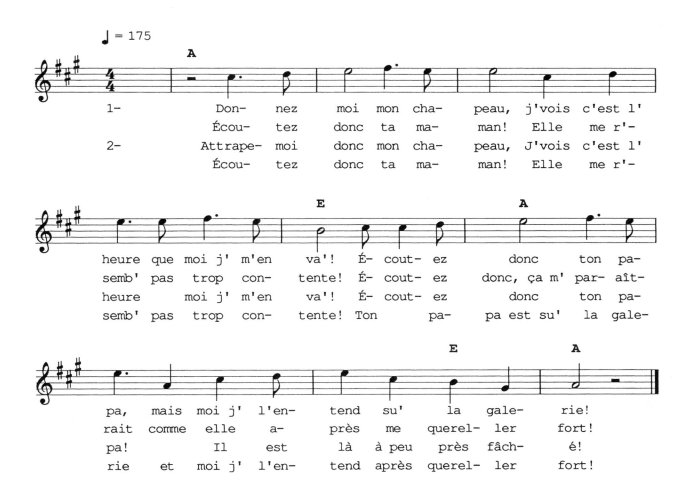

Give Me my Hat

(1)
Give me my hat, I see it's time for me to go!
Listen to your papa, I hear him on the porch!
Listen to your mama! She doesn't seem too happy!
Listen, it seems like she's fussing loudly at me!
(2)
Get my hat, I see it's time for me to go!
Listen to your papa! He is there very angry!
Listen to your mama! She doesn't seem too happy!
Your papa is on the porch and I hear him fussing loudly!

Drunkard's Waltz

Key. A
Pattern. Violin: two Tunes and two Turns; Vocal #1;
Violin: two Tunes and two Turns; Vocal #2; Violin: two
Tunes and two Turns.

Version. Chuck Guillory.
Related song. See: *La Valse d'Ennui* (Aldus Roger
and Phillip Alleman).

Drunkard's Waltz

(1 & 2)
Hey, pretty girl, you said you couldn't love me anymore.
Hey, pretty girl, I took it so hard, I'm going to go get drunk.

Valse de Durald

Key. G
Pattern. Violin: one Tune; Vocal #1; Violin: three Tunes; Vocal #2; two Tunes; Vocal #3; Violin: one Tune.

Version. Iry LeJeune, vocal, and Wilson Granger, violin (©Tek). Raymond François (second instrumental).
Related songs. Also: Duraldo Waltz (Iry LeJeune); Duralder Waltz.

Durald Waltz

(1)
Say goodbye to your dad and your mom, unhappy one, and come meet me in Big Durald.
You had promised, made promises to come meet me, doll. Soon, I'll see you coming back to me.
(2)
For a time you thought your family would always take up for you when you made me leave, my dear.
Thinking clearly, you can see for yourself that all the grief we are causing ourselves doesn't help.
(3)
It's too late for the children to come back and complain for you. You're the one who made the big mistake.
You told me, you, baby, that you never wanted to see me again. It's too late! You'll come back, maybe some day.

Valse de Duson

Key. G
Pattern. Accordion: two Tunes; Vocal #1; Steel Guitar: two Turns; Violin: two Tunes; Accordion: two Turns; Vocal #2; Steel Guitar: two Turns; Violin: two Tunes; Accordion: two Tunes and one Turn.

Version. Don Guillory, vocal, and Aldus Roger, accordion (©Tek).
Related songs. See: *Valse de Bayou Chêne* (Iry LeJeune). Also: *La Valse qui m' Fait du Mal* (Lawrence Walker).

Duson is the name of a town west of Lafayette, Louisiana. The town was named for a Saint Landry Parish sheriff, C.C. Duson, who was involved bringing the railroad to southwest Louisiana and in laying out the town of Duson and selling tracts.

Duson Waltz

(1)
Oh, little one, I'd like for you to come back just one more time before death.
Oh, doll, it's no use for me to be lonesome for you; I know, dear little girl, why you're like that.
(2)
Hey pretty one, I traveled the four corners of the earth trying to find you again.
Oh, little one, some day you'll notice all what you said not long ago. What will I do?

Embrasse-moi Encore

Key. D
Pattern. Violin: three Tunes; Vocal #1; Violin: one Tune and two Turns; Vocal #2; Violin: one Tune and two Turns; Vocal #3; Violin: one Tune and one Turn.

Version. Leo Soileau (OT).
Related songs. Also: *Mets ta Robe Barrée*; *Robe à Parasol*; *Madame Étienne*.

I have not included the vocals because of related songs, which I believe are older.

Valse d'Evangeline

Key. G
Pattern. Accordion: one Tune; Vocal #1 (two Tunes and one Turn); Steel Guitar: one Turn; Vocal #2 (two Tunes and one Turn); Accordion: one Tune; Vocal #3 (two Tunes); Accordion: one Tune.

Version. Lawrence Walker (©La Lou).
Related songs . Also: *Quand Je Suis Bleu* (Leo Soileau, 1935); *Valse du Grand Chênier* (Jimmy Newman); *Cajun Bandstand* (Johnny Janot).

The tune reminds me of Dewey Balfa's *Drunkard's Sorrow Waltz* or *La Valse de Bamboche.* Lawrence Walker's arrangement is a little more complicated than usual because he sings the turn.

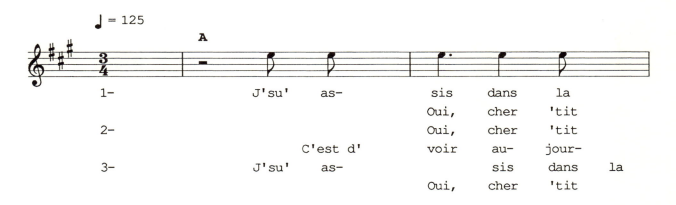

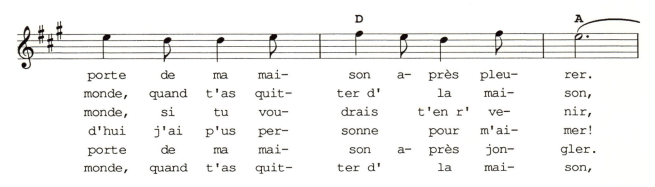

coeur   me   fais   mal.   J'ai   p'us   per-   sonne   à   la   mai-

chère   'tit   bé-   bé!   J'ai   p'us   per-   sonne   à   la   mai-

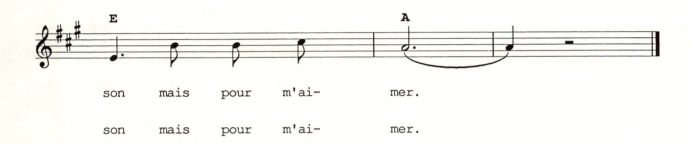

son   mais   pour   m'ai-   mer.

son   mais   pour   m'ai-   mer.

Evangeline Waltz

(1)
I'm sitting in the doorway of my home crying. I'm crying for you to come back to rejoin your lover.
Yes, dear little one, when you left home, you told me that you couldn't love me.
(Turn) Oh, it hurts! My heart hurts me. I have no one at home to love me.
(2)
Yes, dear little one, if you'd want to come back, I'd pardon you for all that you've done to me.
See, today, I have no one to love me. I'm all alone dying in sadness.
(Turn) Oh, baby, my dear little baby! I've no one at home to love me.
(3)
I'm sitting in the doorway of my home wondering. I'm wondering if you'll ever come back.
Yes, dear little one, when you left home, you told me that you couldn't love me.

Faire l'Amour dans l' Poulailler

Key. A
Pattern. Steel Guitar: short introduction; Vocal #1;
Steel Guitar: one tune similar to vocal tune with a
break; Vocal #2; Steel Guitar: one tune to finish. Any
other lead instruments can also be used.
Rhythm. The double rests, except the last pair, can be
filled with a repetition of the previous phrase.

Version. Raymond Tauzin (©Flat Town).

Birouette and *bourouette* are Cajun French forms of the standard French *brouette* "wheelbarrow". We also sing *et fumer en bas l' wagon* instead of *et fumer su' l' palonnier*. *Fumer* has a double meaning. *Palonnier* used here means the long, thick single-tree attached to the base of a wagon tongue, which is connected to the center of the front axel. It was common to go to the barn where the wagon was kept when people didn't have an outhouse or wanted privacy.

There are several other old songs whose words include insults and innuendos. They weren't recorded until after World War II; earlier, the musicians would have received too much criticism. This sense of humor makes me think of some of the stories I've heard about jokes that people used to play on one another.

In the old times they didn't have clubs like we have now, they had to make house dances. Mom and Dad had a house and they had pigs behind the house. The fence was attached to *both sides of the house and the hogs were in back of the house. So my dad made a little dance there, he was playing the violin. I don't know who else was playing, I wasn't even born. My daddy told me this.*

There was a wooden water bucket with a long handled drinking cup. My mama had two buckets like that. What the people did! They went and cut off all my father's pigs' tails and put them in the water buckets. The only light that they had was from old coal oil lamps, two or three lamps, that's all they had in her house. People would go drink water and they never did notice because they couldn't see inside the buckets. When the cup didn't want to go down far enough to fill it, my mother came and saw all the pig tails in the bottom of the bucket. Daddy couldn't find the pigs anywhere, they were hiding all over. They didn't have any more tails! They had cut them, all their tails! No one knew who had done this.

— Bernice Roger

1-   Faire l'a- mour dans   l'pou- laill- er
            Faire l'a- mour dans   l'pou- laill- er
            Faire l'a- mour dans   l'pou- laill- er
2-   Faire l'a- mour dans   l'pou- laill- er
            Faire l'a- mour dans   l'pou- laill- er
            Faire l'a- mour dans   l'pou- laill- er
            Faire l'a- mour dans   l'pou- laill- er

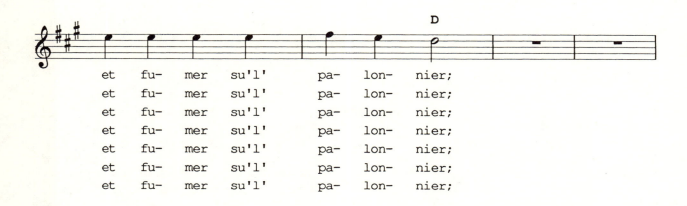

et   fu- mer su'l'   pa- lon- nier;
et   fu- mer su'l'   pa- lon- nier;
et   fu- mer su'l'   pa- lon- nier;
et   fu- mer su'l'   pa- lon- nier;
et   fu- mer su'l'   pa- lon- nier;
et   fu- mer su'l'   pa- lon- nier;
et   fu- mer su'l'   pa- lon- nier;

ma   gran' mère a fait   une   pi-   rouette,
mon grand- père il a   cassé ces   veines
c'est la   fille à   nonc' Hi-   laire
ma   grand' mère a fait   une   pi-   rouette,
mon grand- père il a   fait une pi- rouette,
c'est la   fille à   nonc' É-   douard
c'est la   fille à   nonc' Hi-   laire

elle   a   tom-   bé   dans   la   bi-   rouette.
a- près   cour-   ser   ma'm' selle   Mar-   tin.
qu'a   cro-   chi   ma   'tite   cuill-   ière.
elle   a   tom-   bé   dans   la   bi-   rouette.
il   a   tom-   bé   dans   la   bi-   rouette.
qu'a   frot-   té   mon   'tit   frot-   toir.
qu'a   tou-   ché   ma   'tite   cuill-   ière.

Making Love in the Chicken Coop (Hen house)

(1)
Making love in the hen house and "smoking" on the single-tree;
my grandmother did a pirouette, she fell in the wheelbarrow.
Making love in the hen house and "smoking" on the single-tree;
my grandfather broke his veins chasing Miss Martin.
Making love in the hen house and "smoking" on the single-tree;
it's Uncle Hilaire's daughter who bent my little spoon.
(2)
Making love in the hen house and "smoking" on the single-tree;
my grandmother made a pirouette, she fell in the wheelbarrow.
Making love in the hen house and "smoking" on the single-tree;
my grandfather made a pirouette, he fell in the wheelbarrow.
Making love in the hen house and "smoking" on the single-tree;
it's Uncle Édouard's daughter who rubbed my little washboard.
Making love in the hen house and "smoking" on the single-tree;
it's Uncle Hilaire's daughter who touched my little spoon.

Faire l'Amour dans les Rangs d' Coton

Key. D
Pattern. Violin: last nine bars; Vocal #1; Steel Guitar: last nine bars; Vocal #2; Piano: last nine bars; Vocal #3; Violin: last nine bars.

Version. Dunice P. Theriot (©Flat Town).

Vatican is a town northwest of Lafayette.
Jeanerette is southeast of New Iberia.

Cotton Rows

(1)
Making love in the cotton rows and "smoking" under the wagon;
teasing my little girl-cousin, who's leaning on her little thin legs.
My grandfather broke his veins chasing the old whores;
he thought he could still make love in the cotton rows.
(2)
My grandmother scratched her bottom trying it in the wheelbarrow;
she thought that it was so good making love in the cotton rows.
Yes, my mother had whipped me after she had caught me;
that's the night she made me sleep with the chickens in the chicken coop.
(3)
Yes, the girls from Lafayette had broken his "rated-X;"
they didn't want him to make love anymore with the girls from Jeanerette.
It's the girls from Vatican who had broken his little sticker;
they didn't want him to make love anymore with the girls in the cotton rows.
Making love in the cotton rows and "smoking" under the wagon;
I'll never forget making love in the cotton rows.

1- C'est faire l'a- mour dans les rangs d'co-
2- Ma grand' mère a 'gra- fi- gné ces
3- Ouais, les filles de "La- fa-

ton et fu- mer en bas l'wa- gon; ta- qui-
fesses après 'say- er dans la b'rou- ette; a' cro-
yette" avait cas- sé son "ra- ted X;" a' vou-

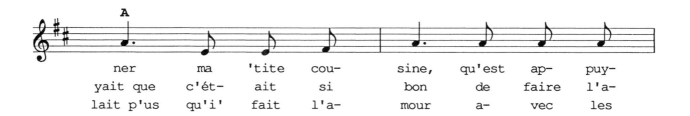

ner   ma   'tite   cou-   sine,   qu'est   ap-   puy-
yait que   c'ét-   ait   si   bon   de   faire   l'a-
lait p'us   qu'i'   fait   l'a-   mour   a-   vec   les

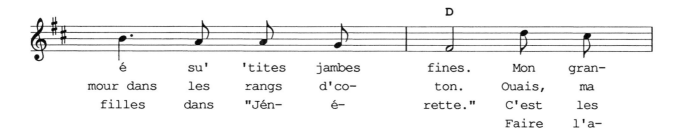

é   su'   'tites   jambes   fines.   Mon   gran-
mour dans   les   rangs   d'co-   ton.   Ouais,   ma
filles dans   "Jén-   é-   rette."   C'est   les
                                                                Faire   l'a-

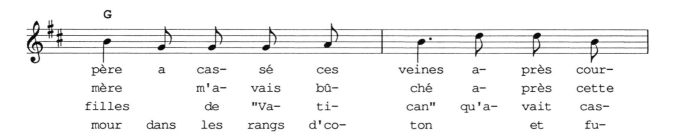

père   a   cas-   sé   ces   veines   a-   près   court-
mère   m'a-   vais   bû-   ché   a-   près   cette
filles   de   "Va-   ti-   can"   qu'a-   vait   cas-
mour   dans   les   rangs   d'co-   ton   et   fu-

ser   les   vieilles   pu-   tains;   I'   croy-   ait   i'   pou-   vait   tou-
vielle m'a-   vait   'tra-   pé;   c'est   ça   le   soir   qu'a   ma   mis   cou-
sé   son   'tit   pi-   quant;   ça   vo-   lait   p'us   qu'i   fait   l'a-
mer   en   bas   l'wa-   gon;   j'va'   ja-   mais   ou-   bli-

jours   faire   l'a-   mour   dans   les   rangs   d'co-   ton.
cher   a-   vec   les   poules   dans   le   pou-   laill-   er.
mour   a-   vec   les   filles   dans   les   rangs   d'co-   ton.
er   fair   l'a-   mour   dans   les   rangs   d'co-   ton.

Valse de Famille

Key. C
Pattern. Accordion: two Tunes; Vocal #1; Steel Guitar: two Tunes; Violins: two Tunes; Vocal #2; Accordion: one Tune. There is no turn in this song.

Version. Aldus Roger (©La Lou).
Related songs. Also: *Big Boy Waltz* (Iry LeJeune).

Family Waltz

(1)
Oh, I used to love you! It's your dad and mom ... for all that happened!
Oh, that hurts me when I see you pass with another at your side!
(2)
Oh, I abandoned my family just for you, little one, and today we don't get along!
Oh, it's not you I'm lonesome for, it's my dear child whom I love so much!

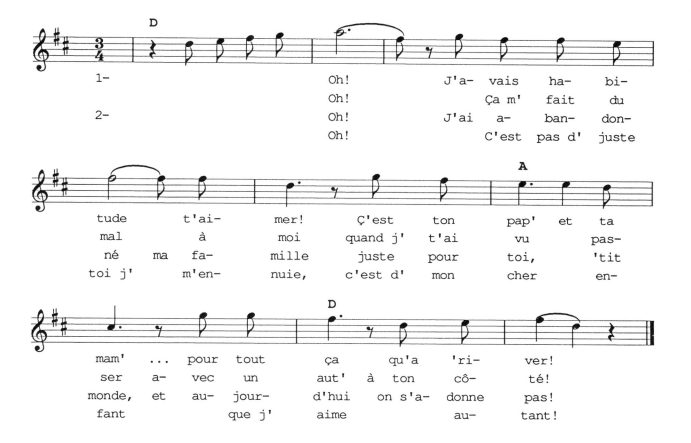

1-
2-

Oh!   J'a- vais ha- bi-
Oh!   Ça m' fait du
Oh!   J'ai a- ban- don-
Oh!   C'est pas d' juste

tude   t'ai- mer!   Ç'est   ton   pap' et ta
mal   à   moi   quand j' t'ai   vu   pas-
né   ma fa- mille   juste   pour   toi,   'tit
toi j'   m'en- nuie, c'est d' mon   cher   en-

mam' ... pour tout   ça   qu'a 'ri-   ver!
ser a- vec un   aut'   à ton cô-   té!
monde, et au- jour-   d'hui on s'a- donne pas!
fant   que j'   aime   au-   tant!

Fi Fi Poncho

Key. G

Version. Raymond François.

Pattern. Violin: one Tune (25 bars), one Turn (9 bars), etc.

Rhythm. The bass beat stays the same (quarter note, quarter rest, etc.) throughout the entire song. Notice the meter which is changed from 3/4 to 4/4 in this unusual two-step full of syncopation.

This is an instrumental. Accordion player Joseph Falcon first recorded this song.

Valse Qu'a Fini Dans l' Coin

Key. F

Version. Dennis McGee (©Flat Town).

Pattern. Violin: two Tunes, one Tune variation and two Turns. Repeat all and end with one Tune.

Rhythm. This is a *valse à deux temps*. It has two dotted quarter notes per measure for rhythm guitar. The bass pattern is: 1st measure, one dotted quarter rest and one dotted quarter note; 2nd measure, one dotted quarter note and one dotted quarter rest; 3rd measure, two dotted quarter notes. Repeat over until the end of the song.

Les Flammes d'Enfer

Key. G
Pattern. Accordion: two Tunes; Vocal #1; Guitar: two Tunes; Accordion: two Tunes; Vocal #2; Accordion: two Tunes. No Turns.

Version. Austin Pitre (©Flat Town).
Related songs. Also: *Two-Step à Tante Adèle* (Austin Pitre, 1960); *Flames Of Hades* (Aldus Roger). Change tempo to 175 for these two songs.

The voices he hears could be sung by another singer. This is a very simple tune but made complicated by its many possible variations within the framework of the chord structure. Austin recorded this song in 1959, but my mother says she heard the song played before she was married in 1922. Originally slow, the tempo has been changed into a faster one after *Flames of Hades* was recorded by Aldus Roger.

The Flames Of Hell

(1)
Oh, mother, you always said I'd cry.
"You killed your little Aunt! She was a young little girl; she was so beautiful! What did you do for a good time?
From what I've seen, you're condemned! You're condemned to the flames of hell."
Pray for me to save my soul. Save my soul from the flames of hell!
(2)
Oh mother, pray for me; I'm condemned to the flames of hell!
Who's at the door — "You killed little Aunt." — calling hello? Who's there?
"It's your nephew!" What do you want? Pray for me, I'm condemned!

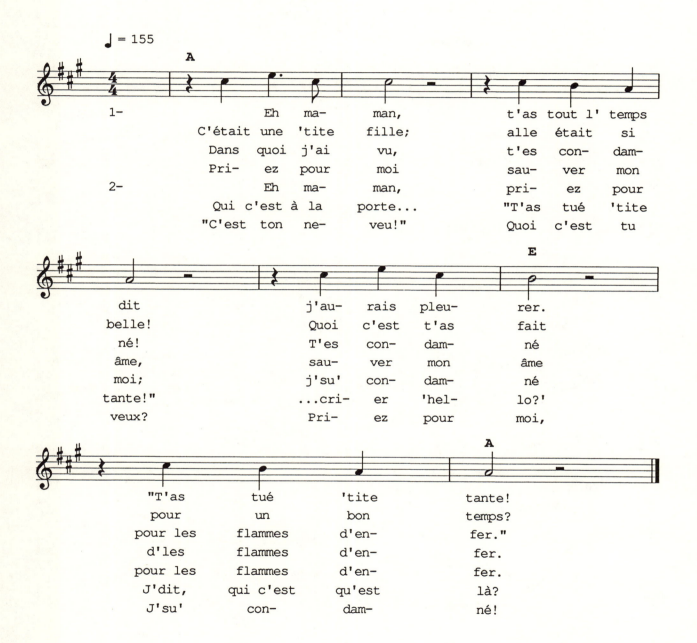

Fond d' Culotte Two-Step

Key. G
Pattern. Accordion: three Tunes; Steel Guitar: two Tunes; Violin: two Tunes; Accordion: two Turns; Steel Guitar: two Tunes; Violin: two Tunes; Accordion: two Tunes.

Version. Reggie Matte (first Tune and Turn); Sidney Brown (last Tune in manuscript, ©Flat Town)).

The Seat of the Pants Two-Step is an old instrumental. We still use the word *culotte* for pants.

Valse des Frugés

Key. G
Pattern. Violins: two Tunes and two Turns; Vocal #1; etc.

Version. Dennis McGee and Ernest Frugé (©Flat Town).
Related songs. Also: *Old Country Waltz*, but not the one Lawrence Walker recorded.

Go ahead and make your own words! This is a beautiful old tune and two violins sound nice. The original lyrics have probably been forgotten; Dennis sings this with strings of clichés, like *Dit 'bye-bye' à ton pap' et ta mam'* and *Tu m'as quitté pour t'en aller, malheureuse*.

Ernest Frugé was one of Dennis' violin partners.

Gabriel

Key. G
Pattern. Vocal#1 (1A-duet, 1B-solo, 1A-duet); Violins: two Tunes; Vocal #2 (2-solo, 1A-duet); Violins: one Tune; Vocal #3 (3-solo, 1A-duet); Violins: one Tune; Vocal #4 (1A-duet).

Version. Leroy "Happy Fats" LeBlanc and "Doc" Guidry (©Jamil); Moïse Robin.
Related songs. See: *Valse d'Amour I* (Austin Pitre). Also: *Valse d'Amour* (Leo Soileau).

The verses of *Les Maringouins Ont Tout Mangé Ma Belle* are also used with this tune.

Gabriel

(1-A)
Gabriel was my godfather and Madeline was my godmother;
Gabriel was no good and Madeline wasn't any better.
(1-B)
Gabriel had some good shoes and Madeline had a good hat.
Madeline had a good hat; it's a pity it had no lining. *(Repeat 1-A.)*
(2)
Madeline had a good hat and Gabriel had some good shoes.
Gabriel had some good shoes; it's a pity they were tennis shoes. *(Repeat 1-A.)*
(3)
Gabriel had some good shoes and Madeline had a good coat.
Madeline had a good coat; its a pity it was all torn up. *(Repeat 1-A.)*
(4) *(Repeat 1-A.)*

Another version of the words has been preserved by Moïse Robin:

(1)
Josephine is in her room and Anna is on the chamber pot.
Leon is watching and Caroline is very angry.
(2)
Uncle Adam broke all his veins chasing the women in the cotton rows
and then he finished his days by making love in the hen house.

1 (A) –   Ga-   bri-   el   c'é-   tait   mon   par-
  (B) –   Ga-   bri-   el a-   vait   des   bons   sou-
2-   Ma-   de-   leine a-   vait   un   bon   cha-
3-   Ga-   bri-   el a-   vait   des   bons   sou-
1-   C'est   Jos-   sé-   phine   qu'est   dans   sa
2-   C'est   nonc'   A-   dam qu'a   tout   cas-   sé   ces

rain   et   Ma-   de-   leine   c'é-   tait   ma   mar-
liers   et   Ma-   de-   leine a-   vait   un   bon   chapeau   et   Ga-   bri-   el a-   vait   des   bon   sou-
liers   et   Ma-   de-   leine a-   vait   un   bon   ca-
chamb'   et   An-   na   est   des-   sus l'   pot d'
veines à course-   aill-   er   les   femmes   dans   les   rang d'   co-

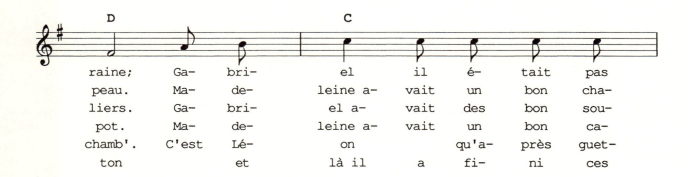

raine;   Ga-   bri-   el   il   é-   tait   pas
peau.   Ma-   de-   leine a-   vait   un   bon   cha-
liers.   Ga-   bri-   el a-   vait   des   bon   sou-
pot.   Ma-   de-   leine a-   vait   un   bon   ca-
chamb'.   C'est   Lé-   on   qu'a-   près   guet-
ton   et   là il   a   fi-   ni   ces

bon   et   Ma-   de-   leine elle   en   va-   lant   pas   mieux.
peau;   c'est   dom-   mage il   a-   vait pas d'   ca-   lotte.
liers;   c'est   dom-   mage c'é-   tait   des   "ten-   nis   shoes."
pot;   c'est   dom-   mage il   é-   tait   dé-   chi-   ré.
ter et   c'est   Ca-   ro-   line   qu'est   bien   fâ-   chée!
jours   à   faire   l'a-   mour   dans   le   pou-   laill-   er!

Valse des Grands Bois

Key. C
Pattern. Violin: two Tunes and two Turns, etc.

Version. Carrie "Mignonne" Royer Miller.
Related songs. See: *La Breakdown la Louisiane* (Walker Brothers) and *Valse à Kathleen* (Sady Courville and Dennis McGee). Also: *Valse de l'Anse Maigre* (Sady Courville and Dennis McGee); *Valse de la Belle* (Shirley Bergeron); *Valse à Will Kegley* (Will Kegley); *Valse de Crowley.*

I have forgotten the words that go with this song, but one verse is about a person walking through the woods late in the evening listening to the owls hooting and, in another verse, swimming across bayous and gullies to reach his sweetheart but failing to win her.

This song is quite different from *Valse des Grands Bois*, recorded by Dewey Balfa.

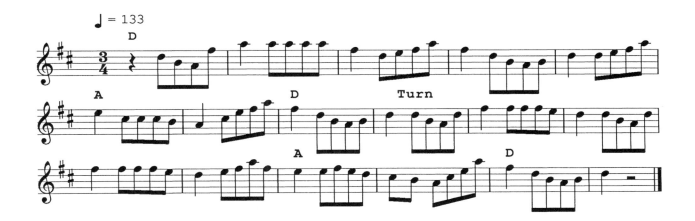

Valse des Grands Chemins

Key. G
Pattern. Accordion: Part 1 twice, Part 2 once; Vocal
#1; Accordion: Part 1 twice, Part 2 once; Vocal #2;
Accordion: Part 1 twice, Part 2 twice and Part 1 once.

Version. Iry LeJeune (©Tek).
Related songs. Also: *The Waltz that Carried Me to
My Grave* (Joseph Falcon); *Mon Coeur est Barré
dans l'Armoire* (Irène Whitfield).

The tune is usually played twice after the
vocals; Parts 1 and 2 are played by the accordion.
Today the switch to the G-chord is used
for entering the vocal and leaving the tune; Iry
didn't use this technique because the
accordion was the main instrument throughout
the song. This technique will give a better
chance for other instruments to be included in
your arrangement. See Ann Savoy's book for
additional information about this song.

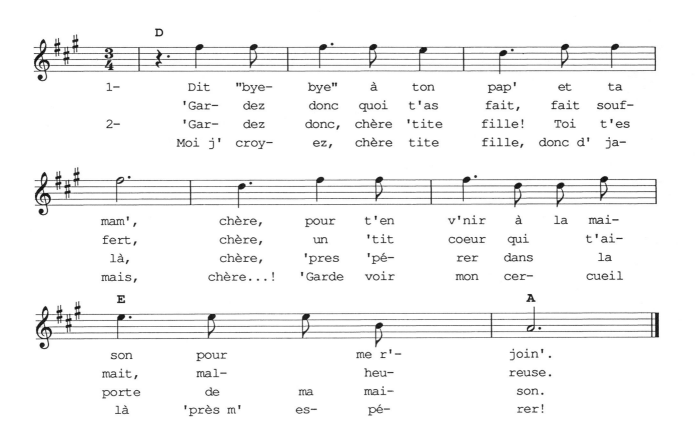

Highway Waltz

(1)
Say goodbye to your mom and dad, dear, so that you can come back home to me.
Look what you've done, dear, caused a loving heart to suffer, unhappy one.
(2)
Look, dear little girl! You're there waiting in the doorway of my home.
I never thought, dear little girl, that I'd ever — look at my coffin waiting there for me!

Grand Mamou Blues

Key. C
Pattern. Accordion: one Tune; Vocal #1; Steel Guitar: two Tunes; Violin: one Tune; Accordion: one Tune; Vocal #2; Accordion: one Tune.

Version. Austin Pitre (©Flat Town).
Related songs. See: *Grand Mamou (variation)* (Varise Connor); *Grand Mamou (in G)* (Wallace "Cheese" Reed; Raymond François). Also: *La Bonne Valse* (Leo Soileau); *Big Mamou* (Link Davis); *Grand Basile* (Mayuse LaFleur, the original recording).

Austin didn't put a turn in his version, but other musicians include it.

Big Mamou Blues

(1)
Well, dear little piece of a person, what do you think you will do when your old lover
will be in that bed in his house, yes, with some candles, yes, around him?
Well, dear little girl, what do you think you'll do when you return?
I've suffered for you, my old lover. You know your old lover won't be there.
(2)
Ah, but dear little piece of a person, what do you think you'll do when your old lover —
you will come to regret, dear little one. You know you will never see him again.
Ah, but dear little piece of a person, yes, when I go,
come back and get on your knees at my tomb and cry until you're tired;
place some flowers to make a wreath for me.

Grand Mamou (in G)

Key. G
Pattern. Violins: one Tune and two Turns ; Vocal #1; Violins: one Turn and one Tune; Vocal #2; one Turn and two Tunes.

Version. Wallace "Cheese" Reed, (vocal); Raymond François (turn).
Related songs. See: *Grand Mamou (variation)* (Varise Connor); *Grand Mamou Blues* (Austin Pitre). Also: *La Bonne Valse* (Leo Soileau); *Big Mamou* (Link Davis); *Grand Basile* (Mayuse LaFleur, the original recording).

I have attempted to write a three part harmony. I have called this version *Grand Mamou in G* to differentiate it from Varise Connor's *Grand Mamou*. I think this is more like the original, or at least played more often.

Grand Mamou (G)

(1)
Oh, I'm going to big Mamou. I'm going so lonely while thinking of what you've done.
If you'd want to come back with me to big Mamou, I'd be happy to have you for my wife.
(2)
Oh, little darling, with your ugly ways, I know you'll cry some day for what you've done.
Oh, I'm wandering the roads, so lonely! Oh, I'm going to Big Mamou.

Grand Mamou (variation)

Key. G
Pattern. Violin: play Tune.

Version. Varise Connor.
Related songs. See: *Grand Mamou Blues* (Austin Pitre) and *Grand Mamou* (in G)Wallace "Cheese" Reed; Raymond François). Also: *Big Mamou* which Link Davis made a national hit; *La Bonne Valse* (Leo Soileau) and *Grand Basile* (Mayuse LaFleur).

This song was first recorded as *Grand Basile* by Mayuse LaFleur. Varise Connor's variation of this song is interesting; there is no Turn.

Mamou is a small town north of Eunice, Louisiana; it was named for the large (mammoth) prairie there. Basile is a small town west of Eunice.

Valse des Grands Pins

Key. G
Pattern. Accordion: one Tune; Vocal #1; Steel Guitar: one Tune; Violin: one Tune; Accordion: one Tune; Vocal #2; Accordion: one Tune.

Version. Blackie Forestier (©La Lou).
Related Song. Also: *La Valse des Grands Pins* (Archange "Coon" Touchet, vocal, and the Louisiana Aces).

It was during this time, when I was growing up, that I was learning to play the accordion and sing. I didn't have a good voice, it was too low and I never had a good voice up to this day. I never had a good singing voice but anyway, I'd do what I could. One of my friends advised me to drink raw eggs and that would cause me to have a beautiful voice. So, I started watching the chicken house and looking for eggs. I watched the hens lay and when they had layed, I'd take the egg and drink it so that I'd have a beautiful voice. My mother started noticing that she wasn't picking any eggs and wondered out loud if it wasn't a chicken snake that was swallowing the eggs. I began laughing and told her that I was the snake that was drinking the eggs so that I'd have a beautiful voice. She made me stop that.
— Moïse Robin

Waltz of the Big Pines

(1)
I didn't listen to your father and mother when they told me that you were no good.
Today, I'm dying of grief; I'm all alone these years in the big pines.
(2)
You broke the promises that you made to me. You mustn't think that I was angry!
Today, I'm dying of grief; I'm all alone these years in the big pines.

1- J'ai pas é- cou- té ton pa- pa et ta mam- an,
2- T'as cas- sé les pro- mises que tu m'as fait.

et quand i' mon dit que toi t'é- tais pas bonne.
I' faut pas tu crois que moi j'é- tais fâ- ché!

Au- jour- d'hui j'su'a- près mou- rir dans l' cha- grin;
Au- jour- d'hui j'su'a- près mou- rir dans l' cha- grin;

su' moi tout seul les an- nées dans les grand pins.
su' moi tout seul les an- nées dans les grand pins.

Valse de Grande Prairie

Key. C

Pattern. Accordion: one Tune; Vocal #1; Steel Guitar: two Tunes; Violin: two Tunes; Accordion: two Tunes; Vocal #2; Accordion: two Tunes.

Version. Joe Bonsall (©Flat Town).

This song has two moods; the first vocal is a happy one and the second vocal an unhappy one. Grand Prairie is located east of Ville Platte, Louisiana.

Grand Prairie Waltz

(1)
I asked your father, I asked your mother, to marry you.
They told me, "You can take her. Be sure to take her back to Grand Prairie."
Today we're married, I'm happy to have her at home.
Don't listen to other people's advice, dear little girl, it will hurt you.
(2)
Today we're separated on account of your father and mother.
You listened to other people's advice, dear little one.
That hurts, baby! Look what I've done, today I'm there thinking; thinking, dear little one.
You know where you're at, that hurts me, baby.

1-   J'ai d'man- dé   à ton pa-   pa, j'ai d'man-
          Au- jour-   d'hiu   on est ma-   rié, j'su' con-
2-   Au- jour-   d'hui on est sé- pa-   ré   par rap-
          'Garde   donc   ça j'ai fait, au- jour-

dé   à ta ma-   man pour te ma-   rier.   Ils mon-
tent oui,   l'a-   voir à la mai-   son.   É- coute
port à ton pa-   pa et ta ma-   man.   Ta é- cout-
d'hui moi j'su'   là a- près jon-   gler;   a- près jon-

dit, "Tu peut la   prendre. Sois   sûre de la rame-
pas   les con-   seils d'un et   l'aut', chère 'tite
ais   les con-   seils d'un et   l'aut', chère 'tit
gler, chère 'tit   monde. Tu con-   nais à où toi

ner   à Grande Prai-   rie.
fille, va t'faire du   mal.
monde. Ca fait du   mal,   bé- bé!
t'est ça m'fait du   mal,   bé- bé!

Valse à Guilbeau

Key. F
Pattern. Violin: one tune one turn, etc.
Rhythm. This instrumental has one half note and one
quarter note per measure. See the sample of the bass.

Version. Dennis McGee.

This is the waltz Guilbeau played for the General. See the story found with *Valse à Napoléon.*

Le Hack à Moreau

Key. A
Pattern. Accordion: two Tunes; Vocal #1; Steel Guitar: two Tunes; Violin: two Tunes; Accordion: two Tunes; Vocal #2 (repeat vocal #1); Accordion: two Tunes.

Version. Raymond François.
Related songs. Also: *La Fille à Jasman.*

When my father was a tenant farmer near Scott, Louisiana, in the 1940's, there were motorized hacks in the form of old buses with merchandise and poultry cages on the top and back. The drivers traded with the farmers along the route. The horse-drawn hack, the kind referred to in this song, preceded the motorized ones and they collected eggs and poultry as well as money for store goods. In other words, a hack was a store on wheels.

C'est le "hack" à Moreau qu'a capoté, cher, qu'a capoté les quat' roues en l'air dedans l'fossé. La 'tite blonde s'a fais prend' sous le "hack," cher, alle s'a planté un écharde dedans la fesse.

Moreau's Hack

(1 & 2)
Moreau's hack turned over, dear, turned over with the four wheels in the air in the ditch.
The little blond got caught under the hack, dear, she was stuck with a splinter in the buttock.

Happy One-Step

Key. G
Pattern. Violin: two Tunes and two Turns, etc.
Rhythm. Two strong half-notes per measure works fine
for bass!

Version. Dennis McGee (MS).

Les Haricots Sont Pas Salés

Key. G
Pattern. Accordion: parts 1, 2, and 1; Vocal #1;
Accordion: parts 3, 4, 5 and 6; Vocal #2; Accordion:
part 1.

Version. Aldus Roger, vocal and accordion (©La
Lou).
Related songs. See: *Les Huppés Taïauts.* Also:
Zydeco Est Pas Salé (Clifton Chenier).

There are many variations; therefore I strongly
urge you to arrange your own version using
the variations here as a guide. This is the song
that gave its name to Zydeco music; see the
Introduction. Green snapbeans are very bland
and the cook shouldn't forget to add salt to
this tasty dish.

The Snapbeans Aren't Salted

(1 & 2)
Oh, mom! What you did to your dinner!
The snapbeans aren't salted! The snapbeans aren't salted!
You stole my sled! You stole my sled!
You stole my sled! You stole my sled!
It's those clever hound dogs! It's those clever hound dogs!
It's those clever hound dogs! It's those clever hound dogs!

Hathaway Two-Step

Key. G
Pattern. Each instrument plays two Tunes with variations

Related song. Pas de Deux Babineaux (Merlin Fontenot).

This instrumental is named for the community of Hathaway, located eight miles north of Jennings, Louisiana.

Les Huppés Taïauts

Key. C
Pattern. Accordion: two Tunes; Vocal #1; Steel Guitar: two Tunes; Violin: two Tunes; Vocal #2; Accordion: two Tunes.

Version. A mixture of Joe Bonsall (©Flat Town) and Jimmy Newman (©La Lou).
Related songs. Also: *Hippy Ti Yo* (Joe Bonsall); *Hippy Ty-Yo* (Jimmy Newman); *Les Filles d'Arnaudville* (Moïse Robin); *Hip et Taïaut* (Irene Whitfield).

This title has been interpreted in several other ways, too. This is my interpretation of what it means. *Huppé*, used colloquially, means clever and *taïaut*, which comes from English tally-ho, simply means a hound dog. Originally, the song blamed only the hound dogs for stealing different articles, but later, other rascals such as *les filles de Bosco* stole articles too. Other stolen articles are often added to the vocals such as *Yo-yo, candi* (candy), etc. I have given two manuscript variations.

To this day, *capot* is used for coat instead of *manteau.*

The Clever Hounds

(1)
It's the clever hounds, hounds, hounds, who stole my sled, sled, sled.
When you saw I was mad, dear, you brought back my sled.
It's the clever hounds, hounds, hounds, who stole my coat, coat, coat.
When you saw I was mad, dear, you brought back my coat.
(2)
It's the girls from Bosco, dear, who stole my vest, dear.
When you saw I was mad, dear, you brought back my vest.
It's the girls from Bosco, dear, who stole my hat, dear.
When you saw I was mad, dear, you brought back my hat.

J.B. Fusilier's Song

Key. G

Pattern. Violin: one Tune and two Turns, etc.

Version. Varise Connor; J.B. Fusilier.

Varise Connor played this song with J.B. Fusilier many times but doesn't remember its name. Here is another "unburied" song. Preston Manuel, who played rhythm guitar with J.B., told me there were lyrics, but he can't remember the words.

Back then, the Great Depression was so bad that they couldn't pay us enough to play dances. You weren't guaranteed a fixed price, you had to play for a certain percentage of the money paid at the door.

I worked hard all the time, all the time. When I stopped playing dances, that's when I started my saw mill. I told J.B. Fusilier, "If you want to play your life for nothing, go ahead. I quit." Not too long afterwards, my brother quit too. For three musicians you'd get fifteen, maybe twenty dollars per night. Then when the depression of the 30's came, you were only guaranteed half or maybe sixty percent of what was collected at the door. The people would come but they didn't even have enough money to pay to enter the dance hall. Things were serious.

— Varise Connor

J'ai Passé Devant Ta Porte

Key. G
Pattern. Accordion: one Tune; Vocal #1; Steel Guitar: one Tune; Violin: one Tune; Accordion: one Tune; Vocal #2; Steel Guitar: one Tune; Violin: one Tune; Accordion: one Tune.

Version. Elton "Bee" Cormier, vocal; Raymond François, tune.

This is a very popular old song about a lover who discovers that his sweetheart had died. My father remembers this song being played at the time the Titanic sank. The tune is even older.

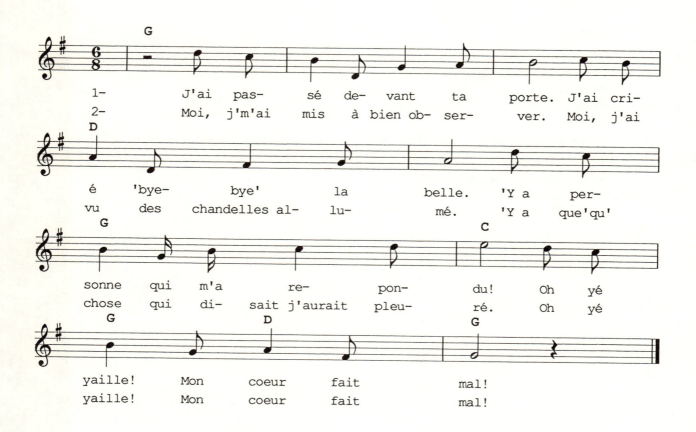

1- J'ai pas- sé de- vant ta porte. J'ai cri-
2- Moi, j'm'ai mis à bien ob- ser- ver. Moi, j'ai

é 'bye- bye' la belle. 'Y a per-
vu des chandelles al- lu- mé. 'Y a que'qu'

sonne qui m'a re- pon- du! Oh yé
chose qui di- sait j'aurait pleu- ré. Oh yé

yaille! Mon coeur fait mal!
yaille! Mon coeur fait mal!

I Passed in Front of Your Door

(1)
I passed in front of your door. I cried good-bye to my sweetheart.
No one answered me! Oh it hurts! My heart hurts!
(2)
I looked closely. I saw (religious) candles were lit.
Something told me I would cry. Oh it hurts! My heart hurts!

J'étais au Bal

Key. G
Pattern. Accordion: two Turns and one Tune; Vocal #1; Accordion: two Turns and two Tunes; Vocal #2; Accordion: two Turns and one Tune; Vocal #3; Accordion: two Turns.

Version. Iry LeJeune (©Tek).
Related songs. Oh, Susannah; Get Along Home, Cindy.

This song is so popular, I've decided to include it here, even though I believe it is borrowed from an American song.

1-   'Tais   au   bal   hier   au   soir;   j'ai r'-
      'Gard- ez   donc   la   jolie   fille,   cette
2-   'Tais   au   bal   heir   au   soir;   alle était
      'Tais   au   bal   à   soir;   alle est
3-   'Tais   au   bal   hier   au   soir;   j'va' r'-
      'Gar- dez   donc   la   jolie   fille!   Per-

venu   en- core   à   soir;   si   l'oc- ca- sion se r'-
la   que j'   aime   au- tant!   Moi j'   con- nais   tout
tout ha- bil- lée   en   noir.   (J'ai)   fait   ser- ment d' ja-
tout ha- bil- lée   en   bleu.   (C'est)   ça   l'ha- bille   que
tour- ner   encore   à   soir;   si   l'oc- ca- sion se r'-
sonne   qui veut m' ai- mer!   'Garde- donc   voir   si

pré- sente,   j'va' r'- tour- ner   demain   au   soir.
l'a- mour   que   moi   j'ai   eu   pour   toi!
mais r'- boire   pour   cour- ti- ser   ma   fille.
moi j'   aime   pour   cour- ti- ser   ma   belle.
pré- sente,   j'va' r'- tour- ner   demain   au   soir.
ça   fait   pas   mi- sé- rab' pour   moi!

I Went to The Dance Last Night

(1)
I went to the dance last night and I've come again tonight;
if the occasion presents itself again, I'll come back tomorrow night.
Look at the pretty girl, the one I love so much!
I know all the love I've had for you.
(2)
I went to the dance last night; she was all dressed in black.
I promised never to drink anymore so I could court my girl.
I went to the dance tonight, she's all dressed in blue;
that's the clothing I like for courting my sweetheart.
(3)
I went to the dance last night and I am going again tonight;
if the occasion presents itself again, I'll go back tomorrow night.
Look at the pretty girl! No one wants to love me.
Look indeed, if that's not miserable for me!

Je Suis Orphelin

Key. C
Pattern. Accordion: two Tunes; Vocal #1; Violin: two Tunes; Accordion: two Tunes; Vocal #2; Violin: two Tunes; Accordion: two Tunes.

Version. Dewey Balfa (©Flat Town).
Related songs. See: *Viens m' Chercher* (Iry LeJeune); *La Valse à Tante Aleen* (Dennis McGee). Also: *L'Orphelin* (Irène Whitfield's book).

1- Mes pa- rents, ils sont pres- que touts
Quand j'su' ma- lade, il faut j' va' chez les é- tran-
2- Les ma- mans m'in- vite au- jour-
Au- jour- d'hui, j'su' tout seul de- dans les

morts; ces là qui reste, y'n a p'us
gers et les souf- frances, il faut j'les
d'hui d'pas é- cou- ter les con-
chemins et mes mi- sères fau- dra j'les

une qui veut me voir.
prends comme ça vient.
seils de un et l'aut'.
prends comme ça vient.

I'm an Orphan

(1) My relatives are practically all dead; those who are left don't want to see me.
When I'm sick, I must go to strangers and I must take suffering as it comes.
(2) Today the mothers advise me not to listen to everyone.
Today I'm all alone in the roads and I must take my misery as it comes.

J' Veux m' Marier

Key. C
Pattern. Tune (and vocal) consists of two parts. Violin:
Part 1 twice; Vocal #1; Violin: Part 2 then Part 1 twice;
Vocal #2; Violin: Part 2 then Part 1; Vocal #3; Violin:
Part 1; Vocal #4; Violin: Part 1 twice; Vocal #5; Violin:
Part 2 then Tune; Vocal #6; Violin: Part 2; Vocal #7;
Violin: Part 2 then Part 1; Vocal #8; Violin: Part 2 then
Part 1 three times.

Version. Leo Soileau, vocal and violin, and Moïse
Robin, bass on accordion (OT).

I Want to Marry

(1)
I want to marry! I want to marry! I want to marry but my sweetheart doesn't.
(2)
My sweetheart wants! My sweetheart wants! My sweetheart wants but the old folks don't!
(3)
My sweetheart wants! My sweetheart wants! My sweetheart wants but the old folks don't!
(4)
Oh, the old folks want! The old folks want! The old folks want but I have no money!
(5)
I have no money! I have no money! I have no money, the hens don't lay! It hurts!
(6)
I want to marry! I want to marry! I want to marry but the old folks don't, dear!
(7)
Oh, the old folks want! The old folks want! The old folks want but I have no money, dear!
(8)
I have no money! I have no money! I have no money, the hens don't lay! Ouch!

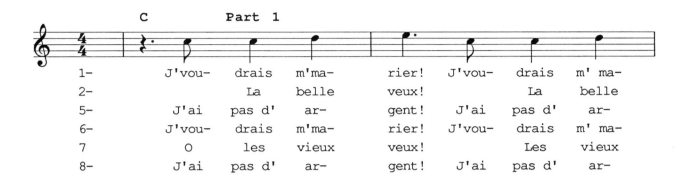

C   Part 1

1-	J'vou-	drais	m'ma-	rier!	J'vou-	drais	m' ma-
2-		La	belle	veux!		La	belle
5-	J'ai	pas d'	ar-	gent!	J'ai	pas d'	ar-
6-	J'vou-	drais	m'ma-	rier!	J'vou-	drais	m' ma-
7	O	les	vieux	veux!		Les	vieux
8-	J'ai	pas d'	ar-	gent!	J'ai	pas d'	ar-

rier!	J'vou-	drais	m' ma-	rier	mais	la	belle	veux	pas,	
veux!		La	belle	veux	mais	les	vieux	veux	pas,	
gent!	J'ai	pas d'	ar-	gent	mais	les	poules	pond	pas,	yé
rier!	J'vou-	drais	m' ma-	rier	mais	les	vieux	veux	pas,	
veux!		Les	vieux	veux	mais	j'ai	pas d'	ar-	gent,	
gent!	J'ai	pas d'	ar-	gent		les	poules	pond	pas,	

Part 2

| ô! | (3) | La | belle | veux! | La | belle | veux! | O la | belle |
| iii! | (4) | O les | vieux | veux! | Les | vieux | veux! | Les | vieux |

yaille!
chère!
chère!
yaille!

| veux | mais | les | vieux | veux | pas! |
| veux | mais | j'ai | pas d' | ar- | gent! |

I was ten years old when I started playing the accordion. A man called Sosthène Saucier was a neighbor. He worked for my grandmother as a tenant farmer. He played some little dances in the country. I liked that man very much! He'd play the accordion. I guess he didn't play very well, but I thought it was good in those days, you know. I learned all those tunes! I watched his fingers move!

There was a dance one night in the country, around our neighborhood, and at nightfall a buggy arrived with someone playing the accordion. He turned in and tied up close to us. My father and others his age liked to drink outside and the younger ones danced in the house. And, my dad went to the buggy and looked under the buggy top and asked, "Who's that playing the accordion?" The guy said, "It's me!" Dad said, "Get down. We'll give you a few drinks and you'll play us a few songs."

There was an old woodpile outside, leftover from the winter; it was in July. They told him, "Sit down on a log there." It was a moonlit night. He sat down and started playing there. I sat down near him, on the fingerboard side; even though I couldn't see his fingers, I wanted to listen. After a while, he pulled out a Bull Durham sack and rolled himself a cigarette. He put the accordion down between him and me. I caught the accordion and played the tune that was very popular during those times, J' Veux m' Marier. It was Mayuse LaFleur and Leo Soileau who had made this tune. I

liked it very much but I had heard it before, before the record was out. I had heard it from Mr. Sosthène. Mr. Sosthène played it, but he didn't sing it. That's how I learned.

The fellow asked me, "Do you have an accordion, cher?" I said, "No." He called my father and remarked, "It's your son who's playing that!" Dad said, "I can't believe it! It's you, son, who's playing that?" I said, "Yes." Dad asked me to play it again. I played it again then Dad asked the fellow, "Would you sell your accordion?" "Oh, no!" the fellow answered. "I'd give you two dollars for it," Dad offered. It was an accordion that sold for three dollars and fifty cents new, I guess. The bellows were of paper and it kinda sounded not too loud. Dad offered again, "I'll give you two-fifty." "No. No," was the reply. "I'll give you three dollars," persisted Dad. "No." was the answer. "I'll give you three-fifty cash!" insisted Dad. The guy said, "Look, if you're crazy enough to give me three-fifty for it, give it to me." Dad gave him the money and I ran home with it.

When they came back from the dance, I was soaking wet with sweat in the kitchen. It was hot, you know. I was pulling on that accordion! Dad exclaimed, "Hot damn, my son! It seemed that there was a big dance going on here since it sounded so pretty!" Dad wanted to encourage me as he liked music very much. Then he bought a violin for my brother. "Oh, yes, we must have the whole band!" he said.
— *Roy Fusilier*

Jeunes Gens de la Campagne

Key. G
Pattern. Violin: two Tunes; Vocal #1; Violin; one Tune and three Turns; Vocal #2; Violin: two Tunes; Vocal #3; Violin: two Turns.

Version. Dennis McGee (MS).
Related songs. See: *Allons à Lafayette* (Joe Falcon) and *Lafayette Two-Step* (Aldus Roger).

Don't confuse this song with the *Country Gentlemen* recorded by Iry LeJeune, which is a different tune altogether and often called *Jeunes Gens de la Campagne* too.

Young Country Lads

(1) Young country lads, don't marry too young. Pleasure is too beautiful; the girls are so pretty.
They all dance so well; they are all so good looking. Listen to my advice, the advice of a miserable man.
(2) Oh, wow, darling heart! Lets go to the dance to see the dear beautiful girls!
They're all so pretty! They're all good-looking; the dear little curls, the dear little dark eyes!
Oh, don't do that! Don't make me hard to please like y'all are doing. Keep them well loved! Oh wow, darling!
(3) You are cute! Say bye-bye to your mother; indeed come with your old lover!
Dear little black curls! Don't do that to your lover!
You know I don't deserve what you're doing to me; those things you want me to believe, dear.

♩ = 175

G   C

1- Jeunes   gens   de   la   com-   pagne,   ma-
   Ça   dance mais tous si   bien;   i'ont
2- Haïe   yaille,   ché- rie   coeur!   Al-
   I'sont   tous mais bien bonnes mines;   les
   Fai-   sez moi pas diffi-   cile   comme
3- Tu   es   mais toi mi-   gnonne! Dis 'bye-
   Fais pas   ça mais avec ton   nèg'!   Tu con-

G

rier   pas vous aut' trop   jeunes. L'agré-   ment   c'est   trop
tous   mais si bonnes   mines. Écou-   tez   mais mon con-
lons   mais aller au   bal   pour   voir les chères belles
chères mais 'tites bou-   clettes, les   chéres mais 'tits yeux
vous   aut' a-   près   faire. Les   tiennes mais bien ai-
bye'   à   ta   mam-   an;   viens   donc avec ton vieux
nais   mais j' mé-   rite   pas   tout   ça   t'a- près me

D   G

belle; les   filles sont trop jo-   lies.
seil,   con-   seil à l'   mi-   sé-   rable!
filles! Elles sont mais   tous si jo-   lies!
noirs! Hé,   fai- sez   donc pas   ça!
mées!   Haïe   yé   yaille,   ché-   rie!
nèg'!   Chère, mais 'tites bou- clettes noires!
faire, ces ac- croires que   tu m' fais, chère.

Jolie Blonde

Key. G
Pattern. Violin: two Tunes; Vocal #1; Violin: one Turn; Vocal #2; Violin: one Turn; Vocal #3; Violin: one Tune.

Version. Varise Connor; Preston Manuel (vocal); Raymond François (second turn variation).
Related songs. See: *Ma Blonde Est Parti* (Amédé Breaux). Also: *Reine de Mon Coeur* (Elton "Bee" Cormier); *La Fille d' la Veuve* (Iry LeJeune).

Varise Connor loves this song, as do most Cajuns; we sometimes call it the "Cajun National Anthem." I have added my own variation to the second turn. The first tune shows the evolution of the "Harry Choats style" made famous in the late '40's. Harry's folks and Varise lived in the same area around Lake

Arthur. The tune variation is from the older and still popular style. Preston Manuel's vocal is typical of this older style. Also included within this song are the vocals for *La Fille d' la Veuve* as sung by Shirley Bergeron which may be an older version of *Jolie Blonde*.

Pretty Blond

(1)
Oh, but pretty blond, you've left me to go away, to go away with that good-for-nothing.
What hope and what future can I have, baby?
(2)
Oh, but dear little heart, to die is nothing, it's staying in the ground for so long!
What hope and what future can I have?
(3)
Oh, but pretty blond, you thought there was only you in the world for me to love and care for!
What hope and what future can I have?

The Widow's Daughter

(1)
Oh, Chic and Joséphine! Going to Madam Do-do (sleepy?)
to steal the plums in the plum trees, but it was to see the widow's daughter.
(2)
Well, the widow's daughter, the one there who was so pretty, so fine, and she had a very well-trimmed forelock.

Jolie Catin

Key. G
Pattern. Accordion: two Tunes; Vocal #1; Accordion: two Turns and one Tune; Vocal #2; Accordion: two Turns and one Tune; Vocal #3; Accordion: one Turn.

Version. Iry LeJeune (©Tek); Maurice Berzas, *Eunice Two-Step* (©Flat Town).
Related songs. Also: *'Tit Ardoin Two-Step* (Moïse Robin); *Bayou Teche Two-Step* (Austin Pitre); *Chère Ici, Chère Là Bas* (Alphonse "Bois Sec" Ardoin); *Jolie Fille* (Ambrose Thibodeaux); *Cypress Inn Special* (J.W. Pelsia, Nathan Menard). There are others, as well.

"Bois Sec" Ardoin has made a recording called *Jolie Catin,* but it has the same tune as the *Choupique Two-Step.* I have also included the lyrics for the *Eunice Two-Step* as sung by Vorance Berzas. Amédé Ardoin first recorded this tune.

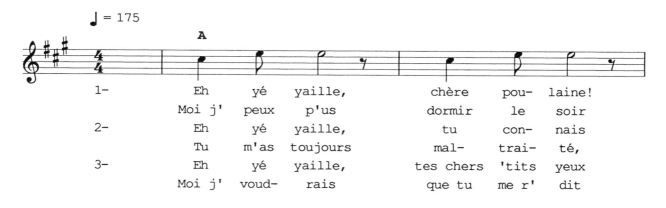

1-   Eh   yé   yaille,   chère   pou- laine!
       Moi j' peux p'us   dormir   le   soir
2-   Eh   yé   yaille,   tu   con-   nais
       Tu   m'as toujours   mal-   trai- té,
3-   Eh   yé   yaille,   tes chers 'tits yeux
       Moi j' voud- rais   que tu   me r' dit

Toi,   ca-   tin   r'gar- dez   donc!
a-   vec   tous   mes jong- le- ments
t'a-   près   sen-   tir   ton   mal
fais   des   choses que j'   méri- té   pas.
q'es aus- si   canailles,   ça   me r' semb'
pour   toi-   même voir   quo' faire que   toi

Moi j' su'   là dans   les   mi-   sères ...
et mon cha-   grin que   j'ai   pour toi.
parce   que   toi t'as   tou-   jours fait
Là   peut- êt' ces   'tites af-   faires
que t'as q'e'que chose que   tu   peux m' dire
tu   m'as   mis dans   autant d' cha- grins

pou-   laine, j'peux pas   t'a-   voir!
Ca-   tin,   ou-   blie   pas   ça!
tout l' temps mal   a-   vec   moi!
sont   toutes tes   grosses er-   reurs.
mais   tu t' sens   pas   ca-   pab'.
que   moi j' su'   toujours de-   dans.

Pretty Doll

(1)
Well it hurts, dear colt! Doll, look! I'm in misery because I can't have you.
I can't sleep at night with all those thoughts and grief I have for you. Doll, don't forget that!
(2)
Well it hurts! You know you're feeling pain because you've always treated me badly.
You always mistreated me, done things to me I didn't deserve, perhaps these small affairs were your big mistake.
(3)
Ah it hurts! Your dear little eyes are so cunning,
it seems that you have something to tell me but you don't know how.
I'd like for you to repeat, for yourself to see, why you've put me through so much grief, which I'm still feeling.

Two-Step de Eunice

(1)
Aïe yé yaille! Chaque fois j' te vois c'est "cher" ici et "cher" là-bas;
si ton nèg' te tourne le dos, tu "beg" trop la banane.
Moi j' voudrais que tu me r'dit, pour toi même,
voir quo' faire que toi tu m'as mis dans autant d' chagrins, que moi j'su' toujours dedans.
(2)
Aïe yé yaille! Et cher vieux nèg', t'es si canaille!
Ça me r'semb' t'as pas qu'que chose que tu peux m' dire sans m' faire des vieilles misères.
Moi j' peux pas dormir le soir avec tous ces jonglements. Mon chagrin que j'ai pour toi, bébé, oublie pas ça!

Eunice Two-Step

(1)
Oh, it hurts! Every time I see you it's "dear" this and "dear" that;
if your lover turns his back on you, you pester him too much.
I'd like for you to repeat, for yourself to understand,
why you've put me through so much grief, which I'm still going through.
(2)
Oh, it hurts! And dear old lover, you're such a rascal!
It seems you don't have anything that you can say
without causing me some old misery.
I can't sleep at night with all these worries.
My grief I have for you, baby, don't forget that!

Jolies Joues Roses

Key. E minor
Pattern. Violin: two Tunes, one Turn and one Tune; Vocal #1; Guitar: two Tunes; Violin: two tunes, one Turn and one Tune; Vocal #2; Violin: one Tune.

Version. Austin Pitre (©Flat Town).
Related song. Also: *Chères Joues Roses* (Dewey Balfa).

This song is transposed to F-sharp minor from A major. The turn variation in the instrumental manuscript is from Dewey's version. Although Austin recorded this song in the 70's, I believe the tune is older.

1-   Same-   di   à   mi-   di,   moi j'   me
     Quand   moi   mais j'   ar-   rive,   ouais,   j'ar-
2-   Jo-   lie   cou-   ro-   née,   tu   con-
     pour al-   ler   te   cher-   cher   et   r'me-

rase   et j'   me   peigne   pour   al-   ler   voir   ma   joues
rive   des   fois   tard,   moi j'   la r'-   garde en   tra-   verse   du
nais   t'es   la   seule   dans   mon   coeur   au-   jour-
ner   a-   vec   lui.   Pauv'   vieux   nèg'   dans   chaque

roses,   ouais,   que   moi j'   aime   au-   tant.
clos,   moi j'   la   vois   su' la   gale-   rie.
d'hui.   Ton   vieux   nèg'   a   par-   ti
jour,   oui,   tou-   jours   mon   tout   seul.

Pretty Rosy Cheeks

(1)
Saturday at noon, I shave and comb myself to go see my Rosy Cheeks, whom I love so much.
When I arrive, sometimes I'm a little late, I see her across the field, waiting for me on the porch.
(2)
Pretty beloved, you know you're the only one in my heart today.
Your lover has left to go get you and take you with him. Poor old lover, each day, is always all alone.

Valse de Joséphine

Key. C
Pattern. Accordion: two Tunes; Vocal #1; Accordion: two Tunes; Vocal #2; Accordion; two Tunes and one Turn; Vocal #3; Accordion: two Tunes; Vocal #4; Accordion: one Turn and one Tune.

Version. Moïse Robin, vocal and accordion, and Leo Soileau, violin (OT).
Related song. See: *Chère Alice* (Lawrence Walker).

In the first two vocals someone is prompting Joséphine; in the last two vocals Joséphine's lover laments his love. I remember the times when a cloud of dust meant someone was coming down the dirt road. There were very few gravel roads, much less paved roads, during the 1930's and '40's. Local transportation usually was by buggy, horseback, and wagons, until after World War II.

Josephine's Waltz

(1)
Unfortunate one, look over there at the little cloud of dust!
Your lover is coming for you on his cantering horse.
(2)
Josephine, look over there in your room and put on your pink dress.
Hurry, your lover is here!
(3)
Oh it hurts! Your father and mother don't want you to receive your old lover.
They won't ever want me, they're all against me. What will I do!
(4)
Dear little girl, I'm going away! I'm going away!
Don't listen to your father and mother, dear.
Come home with me to finish your good days with your old lover.

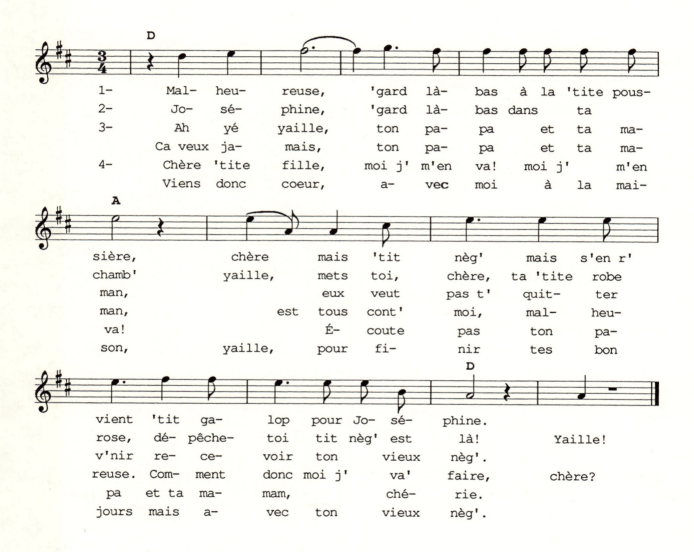

Valse de Kaplan

Key. C
Pattern. Accordion: one Tune; Vocal #1; Violin: one Tune; Accordion: one Turn; Vocal #2; Violin: one Tune; Accordion: one Turn and one Tune.

Version. Nathan Abshire.
Related songs. See: *Kaplan Waltz* (Varise Connor); *Valse de Pointe Noire* (Angélas LeJeune); *Valse de Kaplan variation* (Don Guillory).

(1)- Hé,   cri- mi-   nelle!   La mi- sér-   able!

Hé, j'veux p'us   t'voir! (2)- Oh,   mais tu vas

voire ton er-   reur! Ca s'ra trop   tard pour toi r' ve-

nir! J'veux p'us   t'voir, vi- llaines ma-   nières!

Kaplan Waltz

(1)
Oh, criminal! The miserable one! Oh, I don't want to see you anymore!
(2)
Oh, but you'll see your error! It'll be too late for you to come back!
I don't want to see you anymore, ugly mannered girl!

Valse de Kaplan (variation)

Key. C
Pattern. Accordion: two Tunes; Vocal #1; Steel Guitar: two Turns; Violin: two Tunes; Accordion: two Turns; Vocal #2; Steel Guitar: two turns; Violin: two Tunes; Accordion: two Turns.

Version. Don Guillory, vocal.
Related songs. See: *Kaplan Waltz* (Varise Connor); *Valse de Kaplan* (Nathan Abshire); *Valse de Pointe Noire* (Angélas LeJeune).

See the other versions for the turn. I think the violin sounds much better tuned down with a C-accordion, and it's best for most vocalists too. Kaplan is a town in southwest Louisiana near the Gulf of Mexico and the marshes.

Kaplan Waltz (variation)

(1)
Eh, but I'm going, I'm going to Kaplan, hey, hey, to see my dear little girl, to know if she'll ever come back.
(2)
Oh, but every night I'm there thinking, hey, hey, wondering where you are and if ever you'll come back.

Kaplan Waltz

Key. G
Pattern. Violin: one Tune and one Turn, etc.

Version. Varise Connor.
Related songs. See: *Valse de Kaplan* (Nathan Abshire); *Valse de Kaplan variation* (Don Guillory); *Valse de Pointe Noire* (Angélas LeJeune).

Valse à Kathleen

Key. C
Pattern. Violin: two Tunes; Vocal #1; Violin: one Tune and two Turns; Vocal #2; one Tune, two Turns, two Tunes and two Turns.

Version. Dennis McGee (©Flat Town).
Related songs. See: *Valse des Grands Bois* (Carrie "Mignonne" Royer Miller) and *La Breakdown la Louisiane* (The Walker Brothers). Also: *Valse de l'Anse Maigre* (Sady Courville and Dennis McGee); *Valse de la Belle* (Shirley Bergeron); *Valse à Will Kegley* (Will Kegley); *Pochéville* (Joseph Falcon—a mixture of *Tolan Waltz* in the turn and *Valse des Grands Bois* in the tune); *Valse de Crowley.*

The way Dennis sings this song, the first vocal continues with an A-chord on the seventh bar, while in the second vocal, the chord changes to D on the seventh bar.

Kathleen is the name of one of Sady Courville's daughters.

Kathleen's Waltz

(1)
Yes, unfortunate one, you left me to go so far away. Criminal!
(2)
Hey! Say good-bye, criminal! Unfortunate one!
But you don't want me forever! *(High pitched cry)*

Lacassine Special

Key. A
Pattern. Accordion: two Tunes; Vocal #1; Accordion: two Turns and two Tunes; Vocal #2; Accordion: two Turns and two Tunes; Vocal #3; Accordion: two Turns.

Version. Iry LeJeune (©Tek).
Related songs. Also: *Lacassine Breakdown*; *La Danse de Coulée Croche* (Merlin Fontenot).

Lacassine is about thirteen miles east of Lake Charles, Louisiana. Its name is derived from Spanish and means a small house.

Lacassine Special

(1)
Well, how do you think I will fare all the time in misery,
always suffering because of the words you said to me?
(2)
Well, dear, the ugly ways you've always had,
you'll have to forget all that, if you want to stay with your dear old lover.
Hurry! You can see the road and go!
(3)
Ah, dear, I am speaking the truth to you.
I am always there thinking of you, doll,
because of all the worries that you've put me through.

♩ = 175

A   Intro.

D

1-   Eh,   com-
2-   Eh,   toi,
3-   Eh,

-ment   mais   toi   tu   crois   que
chère,   tes vil-   aines   ma-   nières   que
toi,   chère,   j'parle à   toi   bien!

E

moi   mais   moi   j'   va'   faire   tout   l'   temps   dans   les   mis-
toi   t'as   tout   l'   temps   eu!   I'   fau-   dra   t'ou-   blie   tout
Moi   j'   su'   tout   l'   temps   là   a-   près   jon-   gler   à

A   D

-ères;   tout   l'   temps   a-   près   souf-   fert   juste   rap-
ça   si   toi   tu   veux   res-   ter   a-
toi;   a-   près   jon-   gler   à   toi,   ca-

A

-port   à   tes   pa-   roles,   à   tes   pa-   roles   que
-vec   ton   cher   vieux   nèg'.   Hour-   ra!   Toi   tu   peux
-tin,   c'est   juste   rap-   port   à   tous   mais   ces   jongle-

E   A

toi,   ca-   tin,   tu   m'   a-   vais   dit?
voir   le   ch'min   et   t'en   al-   ler!
-ments   que   toi   tu   m'as   mis   d'   dans.

Lake Arthur Stomp

Key. G
Pattern. Violin: one Turn and two Tunes, etc.

Version. Varise Connor.
Related song. See: *Arnaudville Two-Step* (Johnny Richard, Ray Cormier and "Boy" Frugé).

Instrumental. Varise Connor takes credit for this tune. Here is his version. The turn uses the second position on the violin and has been a challenge to some musicians. I made a special trip to Lake Arthur to get this version from him. Vocals have been added in the *Arnaudville Two-Step*.

When I heard this song, it wasn't played as it is today. I did this by myself. I heard a man play it somewhat like that, but it wasn't like the way I played it. People who heard it around here started recording it and named it Lake Arthur Stomp. *They knew where it came from, too! I started playing it in 1925.*

— *Varise Connor*

Là Tu Attrapes du Sirop

Key. D

Version. Amédé Ardoin (OT).

Pattern. I have made no attempt to find a pattern other than what I've presented.

I've tried to do the rest of the lyrics, but the old scratchy record gave me some problems. This song was recorded as *La Turtape de Saroid*; this is my best guess at what was really meant.

1- Oh yé yaille! Moi j' m'en va'. Oh ouais, moi j' m'en va'. Ouais, moi j' m'en va' à "Church" Pointe. Oh, j'm'en va'!

Là Tu Attrapes du Sirop

(1)
Oh, yé yaille! Moi, j' m'en va'. Oh, ouais, moi j' m'en va'.
Ouais, moi j' m'en va' à Church Pointe. Oh, j' m'en va'!
(2)
Ah, j' m'en va' moi tout seul. Ouais, je m'en va' moi tout seul.
J'en vois pas personne, ouais, qui veut v'nir avec moi à Church Pointe.
Eh, yé yaille! C'est là-bas chez Bellard!
(3)
Oh, yé yaille! Moi j'après m'en aller à Church Pointe.
N'a pas personne qui veut v'nir avec moi pour la voir.
C'est là-bas chez Bellard!
(4)
Oh, yé yaille! Moi j' m'en va' — voir su' la route aujourd'hui.
Peut êt' dimanche matin, j' su' parti. Adieu, belle Ardoin!
Oh, la belle, mais moi j' connais, passe toujours dimanche elle tout seule!

You Get Some Syrup There

(1)
Oh, wow! I'm going. Oh, yes, I'm going.
Yes, I'm going to Church Point. Oh, I'm going!
(2)
Ah, I'm going by myself. Yes, I'm going by myself.
I don't see anyone, yes, who wants to come with me to Church Point.
Well, it hurts! It's over there at Bellard's!
(3)
Oh, wow! I'm going to Church Point.
There's no one who wants to come with me to see her.
It's over there at Bellard's!
(4)
Oh, wow! I'm going — see on the road today.
Maybe I'll go Sunday morning. Good-bye, fine Ardoin!
Oh, I know that my sweetheart always spends Sunday by herself!

Leopold's Song

Key. C
Version. Leopold François.
Pattern. Make your own

This is a song I learned from my father a long time ago. He doesn't remember the name, so I've called it after him. He associates the song with Mayuse LaFleur, so perhaps it's one that Mayuse played, too.

Chanson de Limonade

Key. C
Pattern. Accordion: one Tune; Vocal #1; Violin: one Tune; Accordion: one Tune; Vocal #2; Accordion: one Tune.

Version. Thomas Langly, vocal; Nathan Abshire.
Related song. Also: *Mon Cher Cousin.*

There are other verses as well. I believe this song comes from the New Orleans Creoles.

I went to Lafayette one night last year [1983] and met Leroy Broussard at a saloon while at the bar drinking a few beers. He came over and introduced himself. I was glad, and we started a good conversation. He said, "You made some records?" "Yes," I answered, "and you too?" Leroy said, "Yes, I made Passe Moi le Verre de Limonade." "Aw," I said, "it's not you who made that; it's "Boy" Frugé who made that in 1929." But Leroy said, "I tell you it's me who made the record." I told him, "You're wrong!" He got angry. I said, "Okay, but someday I might find "Boy" Frugé's record, and even if I have to go to your home, I'll find out where you live and I will show you that it's not you who made that record; it's "Boy" Frugé that made it."
— *Moïse Robin*

Lemonade Song

(1)
I like my girl-cousin, and I like my boy-cousin but I like the cook better.
Saturday night I went to the dance, I got drunk as a hog.
Sunday morning I'm kind of sick; pass me the glass of lemonade.
Winter's here! Winter's here! My little boy has no blanket.
Saturday night he went to the dance, he got drunk as a hog.
Sunday morning he's kind of sick; pass him the glass of lemonade.
(2)
I eat some pies and drink my beer and all that costs me nothing.
Saturday night I went to the dance, I got drunk as a hog.
Sunday morning I'm kind of sick; pass me the glass of lemonade.

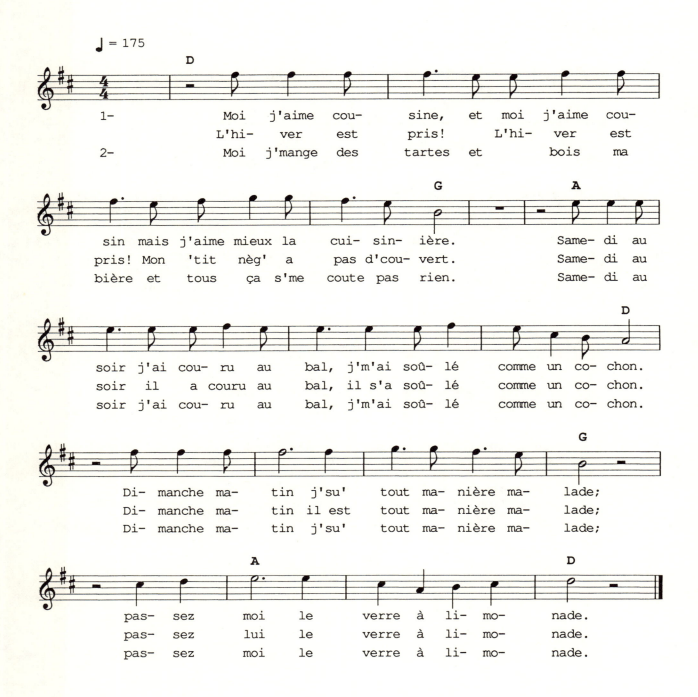

1- Moi j'aime cou- sine, et moi j'aime cou-
   L'hi- ver est pris! L'hi- ver est
2- Moi j'mange des tartes et bois ma

sin mais j'aime mieux la cui- sin- ière. Same- di au
pris! Mon 'tit nèg' a pas d'cou- vert. Same- di au
bière et tous ça s'me coute pas rien. Same- di au

soir j'ai cou- ru au bal, j'm'ai soû- lé comme un co- chon.
soir il a couru au bal, il s'a soû- lé comme un co- chon.
soir j'ai cou- ru au bal, j'm'ai soû- lé comme un co- chon.

Di- manche ma- tin j'su' tout ma- nière ma- lade;
Di- manche ma- tin il est tout ma- nière ma- lade;
Di- manche ma- tin j'su' tout ma- nière ma- lade;

pas- sez moi le verre à li- mo- nade.
pas- sez lui le verre à li- mo- nade.
pas- sez moi le verre à li- mo- nade.

Longue Pointe Two-Step

Key. D
Pattern. Accordion: two Tunes; Vocal #1; Violin: two Tunes; Accordion: two Tunes; Vocal #2; Accordion: two Tunes; Violin: two Tunes; Accordion: two Tunes.

Version. Gervais Quibodeaux, vocal, with Ambrose Thibodeaux (©La Lou).
Related song. Also: *T'as Passé par la Fenêtre.*

When using this vocal, make up your own instrumentals. Long Point is between Iota and Mowata, Louisiana.

1- T'as pas- sé par la fe-
Tu sa- vais tu fais- ais
2- Ta ma- man a- vait peu com-
J'va' r' tour- ner une aut'

nêtre! C'é- tais pour v'nir 'join' ton
mal quand t'as v'nu r' join' ton
pris juste quo' faire moi j' vou- lais t'
fois, met' à genoux et la d' mand-

nèg' au bout d'la manche en ca-
nèg'. Oh chère 'tite fille,
voir. C'é- tais juste pour te d' man-
er en pleu- rant j'va' eu

shette de ta ma- man.
com- ment moi j' t'aime!
der pour te ma- rier!
dire comment j't'aime ma belle!

Long Point Two-Step

(1)
You passed through the window to come meet your lover
at the end of the lane in secrecy from your mother.
You knew you were doing wrong when you came to meet your lover.
Oh, dear little girl, how I love you!
(2)
Your mother had little understood why I wanted to see you.
It was just to ask you to marry me!
I'll go back one more time, get on my knees crying and ask her.
I'll tell them how much I love you, my sweetheart!

We practiced, and when I was thirteen and a half, we played in a hall here in Mamou, Cazo's Hall. My father met him on the street and told him, "Listen, Caz, I have two little boys who play music extremely well. Wouldn't you give them a few dances? Figure out how much you could pay them so that they could enter the dance hall all year long." It cost a quarter to enter the dance hall, and the quarters were rare during that time. Ho, ho! Yaille!

But he said, "Look, tell them to come Saturday and I'll tell my musicians to give them a chance to play three or four songs." We had some good carrying cases, each a flour sack! There were no carrying cases! We arrived with the instruments under our arms, and he told his two musicians, "Look, I have two young men who feel like taking your place for a few songs." They said it was alright and let us play seven or eight songs and when we got off Cazo was right there. He said, "Y'all can come next Saturday." We played until we both got married because the young crowd liked us better than the others. You know, the young ones prefer young musicians. The old musicians, the young don't like that too much, no. That old gray head! They don't like that too much, no! That old gray head? We were young and exciting like the others! And they liked us! We played until we got married.
                                                        — Roy Fusilier

Love Bridge Waltz

Key. A
Pattern. Accordion: two Tunes; Vocal #1; Accordion: one Turn and two Tunes; Vocal #2; Accordion: one Turn and one Tune; Vocal #3; Accordion: two Turns and one Tune.

Version. Iry LeJeune (©Tek).
Related songs. Also: *La Valse Indépendance* (Ambrose Thibodeaux).

These three vocals provide an example of the variations found in many of our Cajun songs. I've tried to standardize most of them into one basic tune.

dit que moi j' pou- vais p'us al- ler t' voir.   Oh, mon 'tit

monde, pour- quoi t'as ou- bli- er   du part où tu m' as

dit... eh moi j' con- nais tu vas braill- er!

Love Bridge Waltz

(1)
Well, little girl, I see myself leaving to go so far away.
Oh, dear little girl, even if you'd want to come back home,
I don't want to see you anymore.
(2)
Well, little dark-haired criminal,
you told me you didn't want to love me anymore, unhappy one.
You know, little girl, that I took it so hard that I traveled the highways.
(3)
Don't forget the advice you listened to!
That's when you said that I couldn't go to see you anymore.
Oh, my little one, why did you forget the part where you told me ...
oh, I know that you're going to cry!

Valse à Macareau

Key. G   *Version.* Dennis McGee.
Pattern. Violin: Play each part twice, etc.

Instrumental. Ken Keppeler and I recorded
this song during a *veillée* at Dennis' home in
1975. Macareau is a person's name.

Madame Young

Key. G
Pattern. Violin: two Tunes; Vocal #1; Violin: one Turn and one Tune; Vocal #2; Violin: one Turn; Vocal #3; Violin: one Turn; Vocal #4; Violin: one Turn.

Version. Dennis McGee (OT).
Related song. See: *Allons Danser Colinda* (Oran "Doc" Guidry and Leroy "Happy Fats" LeBlanc).

Madame Young is similar to *Allons Danser Colinda* but has a different turn. In the old days, a young man had to ask a girl's parents for permission to court her.

♩ = 175

(1)   Ouais,   donc   ouais,   Ma- dame   Young,   don- nez-
        Mais ouais,   oh   ouais,   mais   l'a-   voir.   L'a-   voir,
(2)   Ouais,   donc   ouais,   Ma- dame   Young.   Com- ment
        Ouais,   mais   ouais,   de   l'a-   voir,   a-   vec
(3) De- puis   quand elle é- tait   'tite,   j'a- vais
    Je dé-   sir-   ais   que ça   s'rait elle di-
(4)   C'est   pas qu' elle est si   belle, mais el'est
        Oh   oui,   'garde donc, ché- ri   coeur, mais   fait

moi   la,   vot'   chère   blonde.   Je
oh   ouais, la   grosse   blonde;   pour   moi
ça s'   fait   d'r'- fu-   ser,   pas   mi-
la   chère mais   grosse   blonde.   C'est pour
ché-   ri   la   chère   blonde.   Je   su'
rait   "ouais"d' mon i-   dée   d'a-   voir
si   bonne est   ai-   mable.   La   chère
pas   ça   'vec   ton   nèg'.   Tu   vas

vou-   drais, mal-   heu-   reuse,   a-   vec,
fi-   nir   mes   grands   jours   a-   vant
sèr-   ait?   De m' ma-   rier?   Ah   ouais,
fi-   nir   mes   grands   jours   tou-   jours
a-   près   la   guet-   ter;   oh   ouais,
la   chère mais   grosse   blonde   pour, ouais,
'tite   blonde, j'l'   aim'   rais   dans   tout,
me   faire mais   mou-   rir   pour   toi

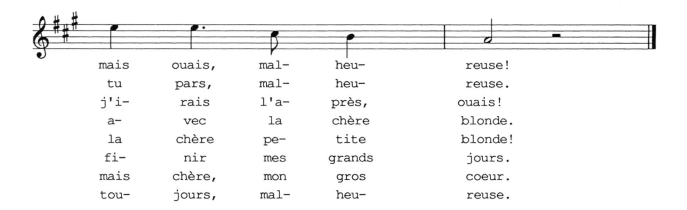

mais	ouais,	mal-	heu-	reuse!
tu	pars,	mal-	heu-	reuse.
j'i-	rais	l'a-	près,	ouais!
a-	vec	la	chère	blonde.
la	chère	pe-	tite	blonde!
fi-	nir	mes	grands	jours.
mais	chère,	mon	gros	coeur.
tou-	jours,	mal-	heu-	reuse.

Madam Young, Give Me Your Most Beautiful Blond

(1)
Yes, indeed yes, Madam Young, give her to me, your dear blond.
I'd like, unfortunate one, but yes, unfortunate one.
But yes, oh yes, to have her. To have her, oh yes, the big blond;
for me to finish my long days before you go, unfortunate one.
(2)
Yes, indeed yes, Madam Young. Why refuse me, make me suffer?
To marry me? Ah yes, I'll go get her, yes.
Yes, but yes, to have her, with the dear, big blond.
To finish my long days forever with the dear blond.
(3)
Ever since she was small, I have cherished the dear blond.
I'm watching for her; oh yes, the dear little blond!
I would desire for her to say "yes" to my idea
to have the dear, big blond to, yes, finish my long days.
(4)
It's not that she's so beautiful, but she's so good and lovable.
The dear little blond, I'd love her in all my big heart, dear.
Oh yes, indeed look, cherished heart, don't do that to your lover.
You'll make me die for you forever, unfortunate one.

Madame Bosco

Key. G
Pattern. Accordion: two Tunes; Vocal #1; Steel Guitar:
two Tunes; Accordion: two Tunes; Vocal #2;
Accordion: two Tunes.

Version. Shirley Bergeron (©JON).
Related song. *Madame Baptiste, Tirez-moi Pas*
(Irène Whitfield).

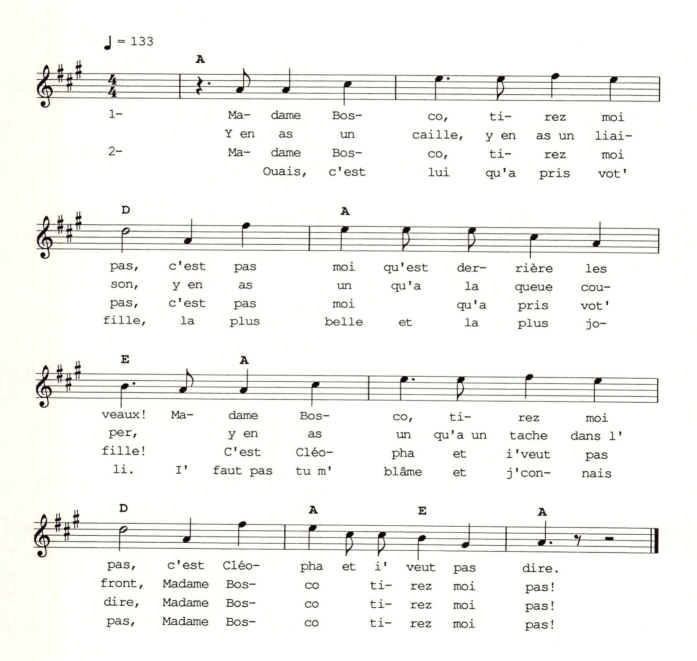

1- Ma- dame Bos- co, ti- rez moi
   Y en as un caille, y en as un liai-
2- Ma- dame Bos- co, ti- rez moi
   Ouais, c'est lui qu'a pris vot'

pas, c'est pas moi qu'est der- rière les
son, y en as un qu'a la queue cou-
pas, c'est pas moi qu'a pris vot'
fille, la plus belle et la plus jo-

veaux! Ma- dame Bos- co, ti- rez moi
per, y en as un qu'a un tache dans l'
fille! C'est Cléo- pha et i'veut pas
li. I' faut pas tu m' blâme et j'con- nais

pas, c'est Cléo- pha et i' veut pas dire.
front, Madame Bos- co ti- rez moi pas!
dire, Madame Bos- co ti- rez moi pas!
pas, Madame Bos- co ti- rez moi pas!

Madam Bosco

(1)
Madam Bosco, don't shoot me, it's not me who's after the calves!
Madam Bosco, don't shoot me, it's Cléopha and he doesn't want to tell.
There's a spotted one, there's a _?_, there's one with the tail cut off,
there's one with a spot on the forehead, Madam Bosco, don't shoot me!

(2) Madam Bosco, don't shoot me, it's not me who took your daughter!
It's Cléopha and he doesn't want to tell, Madam Bosco, don't shoot me!
Yes, it's him who took your daughter, the most beautiful and the prettiest.
You mustn't blame me and I don't know. Madam Bosco, don't shoot me!

Oh, my dear friends, there's a big difference in being young and being old! A big difference! When I was young, anywhere I'd go, I felt and saw myself as having an advantage. When I would've set my eyes on a girl or a widow, they would've looked at me and cracked a smile. That made me so happy! I had feeling down to my toes! My toes tickled! Ha, ha! And now? There's a big difference when I try to find myself a good time. It's all different now. If I look at a girl or a widow and I give her a little smile, she will bow her head or turn her back to me. Oh, yé yaille! That hurts me! It makes me sad! It gives me cramps all the way down to my toes! I can see for myself that my advantage is gone.

— Moïse Robin

Madame Sosthène

Key. A

Pattern. Accordion: two Tunes; Vocal #1; Violin: two
Tunes; Accordion: two Turns; Vocal #2; Violin: two
Tunes; Accordion: two Turns.

Version. Reggie Matte.

Each stanza of the vocals begins with a bar of
rest.

Fourteen was not too young for courting in the
old days. My mother was fifteen, when she
married in the early 1920's.

Madam Sosthène

(1)
Oh, Madam Sosthène, give Alida to me,
the one I've loved since the age of fourteen.
If you don't let me have her, I promise you that I'll steal her.
I'll put her in my wagon and take her home.
(2)
Oh, Madam Sosthène, give me your dear little daughter,
the one I've loved since the age of fourteen.
If you don't let me have her, I promise you that I'll steal her.
I'll pass her through the window and take her home.

Madeleine

Key. G
Pattern. Violin: three Tunes; Vocal #1; Violin: four
Tunes; Vocal #2; Violin: six Tunes.

Version. Balfa Brothers; Rodney Balfa's vocal
(©Flat Town). The original recording was by Adam
Hébert (©Flat Town).

Madeleine

(1)
Oh, Madeline, you slept outside; oh, Madeline, outside in the big fog!
Oh, Madeline, why don't you come back; oh, Madeline, I know you'll make me die!
(2)
Oh, Madeline, you slept outside; oh, Madeline, outside in the big fog!
Oh, Madeline, why do you do that? Oh, Madeline, I know you'll cry!

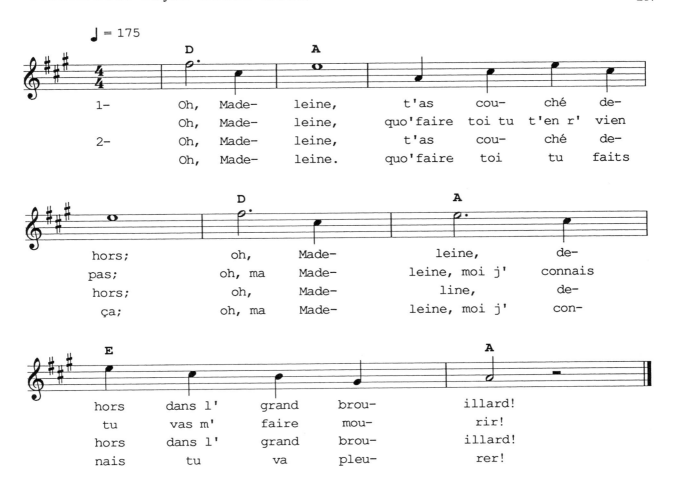

Adam Hébert first recorded this song so I've
included his vocals, too.

(1)
Aïe, Madeleine, toi t'as couché dehors; aïe, Madeleine, dehors dans l' gros brouillard!
Aïe, Madeleine, toi t'es tout l' temps parti; aïe, ma Madeleine, toi tu coursaies trop les hommes!
(2)
Aïe, Madeleine, toi t'as couché dehors; aïe, Madeleine, dehors dans l' gros vent d' nord!
Aïe, Madeleine, toi tu vas m' faire mourir; aïe, Madeleine, si t'arrettes pas de roullaier!

(1)
Oh, Madeleine, you slept outside; oh, Madeleine, outside in the big fog!
Oh, Madeleine, you're always gone; oh, my Madeleine, you chase men too much!
(2)
Oh, Madeleine, you slept outside; oh, Madeleine, outside in the big north wind!
Oh, Madeleine, you will make me die; oh, Madeleine, if you don't stop rambling!

Chanson de Mardi Gras

Key. G minor
Pattern. Violin: play first verse; Vocals: Verses 1 & 2, Turn #1, Verses 3 & 4, Turn #2, Verses 5 & 6, Turn #3, Verses 7 & 8, Turn #4, Repeat first verse; Violin: play first verse.
Rhythm: You could play this song using one chord.

Version. Bee Deshotels (AR).
Related song. See the *Danse de Mardi Gras I.*

Mardi Gras is celebrated forty days before Easter Sunday; it is the day before Lent, which begins with Ash Wednesday. Mardi Gras means Fat Tuesday, and it is the last day on which you were supposed to eat meat, until Easter. Mardi Gras is still an important celebration in southwestern Louisiana, and it is celebrated quite differently in the small towns than it is in New Orleans. Around Mamou, Eunice, and Church Point, masked riders on horseback still go out and solicit food for the community feast, usually a large gumbo, which is served after the dance on Mardi Gras day. It used to be that each little district (*moyeu*, "hub") had its own Mardi Gras; now, it has become a civic event, organized by the various small towns.

Mardi Gras is used to mean both the holiday and the costumed riders. The Mardi Gras are accompanied by an unmasked rider, the captain, who provides some social restraint, if the Mardi Gras get too rowdy, and by a wagon which carries the goods collected, musicians, any Mardi Gras who can't stay on his horse. At each house, the captain asks the householder for permission to visit; if permission is granted, he signals with his flag for the Mardi Gras to approach and dance or perform tricks as they beg for food.

I remember, when I was about four, hiding under my bed because I thought the Mardi Gras might take me away with them. My mother had to bring the rider inside and get him to take off his mask to reassure me that he was really one of our neighbors. The household will contribute ingredients for the communal gumbo: rice, oil, flour, sometimes even a live chicken, which is thrown to the riders; it is their task to catch it, which can lead to more clowning. Finally, the Mardi Gras will remove their masks so you can see who they really are. Then the captain waves his flag to collect the Mardi Gras together and visit the next neighbor.

The words in The Mardi Gras Song describe this custom of "running" Mardi Gras. You should see the costumes! Traditional costumes include a tall pointed hat and a mask made out of painted wire screen. The captain is the only one who doesn't wear a mask and he and a few musicians sing and play this song.

Mamou is a small town about fifteen miles north of Eunice, Louisiana; it is often called Grand Mamou to distinguish it from the community near Evangeline, Louisiana, which is also named Mamou — and called 'Tit Mamou.

Lent in those days was respected very much. There were no dances in Lent, but for Easter I'd always play in private homes for dances. We had played for a dance one night and we'd walk with our girlfriends to the dance then walk back with them afterwards, usually in small groups. The girls' mothers would always walk with us too; the girls were always well chaperoned. This night was the Sunday before Mardi Gras and I had played for the dance and even danced some. When we separated that night, I heard a boy say to his girlfriend in a nasal tone, "Well, this will be a long Lent, eh?" There were no dances in Lent in the old days, that's how it was.
                                                            — Sady Courville

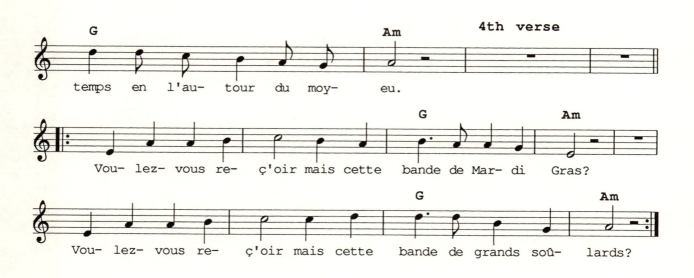

temps en l'au- tour du moy- eu.

Vou- lez- vous re- ç'oir mais cette bande de Mar- di Gras?

Vou- lez- vous re- ç'oir mais cette bande de grands soû- lards?

♩ = 175

5,6,7 & 8th Verses

5- Don- nez- nous aut' une 'tite poule
6- Don- nez- nous aut' un peu d'la
7- On vous invite pour le bal à
8- On vous invite pour le gros gom-

grasse pour qu'on s' fais un gom- bo gras.
graisse, si' vous plaît, mon ka- ra- mi.
soir mais là- bas à Grand Ma- mou.
bo mais là- bas à la cui- sine.

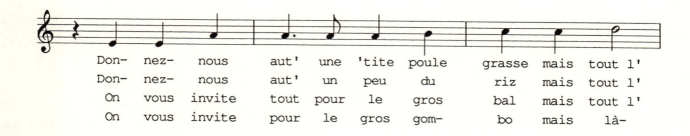

Don- nez- nous aut' une 'tite poule grasse mais tout l'
Don- nez- nous aut' un peu du riz mais tout l'
On vous invite tout pour le gros bal mais tout l'
On vous invite pour le gros gom- bo mais là-

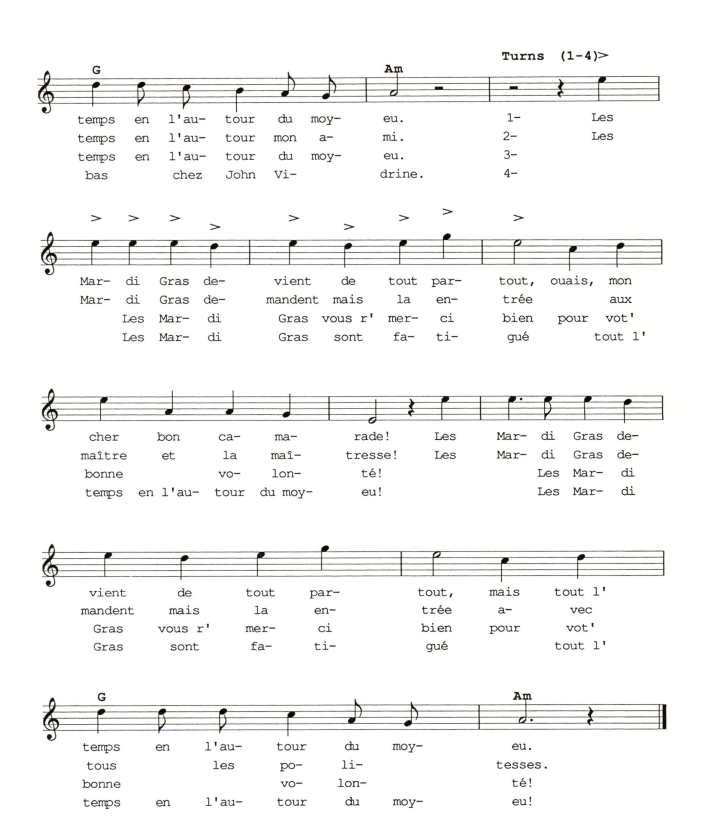

The Mardi Gras Song

Verse (1)
Captain, captain, wave your flag, let's get on the road!
Captain, captain, wave your flag, let's go to the other neighbor!
Verse (2)
The Mardi Gras reassemble once a year to ask for charity.
They will go from door to door always around the hub.
Turn (#1)
The Mardi Gras come from everywhere, yes my dear good
comrade!
The Mardi Gras come from everywhere, but always from around the hub.
Verse (3)
The Mardi Gras come from everywhere, but mainly Big Mamou.
The Mardi Gras come from everywhere, but always from around the hub.
Verse (4)
Would you like to receive this band of Mardi Gras?
Would you like to receive this band of big drunkards?
Would you like to receive this band of Mardi Gras?
Would you like to receive this band of big drunkards?
Turn (#2)
The Mardi Gras ask the master and the mistress to be received.
The Mardi Gras ask to be received with all politeness.
Verse (5)
Give us a little fat hen for us to make a fat gumbo.
Give us a little fat hen, but always from around the hub.
Verse (6)
Give us a little lard, please, my dear friend.
Give us a little rice, but always from around, my friend.
Turn (#3)
The Mardi Gras thank you well for your good will.
The Mardi Gras thank you well for your good will.
Verse (7)
We invite you to the dance tonight, over there in Big Mamou.
We invite you to the big dance, always from around the hub.
Verse (8)
We invite you for the big gumbo over there at the kitchen.
We invite you for the big gumbo over there at John Vidrine's.
Turn (#4)
The Mardi Gras are tired, always from around the hub.
The Mardi Gras are tired, always from around the hub.
Verse (1)
Captain, captain, wave your flag, let's get on the road!
Captain, wave your flag, let's go to the other neighbor!

Chant de Mardi Gras

Key. G
Pattern. All vocal chant.
Rhythm. The first two stanzas and the last stanza use only the last four of the sequence of five accents which I have marked in measures ten and eleven. The other stanzas, which lack a syllable to go with the final accented note, shift the accent to begin one note earlier, using only the first four accents.

Version. Gerald Frugé and the 'Tit Mamou Mardi Gras (a female group).

This song is from Evangeline or 'Tit Mamou in Acadia Parish, Louisiana.

During the Mardi Gras season, a dance hall owner may invite some Mardi Gras to come and amuse the customers. This is the way I've have seen it done, by a male group. Suddenly, there is a great commotion and the Mardi Gras all rush in; they may dance together or grab customers and lead them onto the dance floor. They are followed by the captain, who carries a whip. The Mardi Gras scream and hide under tables, possibly teasing the women who are sitting there by trying to look under their skirts. The captain finds the Mardi Gras, forces them to the center of the dance floor, and pretends to whip them — they wear cardboard or padding under their costumes for protection, but they howl a lot to make a good show. Finally, the Mardi Gras sit in a big circle on the dance floor and chant this song beating on the floor to emphasize the notes which I have marked with accents.

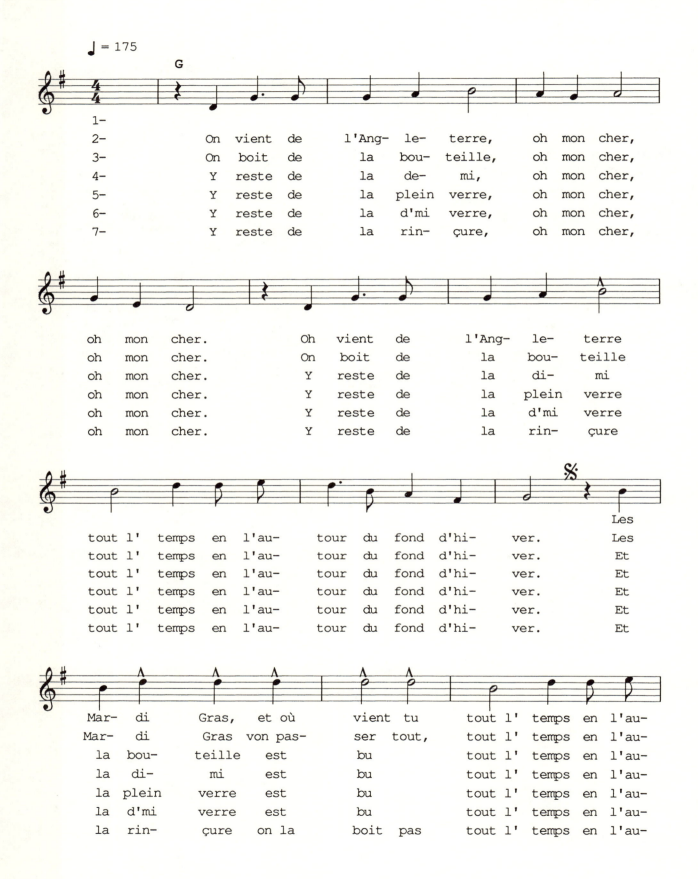

♩ = 175

G

1-
2- On vient de l'Ang- le- terre, oh mon cher,
3- On boit de la bou- teille, oh mon cher,
4- Y reste de la de- mi, oh mon cher,
5- Y reste de la plein verre, oh mon cher,
6- Y reste de la d'mi verre, oh mon cher,
7- Y reste de la rin- çure, oh mon cher,

oh mon cher.   Oh vient de l'Ang- le- terre
oh mon cher.   On boit de la bou- teille
oh mon cher.   Y reste de la di- mi
oh mon cher.   Y reste de la plein verre
oh mon cher.   Y reste de la d'mi verre
oh mon cher.   Y reste de la rin- çure

tout l' temps en l'au- tour du fond d'hi- ver.   Les
tout l' temps en l'au- tour du fond d'hi- ver.   Et
tout l' temps en l'au- tour du fond d'hi- ver.   Et
tout l' temps en l'au- tour du fond d'hi- ver.   Et
tout l' temps en l'au- tour du fond d'hi- ver.   Et
tout l' temps en l'au- tour du fond d'hi- ver.   Et

Mar- di Gras, et où vient tu tout l' temps en l'au-
Mar- di Gras von pas- ser tout, tout l' temps en l'au-
la bou- teille est bu tout l' temps en l'au-
la di- mi est bu tout l' temps en l'au-
la plein verre est bu tout l' temps en l'au-
la d'mi verre est bu tout l' temps en l'au-
la rin- çure on la boit pas tout l' temps en l'au-

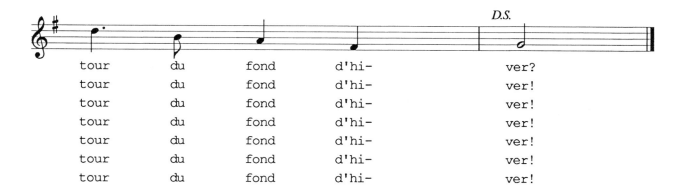

tour	du	fond	d'hi-	ver?
tour	du	fond	d'hi-	ver!
tour	du	fond	d'hi-	ver!
tour	du	fond	d'hi-	ver!
tour	du	fond	d'hi-	ver!
tour	du	fond	d'hi-	ver!
tour	du	fond	d'hi-	ver!

The final verse is spoken, rather than chanted.

Bonjour au maître et la maîtress!
On vous d'mande peu de choses. On veut faire une bonne chose.
On veut faire un bonne chose, on veut faire chauffer les pieds!
(Cris primitifs!)

Mardi Gras Chant

(1)
Mardi Gras, where do you come from, always around the end of winter?
(Repeat)
(2)
We come from England, oh my dear, oh my dear.
We come from England all the time around the end of winter.
The Mardi Gras will pass all, all the time around the end of winter! *(Repeat)*
(3)
We drink from the bottle, oh my dear, oh my dear.
We drink from the bottle all the time around the end of winter.
And the bottle is drunk all the time around the end of winter! *(Repeat)*
(4)
There's half left, oh my dear, oh my dear.
There's half left all the time around the end of winter.
And the half is drunk all the time around the end of winter! *(Repeat)*
(5)
There's a full glass left, oh my dear, oh my dear.
There's a full glass left all the time around the end of winter.
And the full glass is drunk all the time around the end of winter! *(Repeat)*
(6)
There's a half glass left, oh my dear, oh my dear.
There's a half glass left all the time around the end of winter.
And the half glass is drunk all the time around the end of winter! *(Repeat)*
(7)
There's dregs left, oh my dear, oh my dear.
There's dregs left all the time around the end of winter.
And the dregs we don't drink all the time around the end of winter! *(Repeat)*
(8) *(Spoken)*
Good day, master and the mistress!
We ask little of you. We want to do a good thing.
We want to do a good thing, we want to warm our feet!
(Primitive howling screams.)

Marche des Mariés

Key. F
Pattern. Accordion: one Tune; Vocal #1; Violin: one
Turn; Accordion: one Tune; Vocal #2; Violin: one
Turn; Accordion: one Tune. The Turn is vocalized in
each Vocal.

Version. Wallace "Cheese" Reed; Raymond
François.

This wedding march is the first song played at
a wedding dance. The couple link arms and
followed by their entourage, walk around the
dance floor at least twice while this song is
played. Then the first waltz is reserved for the
wedding party; afterwards, anyone who wishes
can dance. Anyone who dances with the bride
will pin money to her veil. "Cheese" told me
that Abe Manuel from Eunice, Louisiana,
made this song popular.

The Wedding March

(1)
You have taken me from the home of my Dad and my Mom.
You have promised to care for and fulfill me for the rest of our lives.
(Turn)
Today you and I are so far away from our parents and I fear that we will suffer.
(2)
You have taken me from home like a poor orphan.
You have promised to care for me till the day of my death, my dear little girl.
(Turn)
Today you and I are so far away from our parents and I fear that we will suffer.

One-Step à Marie

Key. C

Pattern. Accordion: one Tune, one Turn; Vocal #1;
Accordion: one Turn, one Tune, one Turn, one Tune;
Vocal #2; Accordion: one Tune, one Turn, one Tune,
one Turn, one Tune, one Turn.

Version. Breaux Frères (OT).

This is a rare one-step. My father said the first time he saw a one-step danced was about 1916, when he was fifteen; it was danced to the tune of *It's a Long Way to Tipperary*. He gave me a demonstration of dancing a one-step; it is a dance for partners and looks like a slow walk, or like a two-step with one step left out.

Mary's One-Step

(1)
Oh, Mary, I don't see, little girl, the reason, yes, dear, why you're a scoundrel, my old Mary.
(2)
Oh, Mary, you have some little cunning eyes! Because of what you've done, your dress is so very new!
I'm going home because of your lover, and also for you, but I'll never stay with my mother and father. Ah, dear!

Les Maringouins Ont Tout Mangé Ma Belle

Key. D
Pattern. Accordion: two Tunes and Two Turns; Vocal;
Accordion: two Tunes, two Turns and two Tunes;
Vocal; Accordion: two Tunes, two Turns, two Tunes,
and two Turns.

Version. Segura Brothers (OT).

Ouaouaron is a Huron and Iroquois Indian
name for bullfrog; it is used in Canadian and
Louisiana French. *Maringouin* comes from a
South American Indian name for mosquito;
moustique is also used to mean mosquito in
some parts of Louisiana. Saying someone
looks like *un coin d' banquette* probably
means she was angular.

Les ma-rin-gouins a tout mang-é ma belle! I' ons lais-sé que les gros or-teils; c'est pour me faire des bou-chons de liège; c'est pour bou-cher mes de-mi bou-teilles! Et ton pa-pa r' semb' un é-lé-phant et ta ma-man 'r semb' un 'to-mo-bile et ton 'tit frère r' semb' un "oua-oua-ron"* et ta 'tite soeur 'semb' un coin d' ban-quette!

The Mosquitoes Ate Up My Sweetheart

The mosquitoes ate up my sweetheart!
They only left her big toes for me to use as corks to stop up my pints.
Your father looks like an elephant; your mother looks like an automobile;
your little brother looks like a bullfrog
and your little sister looks like the corner of a wooden sidewalk.

Mazurka de la Louisiane

Key. C
Pattern. Play as written (instrumental).
Rhythm. There are two dotted quarter notes per
measure for guitar and one dotted quarter note and one
dotted quarter rest per measure for the bass.

Version. Dudley and James Favor (OT).

Mazurkas are not played anymore in Cajun
music, but a few have been preserved in the
repertoires of older musicians. My mother
remembers, when she was quite small, seeing
her mother at a family party showing how a
mazurka was danced; it was probably already
an old-fashioned dance, because, she says, no
one else at the party knew how to dance it and
my grandmother had to demonstrate it alone,
even though it was originally a dance for partners. She says my grandmother's feet moved
very fast under her long ruffled skirt.

Valse des Mèches

Key. G
Pattern. Accordion: two Tunes; Vocal #1; Violin: two Tunes; Accordion: two Turns; Vocal #2; Violin: two Tunes; Accordion: two Turns and one Tune.

Version. Nathan Abshire (©La Lou); Maurice Berzas (©Flat Town).
Related song. Also: *Ton 'Tit Bec Est Doux* (Ambrose Thibodeaux).

There are huge marshes, with reeds higher than a man's head, in south Louisiana near the Gulf of Mexico where all kinds of wildlife live — muskrats, alligators, ducks and geese, not to mention fish and shrimp. Mosquitoes are jokingly referred to as the state bird. Sometimes the mosquitoes are so numerous they have been known to kill young calves by blocking their nostrils. If just at about sundown you hear a buzzing sound which quickly becomes a roar, you should seek shelter.

1- Hé 'tite fille, mon j' me vois, chère; mon j' me
2- Oh 'tite fille, mais tu vas voir, chère; tu vas

vois m'en a-   ller dans les grands mèches, mais ouais.
voir ton er-   reur, ça s'ra trop tard, bé- bé!

Waltz of the Reed Marshes

(1)
Well, little girl, I see myself, dear, I see myself going in the big reed marshes, baby.
(2)
Oh, little girl, but you'll see, dear, you'll see your error. It will be too late, baby!

I've also included Roy Fontenot's vocal with
Maurice Berzas' band.

(1)
Aïe petite, c'est malheureux, cher 'tit monde, de te voir tout l' temps toi, mais oui, tout seule.
Aujourd'hui, 'tite fille, tu peux r'partir tes manières; c'est pour ça t'es tout seule dans les misères.
(2)
Aïe jolie, tu casses mon coeur, jolie fille, quand toi tu m' dits tu peux p'us mais p'us m'aimer.
Aujourd'hui, jolie, j'ai essayé t' faire comprend'. T'as pas voulu m'écouter, quoi tu vas faire?

(1)
Oh pretty one, it's unfortunate to see you all by yourself.
Today, little girl, you can correct your ways; that's why you're all alone in misery.
(2)
Oh pretty girl, you break my heart when you tell me you can never, never love me.
Today, pretty one, I tried to make you understand. You didn't want to listen, what will you do?

Valse à Napoléon

Key. B flat for tune and F for turn.
Pattern. Violin: two Tunes and one Turn, etc.
Rhythm This is a *valse à deux temps*. It has two dotted quarter notes per measure for rhythm guitar. The bass pattern is: 1st measure, one dotted quarter rest and one dotted quarter note; 2nd measure, one dotted quarter note and one dotted quarter rest; 3rd measure, two dotted quarter notes. Repeat over until the end of the song.

Version. Dennis McGee (©Flat Town).

Instrumental. Dennis claims this song was played by a general to a condemned soldier by the name of Guilbeau whose last request before being executed by a firing squad was to speak, and play the violin. His handcuffs were removed and he sat on his coffin and played a song which Dennis called *Guilbeau's Waltz*. After Guilbeau played his waltz, he asked the general to play a song for him, *Napoleon's Waltz*. Dennis believes this probably happened during the Civil War. See *Guilbeau's Waltz*.

Valse à Napoléon (variation)

Key. B flat for Tune and F for Turn   *Version.* Dennis McGee (©Flat Town).
Pattern. Violin: three Tunes, two Turns, etc.

Instrumental. Written to show the difference
from a *valse à deux temps*.

New Iberia Polka

Key. D
Pattern. Accordion: Repeat all five times.
Rhythm. The rhythm guitar plays two beats per
measure (dotted quarter notes) while the bass has one
dotted quarter note and one dotted rest.

Version. Segura Brothers (OT).

Don't expect this to sound like a traditional
polka played by Lawrence Welk.

No Name Blues

Key. G   *Version.* Leopold François.

Ossun Two-Step

Key. C
Pattern. Accordion: two Turns and two Tunes; Steel Guitar: two Turns; Violins: two Tunes; Accordion: two Turns and two Tunes; Steel Guitar: two Turns; Violins: two Tunes; Accordion: two Turns and two Tunes.

Version. Aldus Roger (©Jamil). Earlier recordings of this song were made by Joseph Falcon and by Lawrence Walker.
Related song. Also: *Opelousas Two-Step.*

Ossun is a small village north of Scott, Louisiana.

There were only two dance halls between Lafayette and Carencro, located between Vatican and Ossun. The entrance fee was ten cents to dance, but for a wedding dance it was fifteen cents. That was something, huh? There were more people and the owner had to pay the wedding couple to celebrate at his place. Yes, he paid the wedding couple ten or fifteen dollars. People were too poor to pin money on the bride's veil. No, they didn't have that kind of money to put on the veil ... They'd sell about 150 or 200 tickets. Oh, there were a lot of people who went to the dance in those days! It was in the country and, if it was too far for them to go on foot, there was a school bus or a truck that'd pass and pick up the people for five or ten cents a head.
— Aldus Roger

Valse à Pap'

Key. G   *Version.* Dennis McGee (MS).
Pattern. Violin: two Tunes and two Turns; Vocal #1;
Violin: one Tune; Vocal #2; Violin: one Tune, three
Turns and one Tune; Vocal #3; Violin: one Turn and
two Tunes; Vocal #4 (Turn); Violin: one Tune.

Dad's Waltz

(1)
Say Good-bye, unfortunate one! Unfortunate one, every day!
Unfortunate one, indeed look what you've done! Unfortunate one, God knows you'll cry!
(2)
Unfortunate one, if you would've never listened to your father and mother,
that would've never happened. Unfortunate one, *le le rai!*
(3)
Indeed look, unfortunate one! Indeed look!
You know I wouldn't do to you what you've done to me on account of you, unfortunate one.
(4)
(Sing the Turn)

Parlez-nous à Boire

Key. G
Pattern. Violin: play Part 1 twice and Part 2 once; Vocal #1-harmonize first stanza Part 1, solo the first stanza Part 2, harmonize first stanza Part 1, solo the second stanza Part 2, harmonize first stanza Part 1; Violin: play Part 1 twice and Part 2 once; Vocal #2- harmonize first stanza Part 1, solo the third stanza Part 2, harmonize first stanza Part 1, solo the fourth stanza Part 2, solo second stanza Part 1, harmonize first stanza Part 1; Violin: play Part 1 twice.

Version. Balfa Brothers (©Flat Town).
Related song. Also: *Parlez-nous à Boire* (Irène Whitfield's book).

Dewey and Rodney alternated on the solo parts of this old drinking song. The second stanza of Part 1 is used only once. It is well worth the effort to get this song right!

Talk to Us of Drinking

(1)
Harmonize: Talk to us of drinking, not of marriage, while always regretting our good times long ago.
Solo: If you should get married to a beautiful girl, you're in great danger of being contradicted.
Harmonize: Talk to us of drinking, not of marriage, while always regretting our good times long ago.
Solo: If you should get married to an ugly girl, you're in great danger of spending all your life with her.
Harmonize: Talk to us of drinking, not of marriage, while always regretting our good times long ago.
(2)
Harmonize: Talk to us of drinking, not of marriage, while always regretting our good times long ago.
Solo: If you should get married to a very poor girl, you're in great danger of working all your life.
Harmonize: Talk to us of drinking, not of marriage, while always regretting our good times long ago.
Solo: If you should get married to a wealthy girl, you're in great danger of being reproached a lot.
Solo: Talk to me, you big good-for-nothing, you wasted all my wealth.
Talk to me, you big good-for-nothing, you wasted all my wealth.
Harmonize: Talk to us of drinking, no, not of marriage, while always regretting our good times long ago.

1- Vas parl- er nous à boire, non,
2- Parle- moi mon grand bon-à- rien, t'as

pas de mari- age, tou- jours en re- gret-
tout gaspiller mon bien. Parle- moi mon grand bon-à-

tant nos jo- lie temps pas- sé. Si que tu t' ma-
rien, t'as tout gas- pill- é mon bien. Si que tu t' ma-
Si que tu t' ma-
Si que tu t' ma-

rie a- vec une jo- lie fille, t'es dans les grands dan-
rie a- vec une vi- laine fille, t'es dans les grands dan-
rie a- vec une fille bien pauv', t'es dans les grands dan-
rie a- vec une fille qu'a d' quoi, t'es dans les grands dan-

gers qu'ils von' te la vo- ler.
gers fau- dra tu fais ta vie a- vec.
gers fau- dra trava- iller tout ta vie.
gers tu vas 'trap- per des grands re- proches.

Patassa Two-Step

Key. D

Pattern. Accordion: two Tunes and two Turns; Violin: two Tunes and two Turns, etc.

Version. Ambrose Thibodeaux (©La Lou).

Ambrose named this song for a place located about two miles south-southeast of Eunice, Louisiana. *Patassa* is a word that Cajun French adopted from the Choctaw Indian word meaning sunfish or perch. My family has lived in that area for several generations — I was born there, too — and there used to be a dam at Patassa that made a good place to fish.

I lived near Patassa and I often went there and played music. The people liked that song very much; they were excited by the two-step and it was very good to dance to. It seemed to me that it deserved the name of their place, Patassa.

— *Ambrose Thibodeaux*

Pauv' "Hobo"

Key. A
Pattern. Accordion: one Tune; Vocal #1; Accordion: three Tunes; Vocal #2; Accordion: one Tune.
Rhythm. Note the meter, which gives each eighth note one beat.

Version. Gervais Quibodeaux first two verses (©La Lou); Austin Pitre last two verses (©Flat Town).
Related songs. Also: *Chère Lisa* (Leo Soileau); *Pauvre Clochard* (Merlin Fontenot).

I've included two versions of the words for this song.

Poor Hobo

(1)
It's sad to see myself like a poor hobo. I don't have any money in my pockets anymore.
What will I do? I'm bumming around today, I don't have anyone to love me anymore.
What will I do, little one, as a poor hobo?
(2)
I'm always bumming around today from one place to another.
I don't know, little girl, how I'll make it. Today I'm alone on the highways all the time.
I'm alone, doll, like a poor hobo.

Poor Hobo

(1)
It's sad to see myself as a poor hobo. It's because of all that, these criminal little bottles.
You're the cause of all that, I'm far from you. I'm there alone all the time like a poor hobo.
(2)
It's sad to see myself as a poor hobo. It's you, the author of that, these criminal little bottles.
Yes, I'm all alone, yes, but at home. It's because of my sweetheart that I'm like this, dear.

♩ = 175

A

1-   Ça m'   fait d'   la   peine   de m'
2-   J'su'   à   la   traine au-   jourd'
1-   Ça m'   fait d'   la   peine   de m'
2-   Ça m'   fait d'   la   peine   de m'

voir   mais   comme   un   pauv'   "ho-
hui   tout l'   temps   d'un   bord   et d'
voir   c'est   comme   un   pauv'   "ho-
voir   c'est   comme   un   pauv'   "ho-

E

bo."   J'ai   p'us d'   ar-   gent   dans   mes
l'aut'.   J'con-   nais   pas,   'tite
bo."   C'est   par   rap-   porte   de   tout
bo."   C'est   toi   l'au-   teur   de   tout

poches.   Com-   ment   mais   moi   j'va'
fille,   com-   ment   moi,   j'va'
ça,   ces   cri-   mi-   nelle 'tites   bou-
ça,   ces   cri-   mi-   nelle 'tites   bou-

A

faire?   J'su'   à   la   train   au-   jour-
faire.   J'su'   tout   seul   au-   jour-
teilles.   C'est   toi d'   la   cause   de
teilles.   Ouais   j'su'   là   tout

d'hui, j'ai p'us per- sonne pour m'ai-
d'hui tout l' temps dans les grands
ça, j'su' loin de toi. J'su'
seul ouais, mais à la mai-

mer. Com- ment j'va' faire, 'tit
chemins. Je suis tout seul, ca-
là moi tout seul tout l'
son. C'est par rap- porte de la

monde, mais comme un pauv' "ho- bo?"
tin, mais comme un pauv' "ho- bo."
temps, mais comme un pauv' "ho- bo."
belle que moi j' su' comme ça, chère.

Two-Step des Perrodins

Key. D
Pattern. Each instrument plays two Tunes and/or two Turns.

Version. Raymond François.
Related song. Also: *Pas de Deux à Elia* (Merlin Fontenot).

The beat and rhythm are extremely important for this tune! If the rhythm for the tune is too confusing, try doing the turn first. Anyone who plays this tune well is considered a good musician. This song is named for the Perrodin family. It was first recorded by Angélas LeJeune, Dennis McGee, and Ernest Frugé.

Valse Pénitentiaire

Key. C
Pattern. Violin: two Tunes and two Turns; Vocal #1; Violin: one Tune; Vocal #2; Violin: one Tune; Vocal #3; Violin: one Tune; Vocal #4; Violin: one Tune; Vocal #5; Violin: one Tune; Vocal #6; Violin: one Tune; Vocal #7; Violin: one Tune and two Turns.

Version. Leo Soileau, vocal and violin; Moïse Robin, bass on accordion (OT).
Related Song. See: *Valse de Tasseau* (Gervais Quebedeaux; Ambrose Thibodeaux).

Angola, the State prison in Louisiana is near Baton Rouge. With good behavior, the man in the song could get out of prison in twenty years.

When I was a child I was told these stories about conditions at Angola. Prisoners had to push wheelbarrows on a six-inch plank and if the wheel slipped off, they were whipped; and also, when the prisoners hoed in the cane fields, those that finished last were whipped. Prisoners were made to agree with the officials by being asked what the color of the wall was. If the prisoner said it was white, the prisoner was struck and the official would say it was black, then the prisoner was asked again and the answer had better be black, even though the wall was white.

1-   Oh,   mam', 'gard- ez
2-   Oh, chère ma- man, m'en al-
3-   Oh, chère ma- man, hier ma-
4-   Oh, chère ma- man, c'est d' traî-
5-   Oh, chère ma- man, J'su' a- près
6-   Oh, chère ma- man, 'gard- ez
7- Moi, j'ai dit, "Chère ma- man, c'est pas la

donc, mal- heu- reuse! J'su'a- près m'en aller au Ba- ton Rouge pour quatre vingt
tin tout'l monde é- tait a- près m' ob- serv-
ner ma brou- ette, ma brou- ette pour
viv'e trop long- temps pour res- ter, oui, là-
donc, mal- heu- reuse! Temps qu' moi, j'ai par-
peine toi tu brailles, j'va' r've- nir quand

ler au Ba- ton Rouge, chère ma- man!
dix- neuf ans, chère ma- man!
er m'en al- ler pour tou- jours!
quat- re vingt- dix- neuf ans!
bas à cô- té d' ma ma- man!
ti, t'é- tais mis à pleu- rer!
même j'su' de- dans vingt ans d' suite!"

Penitentiary Waltz

(1) Oh, mom, look, unfortunate one! I'm going away to Baton Rouge, dear mother!
(2) Oh, dear mother, I'm going away to Baton Rouge to serve ninety-nine years, dear mother!
(3) Oh, dear mother, yesterday morning everybody was watching me go away forever!
(4) Oh, dear mother, I'll drag my wheelbarrow, my wheelbarrow for ninety-nine years!
(5) Oh, dear mother, I'm living too long to stay, yes, over there away from my mother!
(6) Oh, dear mother, look, unfortunate one! While I was leaving, you started crying!
(7) I said, "Dear mother, it's no use for you to cry, I'll come back even if I'm in for twenty straight years!"

Petite ou Grosse

Key. G
Pattern # 1. Violin: four Tunes; Vocal #1; Violin: one Tune; Vocal #2; Violin: three Tunes; Vocal #3; Violin: two Tunes; Vocal #4; Violin: two Tunes.
Pattern #2. Accordion (F): two Tunes; Vocal #1; Steel Guitar: two Tunes; Violin: two Tunes; Accordion (G): three Tunes, (F) two Tunes; Vocal #2 (repeat Vocal #1); Accordion (G) three Tunes.

Version #1. Leo Soileau -1935 (OT).
Version #2. Marc Savoy, accordion, and Rodney LeJeune, vocal-1960's (*Donnez-moi Les,* Cr-Cj).
Related songs. Also: *Two-Step à Tante Adèle* (Austin Pitre); *Lenoir Two-Step* (John Semien); *Madame Édouard.*

Although Leo "turns" this song, I haven't written the manuscript for it. I've included two versions of the words because of the different meanings. In the first version, *petite ou grosse, c'est tout l' même prix* means "it doesn't make any difference," a proverb like *faire ça ou tourner la meule* or *une main lave l'autre.* In the second version, the song is given a more literal meaning.

1-   Pe- tite ou grosse, chère,   c'est tout l'même
         Si tu vou- drais, chère,   oh jo- lie
2-   Pe- tite ou grosse, chère,   c'est tout l'même
         Si tu m'vou- drais, chère,   j'te vou-
3-   Toi, jo- lie fille, chère,   vi- laine ma-
         Toi, 'tit monde,   tu m'as
4-   Pe- tite ou grosse,   c'est tout l'même
         si tu vou- drais, chère,

prix!   Pe- tite ou grosse, chère,
fille,   viens donc res- ter
prix!   Pe- tite ou grosse,
drais.   J't'au- rais avec moi, chérie,
nière,   quoi moi j'peux faire
dit   tu vou- lais p'us
prix!   Pe- tite ou grose,
         t'en r' ve- nir

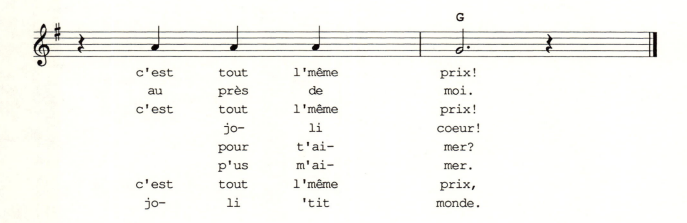

c'est tout l'même prix!
au près de moi.
c'est tout l'même prix!
jo- li coeur!
pour t'ai- mer?
p'us m'ai- mer.
c'est tout l'même prix,
jo- li 'tit monde.

It's All the Same to Me

(1)
It's all the same to me! It's all the same to me!
If you'd want, dear, oh, pretty girl, come stay close to me!
(2)
It's all the same to me! It's all the same to me!
If you'd want me, dear, I'd want you! I'd have you with me, darling, pretty heart!
(3)
You, pretty girl, dear ill mannered girl, what can I do to love you?
You, little one, you told me you couldn't ever, ever love me.
(4)
It's all the same to me! It's all the same to me,
if you'd want, dear, to come back, pretty little one!

Donnez-moi Les

(1 & 2)
Petite ou grosse, Madame Édouard, c'est tout l' même prix.
La 'tite est belle, Madame Édouard, la grosse peut faire.
Donnez-moi les, Madame Édouard, donnez-moi les!
Elle est la seule, Madame Édouard, que moi j' voudrais.

Give Them to Me

(1 & 2)
Small or large, Madam Edward, it's all the same price.
The small one is beautiful, Madam Edward, the large one can do.
Give them to me, Madam Edward, give them to me!
She's the only one, Madam Edward, whom I'd want.

La Pistache à Trois Nanan

Key. D
Pattern. Accordion: two Tunes; Vocal #1; Violin: two
Tunes; Accordion: Two Tunes; Vocal #2; Violin: two
Tunes; Accordion: Two Tunes.

Version. Sidney Brown (©Tek); Raymond François.

This is an old song about a happy farmer whose peanuts produced three nuts instead of the usual two. Sidney Brown changed the words *la pistache à trois nanan* (the three-nut peanut) to *la pistache à tante Nana* (Aunt Nana's peanut). A Mrs. Vasseur from Mamou told me the original words for this song when we played in the New Orleans Jazz Festival in 1975.

Since the peanut was an American plant, the new French colonists could only compare it to a pistachio or *pistache*. Later the new name *cacahouette* (peanut) was added to the French vocabulary, but here in Louisiana the peanut is still called *pistache* by the Cajuns. Now that is isolation! I learned the word *cacahouette* from a Canadian classmate during a summer school session at the Institut National D'Education Populaire at Marly-Le-Roi in France during July 1980. From the time the Acadians arrived in southwest Louisiana from Acadia (Nova Scotia) in 1764 until about 1939, we were relatively isolated in our own little neighborhoods. Even our little neighborhoods could have different French vocabularies, accents, and songs. The new inventions in communication and travel such as the radio and automobile began to change our lives. I think that Cajun music evolved mostly on its own, without much influence from the contemporary music elsewhere until at least 1939.

The Three-Nut Peanut

(1 & 2)
Let's go to Uncle Octave's to see the beautiful crop; some cotton and some corn and the three-nut peanut.
That's what's so good, roasted in the bottom of the stove during a wet rainy day — the three-nut peanut.

La Pointe aux Pins

Key. C
Pattern. Accordion: two Tunes and one Turn; Vocal
#1; Violin: two Tunes; Accordion: one Turn and one
Tune; Vocal #2; Violin: two Tunes; Accordion: one
Turn and two Tunes.

Version. Preston Manuel, first vocal; Moïse Robin,
second vocal.
Related song. Also: *'Tit Galop Pour la Pointe aux
Pins* (Moïse Robin).

I have included Moïse Robin's entire version
of this song too, at the end. I have no idea
where Pine Point was located, but I'm sure the
rider knew. *Cousine* doesn't necessarily mean
they were kin, just acquainted.

Pine Point

(1)
The one I love is the most sociable; I'm glad she has cunning eyes.
And don't tell your mom that I tasted your lips and don't tell your dad because he's goofy.
Oh, mine is the prettiest of the bunch. Canter to Pine Point.
Dear girl-cousin, give me that one; but if it isn't that one, I don't want any at all.
(2)
Canter to Pine Point! Canter to Pine Point!
Dear girl-cousin, give me the young one; but if it isn't that one, I don't want any at all.

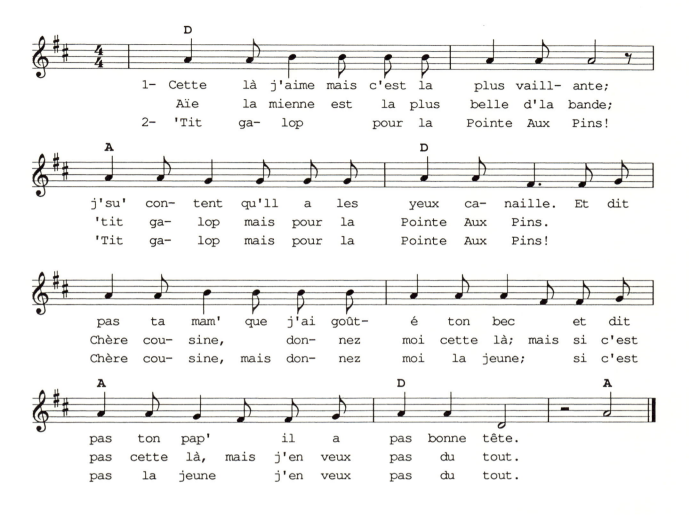

'Tit Galop Pour la Pointe aux Pins

(1)
J'su' après toucher galop mais pour La Pointe Aux Pins! *(Repeat)*
Chère cousine mais donnez moi la jeune! Si c'est pas la jeune, j'en veux pas du tout!
(Addition) Hé, 'tit galop pour La Pointe Aux Pins! Sh-sh-sheew! *(Signal au cheval.)*
(2)
La plus vieille d'la bande c'est la plus jolie! C'est la plus vaillante mais elle a les yeux canaille!
Dis pas à ta mam' que j'ai goûté ton bec et dis pas à ton pap' que j'ai en idée d' t' voler!
(Addition) Oh, pour la belle! Oublie pas moi!

Canter to Pine Point

(1)
I'm riding at a gallop for Pine Point! *(Repeat)*
Dear girl-cousin, give me the young one! If it's not the young one, I don't want any at all!
(Addition) Oh, slow canter to Pine Point! Sh-sh-sheew! *(Signal to the horse.)*
(2)
The oldest one of the bunch is the prettiest. She's the most valiant (sociable) but she has cunning eyes!
Don't tell your mom that I tasted your lips and don't tell your dad that I intend to steal you!
(Addition) Oh, for the sweetheart! Don't forget me!

Pointe Noire Two-Step

Key. A
Pattern. Accordion: two Tunes; Vocal #1; Accordion: two Tunes; Vocal #2; Accordion: two Tunes; Vocal #3; Accordion: two Tunes.

Version. Gervais Quibodeaux, vocal and Ambrose Thibodeaux, accordion (©La Lou).

For information on Pointe Noire see the next song. Make up your own instrumental from the vocal part.

1-   'Garde ton nèg', il a- près ar-ri-ver,
2-   Rap- pelle toi l'aut' mar- di pas-sé,
3-   Moi j' vou- drais tu t'en r' viens avec moi,

chère. Par la fenêtre tu peux l' voir s'en v'nir,
chère. Tu m'as dit tu vou- lais v'nir a-vec moi,
chère, une aut' fois pour re- join' ton nèg',

chère. Ta ma- man est tou- jours cont' moi, ton pa-
chère. Ta ma- man vou- lait pas on se r' join' et
chère. 'Garde donc bien, moi j' vou- drais te voir. Moi j' vou-

pa a l' aire de pour en êt' dur.
droit de- vant la porte de ton pap'!
drais que tu t'en r' vien a- vec moi.

Pointe Noire Two-Step

(1)
Look, your lover is coming, dear. Through the window, you can see him coming, dear.
Your mother is always against me, your father seems to be tough.
(2)
Remember last Tuesday, dear. You told me that you wanted to come with me, dear.
Your mother didn't want us to meet right in front of your father's door!
(3)
I'd want you to come back with me, dear, one more time to meet your lover, dear.
Please understand, I'd want to see you. I'd want you to come back with me.

Valse de Pointe Noire

Key. D
Pattern. Accordion: one Tune; Vocal #1; Accordion: two Tunes; Vocal #2; Accordion: one Tune and two Turns; Vocal #3; Accordion: one Tune; Vocal #4; Accordion: one Tune and two Turns; Vocal #5; Accordion: one Tune and two Turns.

Version. Angélas LeJeune (OT).
Related songs. See: *Kaplan Waltz* (Varise Connor); *Valse de Kaplan* (Nathan Abshire); *Valse de Kaplan variation* (Don Guillory).

I've transposed this song to A, because otherwise the turn on the violin would have to drop an octave or play in the second position on the E-string. This song was named for a place called La Pointe Noire because the point of woods looks dark or black when viewed from the north, at the site of an old forge near the present community of Richard. The area had a reputation for some terrible knife fights in the old days; it was the sort of place you would visit only if you were invited. This area produced many fine musicians: Angélas LeJeune, Iry LeJeune, Rodney LeJeune, Vinus LeJeune, Hilbert Dies, Ervin "Dick" Richard and many others.

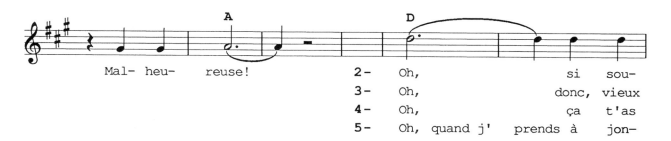

Black Point Waltz

(1)
Oh, unfortunate! Criminal, dear! Unfortunate one!
(2)
Oh, so often, I don't see your dear little eyes, which are so sweet, looking at me anymore.
(3)
Oh, then, old dog, you'll see your error of doing what you did, unfortunate one.
(4)
Oh, what you did to your lover; you know I take it so hard.
(5)
Oh, when I start thinking of all that, I could cry day and night for you.

La Porte du Nord

Key. C

Version. Adam Hébert (©Flat Town).

Pattern. Violin: two Tunes; Vocal #1; Violin: two Tunes; Vocal #2; Violin: two Tunes; Vocal #2; Violin: two Tunes; Vocal #3; Violin: two Tunes.

1- Moi et ma belle on a é- té au bal; on a r've-
2- On a en- tré par la porte du nord; on a é-

nu su' l'a- vant jour. On a pas- sé par la porte du
té dans la grand cui- sine. Elle a- vait sa 'tite robe

nord et sa mam- an é- tait a- près querel- ler fort.
brune; puis on a bû d'la li- mo- nade.

3- Pas- sez les par la porte du nord; ame- nez

les dans la grande sa- vane. Oui, mais moi j'v'al- ler la

r'join' dans l'coin du clos à tante Far- ro.

The North Door

(1)
My sweetheart and I went to the dance; we came back just before daybreak.
We passed through the north door and her mother was fussing loudly.
(2)
We entered through the north door; we went into the large kitchen.
She had on her little brown dress and we drank some lemonade.
(3)
Sneak her through the north door; take her to the big pasture.
Yes, I'll go meet her in the corner of the field at Aunt Farro's.

Quand J' su' Loin de Toi

Key. D

Pattern. Make your own.

Version. Leopold François.

This old song has words, but my father doesn't remember them exactly. It is a blues type song with a very slow tempo and the words ask how the child will fare when the parent is far away. Other versions also include older persons, usually the wife or sweetheart.

Valse de Quatre-vingt-dix-neuf Ans

Key. C
Pattern. Accordion: two Tunes; Vocal #1; Accordion: two Tunes; Vocal #2; Accordion: two Tunes; Vocal #3; Accordion: two Tunes.

Version. Iry LeJeune (©Tek).
Related songs. See: *Mermentau Waltz* (Dunice Theriot, vocal; Bobby Leger, accordion). Also: *Convict Waltz* (Iry LeJeune); *Valse du Vieux Homme* (Ambrose Thibodeaux).

This is the *Convict Waltz*, but the title we often use in French is *Valse de Quatre-vingt-dix-neuf Ans*. It is usually sung an octave higher.

Convict Waltz

(1)
Oh, I am on my way, sentenced for ninety-nine years.
It's only on account of your word that makes me suffer so long as that.
(2)
Oh, every night I go to bed with tears in my eyes.
It's not so much you, baby, that I am lonesome for,
it's those dear children who I know are suffering.
(3)
Oh, little girl, it's useless; your lies will stay on your conscience.
The truth might hurt you, but someone will always pay you back.

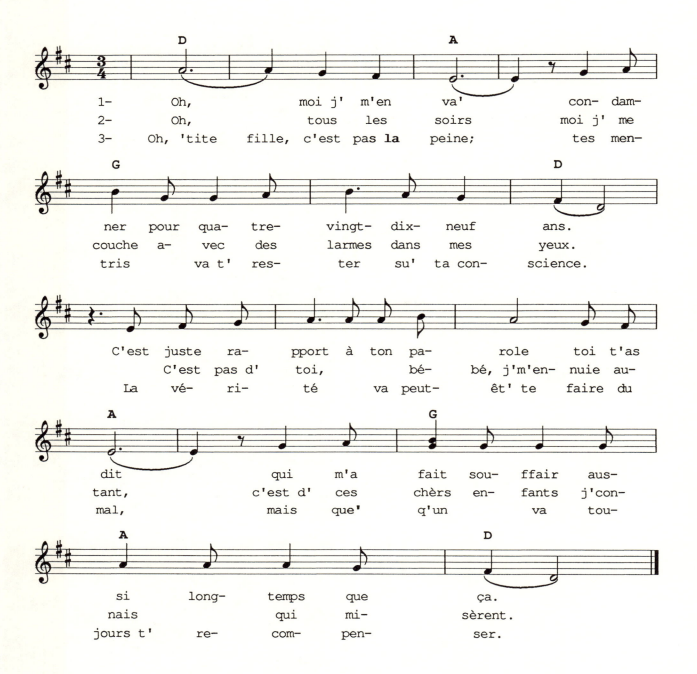

1-   Oh,   moi j' m'en   va'   con- dam-
2-   Oh,   tous   les   soirs   moi j' me
3- Oh, 'tite fille, c'est pas la peine;   tes men-

ner pour qua- tre-   vingt- dix- neuf   ans.
couche a-   vec   des   larmes dans mes   yeux.
tris   va t' res-   ter   su' ta con-   science.

C'est juste ra-   pport à ton pa-   role   toi t'as
C'est pas d' toi,   bé-   bé, j'm'en- nuie au-
La   vé- ri-   té   va peut- êt' te faire du

dit   qui m'a   fait sou- ffair aus-
tant,   c'est d' ces chèrs en- fants j'con-
mal,   mais que' q'un va tou-

si   long- temps que   ça.
nais   qui mi-   sèrent.
jours t' re- com- pen-   ser.

La Queue d'Tortue

Key. G
Pattern. Accordion: two Tunes; Vocal #1; Accordion: two Tunes; Vocal #2; two Tunes; Vocal #3; Accordion: two Tunes.

Version. Moïse Robin.
Related songs. Also: *Allons Tuer la Tortue* (Nathan Abshire); *Cimetière* (Reggie Matte, vocal; Ambrose Thibodeaux).

Queue de Tortue (turtle's tail) is believed to be the name of an Indian family who lived on what is now called Bayou Queue de Tortue between Crowley and Kaplan, Louisiana.

Here is the recipe for *pain perdu* (lost bread or French toast) mentioned in this song. It is delicious and very rich in calories.

2 eggs, beaten
stale sliced regular or French bread
1 cup milk
1/2 cup cooking oil or butter
vanilla (a few drops)
Mix all these ingredients in a bowl and dip the slices of bread in the mixture. Fry the coated bread in a skillet until the bread turns golden brown. Serve with cane syrup and a glass of milk.

Queue Tortue

(1)
Little girl, when I die don't bury me in the cemetary!
Bury me in the corner of the yard, in the corner of your father's yard!
Bury me with my eyes sticking out so I can see your dear little eyes
which will remain so cunning, yes, all your life, darling!
(2)
Every morning when I pass in front of your father's door,
your father is standing there laughing with a pipe in his beak, ha-ha!
(3)
Mean, criminal little bottle!
It's your fault, if my sweetheart doesn't want me anymore!
Let's go to Queue Tortue, to live on French toast!
Let's go to Queue Tortue, to live on French toast!

moi 'vec les yeux sor- ti; c'est pour voir tes chers 'tits

yeux qui vont res- ter si ca- nille, ouais tout l'

temps d'ta vie, chér- ie! (2)-Tous les ma- tins quand moi je

passe de- vant la porte de ton pa- pa, ton pa- pa il est plan-

té a- vec la pipe au bec qui rit! (3)- Mau- di' 'tite cri- mi-

nelle de mau- di' pe- tite bou- teille; c'est toi

bien qu'est la cause si la belle veut pu's de moi. Al-

lons à la Queue Tor- tue, c'est pour viv'e su' le pain per-

du! Al- lons donc à la Queue Tor- tu; c'est pour

viv'e su' le pain per- du!

Les Rangs de "Soybean"

Key. G
Pattern. Accordion: two Tunes and two Turns; Vocal
#1; Steel Guitar: two Tunes; Violin: two Tunes;
Accordion: two Turns; Vocal #2 (repeat vocal #1);
Accordion: two Tunes and two Turns.

Version. "Shorty" Sonnier; *Fais Do-do* (Shirley and
Alphée Bergeron, ©JON).
Related songs. *Plus Tu Tournes Plus J' t'aime*
(Leopold François); *Fais Do-do, Mignonne* (Irène
Whitfield's book).

T'as gue- tté ton pap' et t'as gue- tté ta mam' s'en a- ller, bé- bé, dans les bras d'ton nèg'. Fais do- do bé- bé, fais do- do mig- nonne, fais do- do bé- bé, dans les rangs d'"soy- bean."

Soybean Rows

(1 & 2)
You left your dad and you left your mom.
You've gone, baby, in the arms of your lover.
Sleep, baby, sleep, beautiful, sleep, baby, in the soybean rows.

One-Step de Riché

Key. G

Version. Lawrence Aguillard.

Pattern. Each instrument plays the Tune and Turn once between vocals

Dad gave me the vocal and tune for this song, which he learned from Lawrence Aguillard who played dances at Riché, a community several miles southwest of Eunice, Louisiana. The "ch" is always given the English pronunciation, so it probably comes from the name Ritchey. This song was never recorded and not very many people know it. *Femme* can mean either wife or woman.

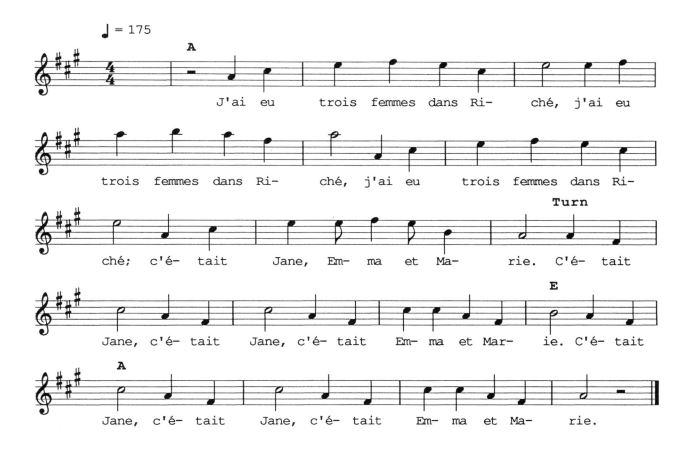

Riché One-Step

(1 & 2)
I had three wives in Riché, I had three wives in Riché, I had three wives in Riché;
it was Jane, Emma and Marie. It was Jane, it was Jane, it was Emma and Marie.
It was Jane, it was Jane, it was Emma and Marie.

Two-Step de Riché

Key. G
Pattern. Each instrument plays two Tunes between vocals.

Version. Lawrence Aguillard.
Related song. Also: *Le Two-Step de Riché* (Ambrose Thibodeaux).

My Dad gave me this tune and words too. Lawrence Aguillard played the accordion at house dances in Riché.

I learned the Riché Two-Step from the late Lawrence Aguillard, one of my first cousins. We traveled a lot together. He was a little older and we both played the accordion. He's the one who made that song. No one had ever recorded it, so when I made my albums, I recorded it. Very few people knew it. It's about the women of Riché.

— Ambrose Thibodeaux

♩ = 175

J'ai é- té à la veille hier au soir; O- li-
J'ai pas- sé en tra- vers d'la fe- nêt' et j'ai sau-

vie é- tait pas là. É- mi- lie é- tait cou-
té en tra- vers su'l lit; elle a sau- té en tra- vers su'

ché, a(lle) vou- lait pas m'ou- vert la port.
moi. J'va' pas vous dire quoi on a fait.

Riché Two-Step

(1 & 2)
I went for an evening visit last night; Olivia wasn't there.
Emily was in bed; she didn't want to open the door to me.
I passed through the window and I threw myself across the bed;
she jumped crosswise on me. I won't tell you what we did.

Saute, Crapaud

Key. G
Pattern. Harmonica: two Tunes and one Turn, two Tunes and one Turn; Vocal #1; Harmonica: two Tunes and one Turn, two Tunes and one Turn; etc.
Rhythm. The rhythm guitar has two beats per measure and the bass one beat per measure.

Version. Isom J. Fontenot (AR).

This is a very old song.

Yes, me and "Boy" Frugé went to Memphis, Tennessee to make some records. "Boy" had no musicians with him. When we arrived there, he found a pop bottle case made of wood and turned it upside down and stomped on that for his drum effect while recording. The first song he recorded was Saute, Crapaud.

—Moïse Robin

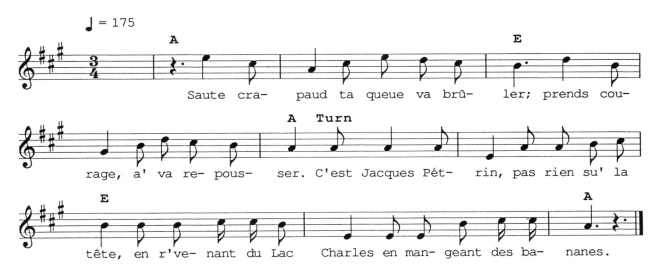

Saute cra- paud ta queue va brû- ler; prends cou- rage, a' va re- pous- ser. C'est Jacques Pét- rin, pas rien su' la tête, en r've- nant du Lac Charles en man- geant des ba- nanes.

Jump, Toad Frog

(1)
Jump, toad frog, your tail will burn; take courage, it'll grow back.
It's Jacques Pétrin, bareheaded, coming back from Lake Charles, while eating bananas.

Valse de Séparation

Key. C
Pattern. Accordion: two Tunes; Vocal #1; Accordion: two Tunes; Vocal #2; Accordion: two Tunes; Vocal #3; Accordion: two Tunes.

Version. Iry LeJeune (©Tek).
Related songs. Also: *Parting Waltz* (same song, Iry LeJeune); *Ridge Road Waltz* (Ambrose Thibodeaux).

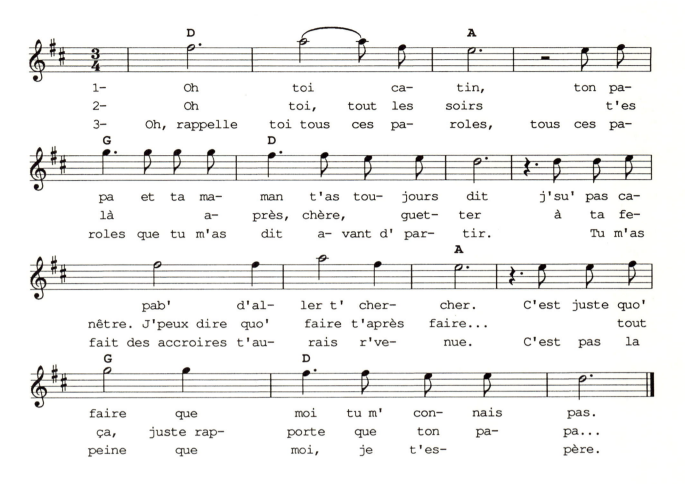

Parting Waltz

(1)
Oh you doll, your father and mother always told you that I wasn't
capable to go get you. That's just why you don't know me.
(2)
Oh, every night you're watching at your window.
I can tell why you're doing all this, just because your father —
(3)
Oh, remember all these words that you told me before you left.
You made me believe that you'd come back. It's no use for me to wait.

Valse à Tante Aleen

Key. C
Pattern. Violin: two Tunes and two Turns. Vocal #1.
Violin: two Tunes, two Turns and two Tunes. Vocal #2.
Violin: two Tunes and two Turns.
Rhythm. This song is a *valse à deux temps* as it has two
dotted quarter notes per measure for rhythm guitar. The
bass pattern for all four of Dennis McGee's *valse à deux
temps* is a sequence of two dotted quarter notes and one
dotted rest; however the starting point for this sequence
is different in this particular song: 1st measure, one
dotted quarter note and one dotted quarter rest; 2nd
measure, two dotted quarter notes; 3rd measure, one
dotted quarter rest and one dotted quarter note.

Version. Dennis McGee (©Flat Town); Amédé
Ardoin.
Related songs. See: *Viens m' Chercher* (Iry LeJeune)
and *Je Suis Orphelin* (Dewey Balfa). Also:
L'Orphelin (Irène Whitfield's book); *Valse des
Musiciens.*

I didn't include the vocals in the manuscript,
but here they are.

La Valse à Tante Aleen

(1)
Hé, chère catin! Malheureuse!
Tu connais moi j' t'aime avec tout mon coeur, malheureuse.
Tu devrais mais pas faire ça mais t'après faire mais malheureuse.
C'est pour ça, cher 'tit monde, tu fais du mal à mon coeur.
(2)
Malheureuse! Tu connais, chère 'tite fille, tu vas pleurer —
pour ça toi t'es après faire. Tu m'as dit, chère 'tite fille, mais criminelle!
Malheureuse! Tu connais tu vas pleurer, mais malheureuse!

Aunt Aleen's Waltz

(1)
Hey, dear doll! Unfortunate one!
You know I love you with all my heart, unfortunate one.
You shouldn't do what you're doing, unfortunate one.
That's why, dear little one, you hurt my heart.
(2)
Unfortunate one! You know, dear little girl, you'll cry —
for what you're doing. You told me, dear little girl, criminal!
Unfortunate one! You know you'll cry, unfortunate one!

Valse de Tasseau

Key. D
Pattern. Accordion: two Tunes; Vocal #1; Accordion: four Tunes; Vocal #2; Accordion: two Tunes.

Version. Gervais Quibodeaux, vocal, and Ambrose Thibodeaux, accordion (©La Lou).
Related song. See: *Valse Pénitentiaire* (Leo Soileau and Moïse Robin).

Tasseau is a Cajun French word for sun-dried strips of meat; it comes from the Spanish word *tasajo*. Today pork or beef tasseau is well-seasoned and smoked like sausage. *Tasseau*, usually labeled as *tasso*, can be bought in local grocery stores today and is used to season chicken, pork or beef sauce piquante, gumbo, beans or okra étouffée (smothered). It is also the name of a community seven miles southeast of Eunice where a long time ago Indians used to dry their strips of meat (jerky).

Tasseau Waltz

(1)
Oh, it hurts! Today I'm condemned! Oh, little one, no one to love me anymore!
Oh, it hurts! I came back last night! Why, dear little girl, are you always selfish?
(2)
Oh, little one, look! Remember how, dear little girl, you're always thinking of yourself.
Oh, little girl, look! Come meet me, I'm always at home crying for you anyway.

1- Oh yé yaille, au jour- d'hui j'su' con- dam-
Oh yé yaille, Moi j' m'en r' vien hier au
2- Oh 'tit monde, 'garde donc! R'ap- pelle
Oh 'tite fille, 'garde donc! Viens me r'

né! Oh cher 'tit monde, p'us per-
soir! Com- ment, chère 'tite fille, que
toi com- ment, chère 'tite fille, que t'es a-
join', j'su tout l' temps à la mai- son 'près pleu-

sonne mais pour m'aim- er!
t'es tout l' temps pour toi?
près jon- gler à toi.
rer pour toi quand même!

T'es Petite et T'es Mignonne

Key. G

Version. Dudley and James Favor (OT).

Pattern. Violin: two Tunes and two Turns; Vocal #1
(two Tunes and one Turn); Violin: two Turns, two
Tunes and two Turns; Vocal #2 (repeat vocal #1);
Violin: two Turns.

In this song, the turn is sung.

You're Small and You're Cute

(1)
You're small and you're cute. You're jealous, but I love you anyway.
You're small and you're cute. You're too mangy to be my wife.
(Turn)
Oh, sweetheart, you're not washed! Oh, sweetheart, you can go wash yourself!
Oh, sweetheart, you're not washed! I'll have to forget my sweetheart!
You can go wash yourself!

Teche Special

Key. G
Pattern. Accordion: two Tunes; Vocal #1; Accordion: two Tunes; Vocal #2; Accordion: three Tunes; Vocal #3; Accordion: three Tunes.

Version. Iry LeJeune (©Tek).
Related song. Also: *Quo' Faire?* ("Bois Sec" Ardoin); *How Come?* (Ambrose Thibodeaux).

Although this song was recorded in 1948, Iry was playing this song as early as 1944. I believe it is based on the traditional music he learned from Angélas LeJeune. Iry did not attend school because his eyesight was so poor, and he spent a great deal of time with the older generation at La Pointe Noire, while the others his age were in school.

When I was in the sixth grade at Richard (always pronounced in the French way, Ree-shard), a small community between Eunice and Church Point, there was a girl in my class that I thought was pretty nice, but I could never get her to pay much attention to me. After a while I learned that she was only interested in Iry. I remember being quite surprised that she was interested in an old fellow like that — he was three or four years older than I was — and I also remember one of her girlfriends would bring her messages from him. I think the third vocal of this song is about this early courtship.

Iry told a story when he'd sing. It wasn't You-left-me-to-go-away, You-went-away, You-left-me-to-go-away all the time!
— Roy Fusilier

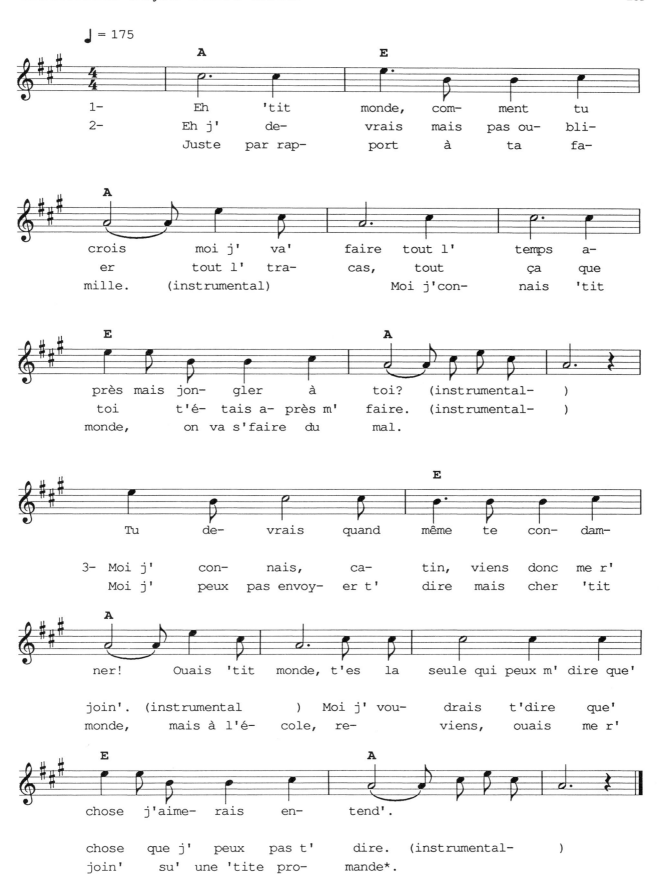

Teche Special

(1)
Oh, little one, how do you think I'll fare,
thinking of you all the time?
You should at least blame yourself!
Yes, little one, you're the only one
who can tell me something I'd like to hear.

(2)
I shouldn't forget all the trouble,
all that you were doing to me just because of your family.
I know, little one, we'll hurt each other.

(3)
Darling, come meet me. I want to tell you something.
I can't send you a message at school,
but come meet me and we'll take a little walk together.

'Tit Galop Pour Mamou

Key. G
Pattern. Violin: two Tunes; Vocal #1; Violin: two Tunes and two Turns; Vocal #2; Violin: two Tunes and two Turns.

Version. Dewey Balfa (©Flat Town).
Related song. *Tit Mulet Coton-Maïs* (Leopold François); *The Games People Play*.

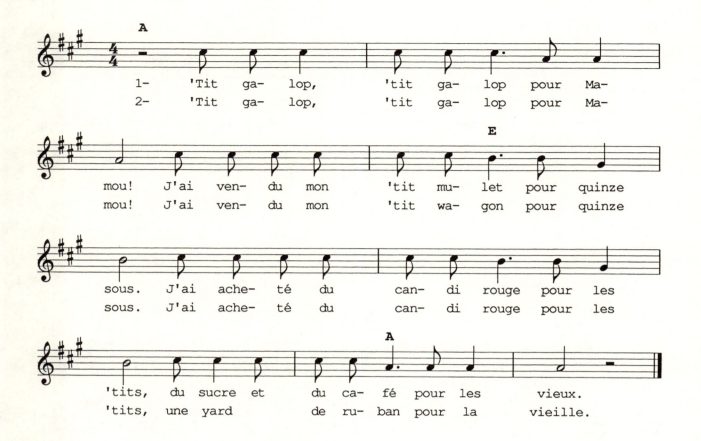

Canter to Mamou

(1)
Canter, canter to Mamou! I sold my little mule for fifteen cents.
I bought some red candy for the kids, some sugar and coffee for the old folks.
(2)
Canter, canter to Mamou! I sold my little wagon for fifteen cents.
I bought some red candy for the kids, and a yard of ribbon for my wife.

'Tit Monde

Key. C

Version. Iry LeJeune (©Tek).

Pattern. Accordion: one Tune; Vocal #1; Accordion: two Turns; Steel Guitar: one Tune; Accordion: one Tune; Vocal #2; Accordion: one Turn.

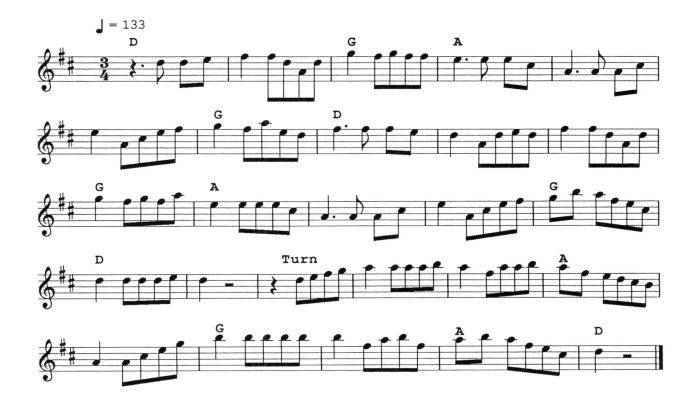

1- Hé, quo' faire toi tu crois moi j' su'
2- Hé, quo' faire t'es comme ça, près 'spé-

là tout l' temps 'près t'e- spé- rer, chère? Tu de-
rer juste pour moi mais jour et nuit juste pour

vrais mais pas m' ou- bli- er. Yé yaille, tant
me faire des mi- sères, 'tit monde,

loin que moi j' m'é- loigne de toi.
des mi- sères que j' mé- rite pas?

Little One

(1)
Well, why do you believe that I am always there waiting for you?
You should not forget me. It hurts to see that I am moving far away from you.
(2)
Well, why are you like that, waiting just for me day and night,
only to cause me miseries, little one, miseries that I don't deserve?

'Tite Canaille

Key. G
Pattern. Accordion: four Tunes; Vocal #1; Violin: one
Tune; Accordion: four Tunes; Vocal #2; Violin: one
Tune; Accordion: four Tunes.

Version. John Semien (©La Lou).

The accordion is played Zydeco style with many variations on the tune, while the violin is always steady on the tune. Notice that the song doesn't change chords. Very few black bands play Cajun music. Nolton Semien and the St. Landry Playboys, John Semien and his band, Bois Sec Ardoin and Canray Fontenot and a few others are the main exceptions. Zydeco music is very different in style, and this song has elements of both Cajun and Zydeco music. The yell *Heyeee* is made up of two syllables; the *eee* part goes to falsetto.

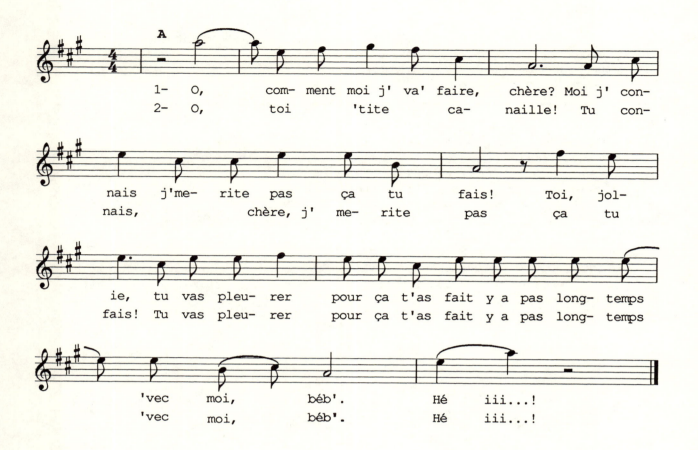

1- O, com- ment moi j' va' faire, chère? Moi j' con-
2- O, toi 'tite ca- naille! Tu con-

nais j'me- rite pas ça tu fais! Toi, jol-
nais, chère, j' me- rite pas ça tu

ie, tu vas pleu- rer pour ça t'as fait y a pas long- temps
fais! Tu vas pleu- rer pour ça t'as fait y a pas long- temps

'vec moi, béb'. Hé iii...!
'vec moi, béb'. Hé iii...!

Little Scoundrel

(1)
Oh, what will I do, dear? I know I don't deserve what you're doing!
You, pretty one, you'll cry for what you did recently with me, babe! Heyeee!
(2)
Oh, you little scoundrel! You know, dear, I don't deserve what you're doing!
You'll cry for what you did recently with me, babe! Heyeee!

Valse à Tolan

Key. C
Pattern. Violin: two Tunes and one Turn; Vocal #1; Piano: two Tunes; Steel Guitar: two Turns; Violin: two Tunes and two Turns; Vocal #2; Steel Guitar: two Tunes; Violin: two Turns.

Version. Chuck Guillory.
Related song. Also: *Pochéville* recorded by Joe Falcon in the 1920's is a mixture of *Valse des Grands Bois* for the lyrics and *Tolan Waltz* for the turn.

This song was named for a bartender in Eunice, Louisiana.

Tolan Waltz

(1 & 2)
I know, darling, someday you'll come back; you'll be too late.

Tous les Deux Pour la Même

Key. C

Pattern. Accordion: one Tune and one Turn; Vocal #1; Steel Guitar: one Tune; Vocal #2; Steel Guitar: one Tune; Accordion: last 9 measures of the Tune.

Version. Lawrence Walker (©La Lou).
Related songs. Also: *La Valse de Sainte Marie* (Leroy "Happy Fats" LeBlanc; Ervin "Vin" Bruce); *All for the Same* (Blackie Forestier); *Les Maringouins* (Merlin Fontenot).

I stayed with Theodore McGee and one day he said, "Well Mac, I believe I'll buy a violin for you. I'm going to Ville Platte." I asked, "You'll buy me a violin?" He answered, "Yes! Boy, you'll do something that I'll like very much."

He went to Armand Coreil, where he bought my violin. No strings! There was nothing on it. He bought some strings and the pegs. When he got back, he sat down and put it all together. He knew how to play a little. He knew how to set the violin. He tuned it up and played, Tout les deux pour la même, ni un ni l'aut' qui l'aura. Ça sera moi, l 'tit 'Cadien, qu'aura, la jolie petite fille. *He said, "Now, you're on your own." I said, "Not really!" "Yes, here!" he said, "Go! Go play!" I went to my little room. I had a little room in back. I sat on the side of my bed and you know what? Before nightfall I played the waltz,* Tout Les Deux Pour La Même. *Oh yes, I learned it during the day. Oh yes!*

— Dennis McGee

Both For The Same One

(1)
Both for the same one, neither I nor you will win her.
Both for the same one, neither I nor you will win her.
It's no use for you to say "no," you'll still have to say "yes."
It's no use for you to say "no," you'll still have to marry me.
(2)
I left home with my jug hanging from the pommel,
the pistol in my pocket and my life in my hand.
I'm going to get you and take you home.
To tell me "no" is useless, you'll still have to say "yes."

My True Love

Key. C
Pattern. Accordion: two Tunes and two Turns; Vocal
#1; Violin: two Tunes; Accordion: two Turns; Vocal
#2; Accordion: one Tune.

Version. Hadley Fontenot, vocal; the Balfa Brothers
(©Flat Town).

♩ = 175

D

1- J'ai eu nou- velles de ma belle alle 'tais
J'ai ar- ri- vé à Ba- sile et moi j'
2- Quand j'ar- ri- vé au Lac Charles moi j'ai
J'ar- ri- vé à sa mai- son c'est là
Alle 'tait 'près m'es- pé- rer a- vec

là- bas au Tex- as. J'ai par- ti par Eu-
m'ai ache- té un "can" sar- dines, c'é- tait pour faire grand voy-
man- gé la moi- tie. J'ai quit- té l'aut' moi-
où mon j'ai vu que une veille a- mi-
des larmes dans ces yeux A'* m'a dit, "Mon cher

A   D

nice et moi j' m'ai ache- té un pain d' cin' sous.
age; c'é- tait là- bas au Tex- as.
tie; c'é- tait pour mon dé- jeu- ner.
tié, ça va ja- mais êt's ou- bli- er.
nèg', mais toi t'es v'nu pour m'cher- cher!"

My True Love

(1)
I had some news from my sweetheart; she was over there in Texas.
I went by Eunice and I bought myself a five-cent loaf of bread.
I arrived in Basile and I bought myself a can of sardines to make a big trip over there to Texas.
(2)
When I arrived in Lake Charles, I ate half of it. I saved the other half for my breakfast.
I arrived at her house, that's when I saw that an old friendship will never be forgotten.
She was waiting for me with tears in her eyes and she said, "My dear lover, you've come for me!"

T'en As Eu, T'en N'auras P'us

Key. G
Pattern. Violin: two Tunes and two Turns; Vocal #1;
Violin: two Tunes and two Turns; Vocal #2; Violin: two
Tunes and two Turns.

Versions. Amédé, Ophy and Cleoma Breaux
(instrumental, OT); Moïse Robin (vocal); Raymond
François (vocal).
Related Songs. Also: *Vas Y Carrément* (Amédé,
Ophy and Cleoma Breaux); *Step it Fast; Steppin'
Fast* (Aldus Roger); *Robe à Joséphine; Canadi
Canada; Boui de Peau d' Lapin.*

I've gathered the vocals from different sources
and there are still others not included here.
Even though there are only five measures for
some variations, the turn or tune should be
repeated so that there are nine measures each
when playing this song. I have included the
full nine measures for one tune and one turn,
too. Pick out your favorite ones. The first
vocal consists of *La Robe à Joséphine* and
T'en As Eu, T'en n'Auras P'us. The second
vocal consists of versions from Moïse Robin
and *Canadi Canada.*

You Had Some, You Won't Have Any More

(1)
Josephine's dress is torn (split) all the way! Uncle Homer's fly buttons are too large!
You had some, you won't have any more! You tasted, you won't taste any more!
You tasted, you won't taste any more! What's left is all for me!
(2)
Grandpa and Grandma went to the cypress grove to spear bullfrogs with a hand axe.
Grandpa and Grandma had bad tempers! They chewed barbed wire and crunched single-trees!
Hi-ho! Let's go cut some wood to make axe handles to spear bullfrogs!

1-   C'est   la   robe   à   Jo- se-
                    T'en   as   eu   t'en au- ra
2-   C'est   pé-   père   et   mé-
                    C'est   pé-   père   et   mé-
                    Ca-   na-   di   ca-   na-

phine   qu'est   fen-   due   mais   tout   du
p'us!   T'as   gou-   té   tu r' gou-   tera
mère   qu'a   é-   tait a la   cy-   pri-
mère   qu'a-   vait   une   mau-   vaise co-
da,   al-   lons   cou-   per   du

long!   C'est la   bra-   guette à   nonc' Ho-
p'us!   T'as   gou-   té   tu r' gou-   tera
ère   pour   dar-   ter   des   oua-   oua-
lère!   I'ont   chi-   qué   des   fils   de
bois!   C'est   pour   faire des   manches de

mer   qu'a   ni   fill   et   ni   bou-   tons!
p'us! Ça   qui rest   c'est tout pour   moi!
rons   a-   vec   une   hache à   main!
fer,   i'ont cro- qué   des   pa-   lon-   niers!
haches pour   dar- ter   les   oua- oua-   rons!

Ton Papa et Ta Maman m'a Jeté Dehors

Key. D
Pattern. Accordion: Part 1 and Part 2 once then Turn twice; Vocal #1; Accordion: Part 2 and Turn twice; Vocal #2; Accordion: Part 2 and Turn twice; Vocal #3; Accordion: Part 2 and Turn twice.

Version. Lawrence Walker with Mitch D'Avy, vocals (©Flat Town).
Related song. Ton Père m'a Mis Dehors (Mayuse LaFleur).

Part 1 and the vocal are fairly simple, but the last few measures of Part 2 and the beginning of the turn can be difficult. This tune was among the first ones recorded in the late 1920's by Mayuse LaFleur and Leo Soileau.

1- Hé, ton pa- pa et ta ma- man m'a jet' de-
2- Hé, chère 'tite fille, mais pour quoi donc mais tu fais
3- Hé, mal- heu- reuse, j'con- nais un jour a

hors, m'a jet' dehors de ma mais- on, ma mai-
ça? Moi j' con- nais j'mé- rite pas mais tous
v'nir t'au- ras du r'- gret pour ça t'as fait à ton vieux

son moi j'aime si tant.
ça que t'as 'près faire.
nèg' y a pas long- temps.

Your Dad and Your Mom Threw Me Out

(1)
Oh, your papa and your mama threw me out, threw me out of my house, my house I love so dear.
(2)
Oh, dear little girl, why do you do that? I know I don't deserve all that you're doing.
(3)
Oh, wretched one, I know someday you'll regret what you've done to your old lover not long ago.

Tu Vas m' Faire Mourir

Key. C
Pattern. Accordion: play Part 1 once and Part 2 three times; Vocal #1; Steel Guitar: Part 2 twice; Violin: Part 2 and Part 1; Accordion: Part 1 once, Part 2 twice, Part 1 once and Part 2 once; Vocal #2; Accordion: Part 1 once, Part 2 twice and Part 1 once.

Version. Wallace "Cheese" Reed, vocal and violin, Marc Savoy, accordion (©La Lou).
Related songs. Also: *La Danse de Port Arthur* (Rufus Thibodeaux); *Lake Arthur Stomp* (Ed Juneau). (This is nothing like the *Lake Arthur Stomp* in this book.)

1- Eh yé yaille, mal-heu-reuse, tu con-
2- Tu m'as dit, mal-heu-reuse, tu pou-

nais j'mé-rite pas ça mais ça t'as fait y a pas long-
vais p'us m'ai-mer, ça ça m' fait...

temps a-vec ton nèg'.
ouais, mais j'va' mou-rir!

You'll Make Me Die

(1)
Well, it hurts, unfortunate one,
you know I don't deserve that,
what you did not long ago with your lover.
(2)
You told me, unfortunate one,
you couldn't love me anymore,
that, yes, you'll make me die!

Valse des Vachers

Key. C
Pattern. Violin: two Tunes; Vocal #1 (A & B); Violin: two Turns; Vocal #2; Violin: one Turn, one Tune (low) and one Tune; Vocal #3 (A & B not included); Violin: one Tune; Vocal #4 (not included); Violin: one Turn.

Version. Dennis McGee (MS; ©Flat Town).
Related songs. Also: *Valse du Passé* (Shirley Bergeron); *My Rope and Spurs* (Adam Hébert).

Some musicians sing about going out to find their *belle* (girlfriend) instead of *bêtes* (cattle). Notice that Dennis stretches the second vocal to twelve measures. He recorded this song twice; both sets of lyrics are included, mostly without manuscript but sufficient to serve as a guide.

♩ = 133

1-(A) Mal- heu- reuse, at- trape moi mon
(B) 'Garde moi mi- sér- er. C'est malheu-

cab' et mes é- perons pour moi al- ler voir à mes bêtes.
reux de m' voir m'en al- ler moi tout seul ma ché- rie!

2- C'est mal- heu- reux de m' voir m'en a- ller au si

loin moi tout seul pour trou- ver que' chose que j'peux pas, per-

du mais dans l' bois, mal- heu- reuse.

Valse des Vachers I

(1)
Malheureuse, attrape moi mon cab' et mes éperons pour moi aller voir à mes bêtes (belles).
'Garde moi miserer! C'est malheureux de m' voir m'en aller mon tout seul, ma chérie!
(2)
C'est malheureux de m' voir m'en aller aussi loin moi tout seul pour trouver
que' chose que j' peux pas, perdu mais dans l' bois, malheureuse.
(3)
Dit 'bye-bye', chérie! Ma chérie, chère, dans les chemins, chère, moi tout seul!
Yaille! Comment je va' faire, malheureuse? Yaille! Toujours moi tout seul, malheureuse! Chérie!
(4)
Ma chérie, viens donc me r'join', chère! Aussi loin que moi j' su' de toi, belle!

Cowboy Waltz I

(1)
Unfortunate one, fetch me my rope and spurs for me to go tend my cattle (sweethearts).
Look at me suffer! It's unfortunate to see myself go away all alone, my dear.
(2)
It's unfortunate to see myself going away so far all alone to find
something I can't, lost in the woods, unfortunate one!
(3)
Say goodbye my darling, darling, dear. On the roads, dear, all by myself!
Ouch! What will I do, unfortunate one? Ouch! Always all alone, unfortunate one! Darling!
(4)
My darling, come meet me, dear! So far away as I'm from you, sweetheart!

This is the same tune as his original version and
is an example of singing whatever comes to
mind.

Valse du Vacher II

(1)
C'est tout l' bal, chère! J' su' parti à cause à lui, pour mourir mais aussi loin moi tout seul.
'Gardez donc, chère, j' m'ennuie! C'est d' part de lui; pour ton nèg' a pas longtemps, criminelle!
(2)
J' su' parti m'en aller, criminelle, malheureuse, pour mourir mais moi tout seul aussi loin.

Cowboy Waltz II

(1)
The dance is over, dear! I'm leaving because of him, to die so far away all by myself.
Look, dear, I'm lonesome! It's partly because of him; for your lover doesn't have much time, criminal!
(2)
I'm going to go, criminal, unfortunate one, to die all by myself so far away.

Veuves de la Coulée

Key. D
Pattern. Violin: two Tunes; Vocal #1; Violin: two
Turns and two Tunes; Vocal #2; Violin: two Turns and
two Tunes; Vocal #3 (repeat vocal #1); Violin: two
Turns.

Version. Lcroy "Happy Fats" LeBlanc and Oran
"Doc" Guidry (©La Lou).

Coton jaune is a variety of cotton which is still
grown in southwest Louisiana. It has a brown-
ish yellow color.

Widows of the Gully

(1 & 3)
All the widows of the gully are gone to town to buy some yellow cotton at the store,
to buy some yellow cotton to make some little bloomers for the beautiful little girls of the gully to finish.
(2)
All the widows of the gully are gone to town to buy some yellow cotton at the store.
Going to the gully! Going to the gully to take the beautiful little girls over there at Joe's!

La Vie Malheureuse

Key. C

Version. Walker Brothers (OT).

Pattern. Accordion: 1st and 2nd Tune, one Turn; Vocal
#1; Accordion: 2nd Tune and Turn; Vocal #2;
Accordion: 2nd Tune and Turn, 1st and 2nd Tunes.

The Unfortunate Life

(1)
Little girl, you make me feel pity when I see you crying, crying in misfortune.
It's me, it's my fault if your heart is broken; have courage, little girl, don't take it so hard.
(2)
Little girl, have courage and come with me. Little girl, I'll take care of you till your dying day.
What will I do, I'm so very lonely? Little girl, have courage, don't take it so hard.

Viens m' Chercher

Key. C
Pattern. Accordion: two Tunes; Vocal #1; Accordion: two Turns and two Tunes; Vocal #2; Accordion: two Turns and two Tunes.

Version. Iry LeJeune (©Tek).
Related songs. See: *Valse à Tante Aleen* (Dennis McGee); *Je Suis Orphelin* (Dewey Balfa). Also: *Valse des Musiciens* (Rodney LeJeune); *L'Orphelin* (Irène Whitfield's book).

Sometimes Iry recorded the same song with different vocals. I've included another version without manuscript.

1- Oh yé yaille! Viens m' cher- cher, bé-bé! À où t'es "gone" tu con- nais t'as pas bien fait a- vec moi. D'hors que toi tu sois a- près m' faire ça, yé yaille; quit- ter tout seul, per- sonne pour me soi- gner.

2- Eh quo' faire t'as mal- fait comme ça? Mais c'est d' jon- gler j'ai fait pa- reil comme toi, 'tite fille. Ca s' fait a- lors al- lons donc pas s' blâm- er, 'tit monde, tu vas voir qu'on se- ra mieux plu- tôt qu'on est.

Come Get Me

(1)
Oh it hurts! Come get me, baby! Where you're gone, you know you didn't do right by me.
Instead of doing that to me, it hurts, leaving me by myself, no one to take care of me.
(2)
Well, why did you do wrong like that? But to think I've done the same as you, little girl.
So then, let's not blame each other, little one; you'll see that we're better off than as we were.

Viens m'Chercher II

(1)
Oh yé yaille, chère 'tit monde! Catin, mets donc voir à jongler ça t'as fait.
Pas la peine que tu lamentes, viens donc m' chercher. Yé yaille! Ton papa et ta vieille maman v'aller t'après.
(2)
Oh 'tite fille, c'est tous les soirs j' me couche, j'embrasse mon oreiller des fois en jonglant.
Ça fait accroire que ça serait toi qui serais là, yé yaille, mais j' peux voir tu t'en r'viendras pas me voir.

Come Get Me II

(1)
Oh, it hurts, darling! Think about what you've done.
It's no use to complain, come get me. Your father and your old mother will go get you.
(2)
Oh, little girl, every night when I go to bed, sometimes I hug my pillow while thinking of you.
I pretend you're there, but I can tell that you will not come back to see me.

Ville Platte Two-Step

Key. D
Pattern. Violin: two Tunes and two Turns; Vocal #1 (Tune); Violin: two Tunes and two Turns; Vocal #2 (Tune); Violin: one Tune; Vocal #3 (Turn); Violin: one Turn; Vocal #4 (Tune); Violin: one Tune; Vocal #5 (Turn); Violin: one Turn and one Tune.

Version. Dennis McGee (MS).
Related song. Also: *Valse d'Amour* (Leo Soileau, recorded c. 1937).

This song was recorded about 1930. It is really a waltz, but can easily be danced as a two-step.

Ville Platte Two-Step

(1) Since the age of fifteen you promised me your little heart. Ouch! At the age of sixteen you abandon me.
(2) Unhappy one, just look what you've done. Unhappy one, you've made me walk all the days and the nights.
(3) Unhappy one, you made me waste my time for one year to go to your home, unhappy one.
(4) Mama, what do you want me to do for you? It hurts! It's too hard! That will make me old quick.
(5) Unhappy one, I want to do as they wish for my life's family, for your life, unfortunate one, my pretty one.

Valse de Ville Platte

Key. F
Pattern. Accordion: one Tune; Vocal #1; Steel Guitar: one Tune; Violin: one Tune; Accordion: one Tune; Vocal #2; Accordion: one Tune.

Version. Wallace "Cheese" Reed, vocal and violin (©La Lou).
Related song. Also: *Lawtell Waltz* (Harry Choates).

Ville Platte Waltz

(1)
Well, you know I don't deserve that, what you did not long ago, with your ugly ways.
If you'd want to promise to come back with me — oh to stay with me in Ville Platte!
(2)
Oh, dear little girl, I don't deserve that, what you did, little girl, not long ago.
Oh, I know I don't deserve what you've done. Oh, baby, come with me to Ville Platte!

1-   Eh, tu con-   nais j'mé- rite pas   ça;   oh mais ça t'as
2-   Oh chère 'tite   fille, j'mé- rite pas ça;   oh mais ça t'as

fait y a pas long-   temps, vi-   llaines ma-   nières.
fait,   'tite   fille,   y   pas   long-   temps.

Si tu vou- drais pro-   mette de r' ve-   nir a- vec   moi...
Oh   moi j'   con-   nais j'mér- rite pas ça t'as   fait...

Oh   res-   ter a- vec   moi dans la Ville   Platte!
Oh   bé-   bé, viens avec moi à   la Ville   Platte!

More Songs

The songs in this section are mainly from the 1940's and 50's, with a few from the 1960's; there may also be earlier material that I have not been able to classify.

Musicians were exposed to many more outside influences by the 40's. I remember my Uncle Sullivan's phonograph which he got around 1932. I loved to visit his house and listen to his French records, but he had American records, too. My parents got their first radio about 1940 and of course we could hear all kinds of music on it. World War II brought changes, also; many young Cajuns traveled far from home for the first time and many American soldiers visited Cajun dance halls. There was suddenly more money to spend, too. Roy Fusilier's story captures some of this excitement.

Yes, I started playing very young. Then, when I got married, the accordion died. All they wanted were some string bands. It died, pat, all over. For five years I was a sharecroper, far out in the country. I was living about eight miles from Basile. Then there were four guys who came. They wanted me to play the accordion with them. I asked, "What's the matter with your string band?" They replied, "The accordion is out and they're eating us up! You were good on the accordion when you were young."

"But," I said, "I don't know one song any more since I've married, and my accordion, my kid finished with it in the yard." I had a good accordion, though, a good D from Germany. A good accordion! Flop, flop, he played with it. Flop, flop, in the mud and everywhere. And every now and then, I'd trip over it. It was in my way. I was right in front of the barn fooling around with some cows. We wanted to sell some calves and they were mixed with the cows. I tripped over the accordion and fell in the mud. The barn had an upstairs door almost seven or eight feet high. I caught the accordion and tossed it into the loft. The accordion had been in the top of the barn for years, when these people came.

I said, "There are no more accordions. How much do y'all make playing music?" They said, "We can give you fifteen, twenty dollars." I repeated, "Fifteen, twenty dollars!" I used to play for three dollars. They said, "Sure! The more we practice, the better we'll be, the more we'll charge." I said to my wife, "What do you think?" And things were bad. We didn't have any money. "Well," she said, "Let's try." We had an old car. I said to them, "My car is a little old to go far." But they said, "We have some good cars. We can pick you up, you and your wife." I said, "Humph! It'll be hell to get an accordion! That's the thing! If it isn't a good accordion, I will not play.

They asked, "You don't know where there's an old accordion?" I replied, "What do you want me to do with an old accordion?" "Ah," they said, "but there's a man over there in Houston, Texas, who renews old accordions." My wife said, "Your old accordion is in the barn. I saw it there. Some hens are laying in it. It's in the loft." They asked, "You have an accordion in the loft?" I said, "That's where I threw it, but it's all rotten." They said it didn't matter and, Jack, they climbed into the loft.

I had put up some hay and there was loose hay there. They started stirring in the hay and found one side of the accordion and threw it down to me. I said, "Oh, that! That will sound good, half an accordion!" "Don't worry," they said, "we're coming with the other half." They had stirred the hay till they came up with the other half. It was all unglued but the reeds were there and they were some good reeds from Germany. They told me, "That's all we need." I told them, "Don't send that over there; if the accordion isn't good, I will not take it." They said, "It can't miss; the reeds here are good. The man will repair it just like the day you bought it."

Hé, I didn't have very much money. I asked, "How much will it cost?" They said, "Climb in with us, we'll go to Basile and see."

"Alright," they said, "we want to know how much it'll cost to repair that accordion. There are only the reeds." We called the man over there in Houston. "Well," he said, "it'll go to a hundred dollars." And I had paid twenty dollars for it. Things were better, you know. I thought a while and said, "Well ... a hundred dollars!" They said, "You'll make more than that in a week! When we start playing, we'll play some dances, yes!" "Well, good!" I said, "Send it."

About five or six weeks after that, it came back. They came to tell me the accordion was there. I went for it and, listen! It seemed to be in the same box I had bought it in when it was brand new! The cardboard box, with the thin paper on it. I opened it. It was bright! "Boy, if it sounds like it looks, we're going to play some dances!" I grabbed it and made some sounds. You talk about a pretty sound! Well tuned! That fellow over there in Houston is good! I climbed on it and started a song I still knew pretty well, you know. Woooooo! These D's and C's and all that were true, true, true!

...We went to play on KSLO radio. It was Floyd Cormier who was there. So when we stopped playing, Floyd said, "You have five calls!" I told Ulysses, "Take the ones who pay more, the larger clubs!" There were some calls for the same nights, you know. We couldn't take all of them.

... There was a club that had been a potato kiln in a large field near Scott. They made a pretty club with it! Beautiful, beautiful club! We played on Sunday afternoons. Gentlemen, there were some people there! They had some money! They were sweet potato farmers. They were stuffed with money. You talk about spending money! They spent money! We were told by the proprietor that we didn't have enough with four. He wanted five musicians when we played for the first time. I asked, "Do you think it'll make better music?" "No," he replied, "you make good music, but it would look better." He had some money, I think. So I said, "We'll find him a fifth musician."
— *Roy Fusilier*

We began to have better roads in the 1930's. Cars became more common too, even though there weren't many available for purchase during the War. I can remember seeing more buggies than cars in the church parking lot in Richard about 1943, but not since then. About the last time I saw a buggy in use was in 1951. It had been demolished by a car near Carencro and pieces of it were in the ditch along with a dead horse. Better roads and more cars made it possible for musicians to travel farther and schedule more dances. It could be exciting as well as stressful.

J.B. Fusilier was coming back from playing a dance in Church Point on a Sunday afternoon The gravel road had some loose gravel on a curve and there was a lot of dust. Before hard surface roads, there was always a lot of dust or a lot of mud. He was turning the curve too fast in the loose gravel and the car turned over with the four wheels spinning in the air. They gathered a few more people and turned it over on its wheels again. It had flattened the top a little, but he went on to do another dance that was scheduled for 8 pm the same day ... It was a 1941 Mercury. None of the musical instruments were broken. The battery hadn't leaked, so he started the car and left. The top was dented about six inches in the middle. These old cars had some good iron then.
— *Shelton Manuel*

Holding a regular job and playing several dances a week is hard on most musicians, too. A dance lasts four hours, and you can easily spend an hour on either side of it traveling there and setting up and taking down the instruments and amplifiers. No matter how much you love playing or how handy a little extra money might be, you can get tired of this kind of schedule real easily. Many musicians just stop playing, at least temporarily.

... There was a long time I hadn't seen him. I asked, "Do you still play?" "No." I asked him why. "Oh, I don't know the reason. I don't like it as much anymore. It's too much," he replied. And, he's younger than I. He's in good health. He told me he didn't need that. "Nor do I," I said, "but I still like it. I like to play."
— *Roy Fusilier*

Acadiana Two-Step

Key. G

Pattern. Accordion: two Tunes; Steel Guitar: two
Tunes; Violin: two Tunes; Accordion: two Tunes; Steel
Guitar: two Tunes; Violin: two Tunes; Accordion: two
Tunes.

Version. Aldus Mouton (©La Lou).

This is an instrumental.

Valse à Alida

Key. C
Pattern. Accordion: two Tunes; Vocal #1; Steel Guitar: two Tunes; Violin: two Tunes; Accordion: two Tunes; Vocal #2; Accordion: one Tune. There is no turn in this song.

Version. Aldus Roger with Phillip Alleman, vocal (©Flat Town).
Related songs. See: *Valse de Carencro.* Also: *Valse de Prairie Ronde* (Marc Savoy and Gerald Broussard); *Valse de Midway* (Aldus Roger); *T' as Volé Mon Idée* (Leopold François).

Alida's Waltz

(1)
Oh, Alida, remember, little one, what you did with me not long ago. How will I live?
Oh, little one, but I'd want, little girl, for you to come back with me at home but for always.
(2)
Oh, your little heart is promised to someone else. I'd like, little girl, for you to come back, but I know.
Oh, little one, but remember, little girl, what I did with you. You no longer want to stay in Lafayette.

1-   Oh, A- li-   da,   mais rap- pelle
                                              Oh,   'tit   monde, mais moi j' vou-
2-   Oh, ton 'tit   coeur il   est pro-
                                              Oh,   'tit   monde, mais rap- pelle

toi,   'tit   monde,   ça   t'as   fait a- vec
drais,   'tite   fille,   tu   t'en r'   viens a- vec
mis à un aut' que   moi. Moi j' aime-   rais,   'tite
toi,   'tite   fille,   ça   j'ai   fait a- vec

moi   i'a   pas long-   temps. Com- ment j'va' viv'e!
moi   à la mai-   son   mais pour tout l' temps.
fille, toi tu t'en r'   viens, mais moi j' con- nais.
toi. Tu veux p'us res-   ter   à La- fa-   yette.

Valse d'Alléman

Key. E standard, as originally recorded by Leeman Prejean with violin only.
Pattern. Violin: two Tunes; Vocal #1; Violin: Turns #1 and #2 and one Tune; Vocal #2; Violin: one Tune and Turns #1 and #2.

Versions. Leeman Prejean (vocal and first instrumental, ©Flat Town); Raymond François (second instrumental).
Related song. Also: *Valse des Grands Bois* (Dewey Balfa).

Alléman Waltz

(1)
When I left home last night, my dear little wife, my dear children started crying.
They asked, they begged to know where I was going. I'm gone to ramble with another (woman).
"Why don't you come back and meet us; yes, meet us — these dear children who are crying?"
(2)
When I returned this morning at daybreak, the old mother, my dear children started crying.
They begged me, "Why are you like that? Why don't you come back to meet us?"
These little children, the little old woman are crying; they're asking for you to come back.

Valse d'Alléman (variation)

Key. C tuned down, to preserve violin position with a C-accordion.
Pattern. Each instrument plays Tune twice between the vocals; no Turns.

Version. "Shorty" Sonnier, vocal with C-accordion.
Related song. Also: *Valse des Grands Bois* (Dewey Balfa).

Alléman is a family name.

Alléman Waltz

(1 & 2)
When you left last night from the house, you said you couldn't love me anymore.
I don't see what in the world I will do, I don't have anyone at the house to caress me anymore.
The little children are asking for their mother; she's left and will never come back.

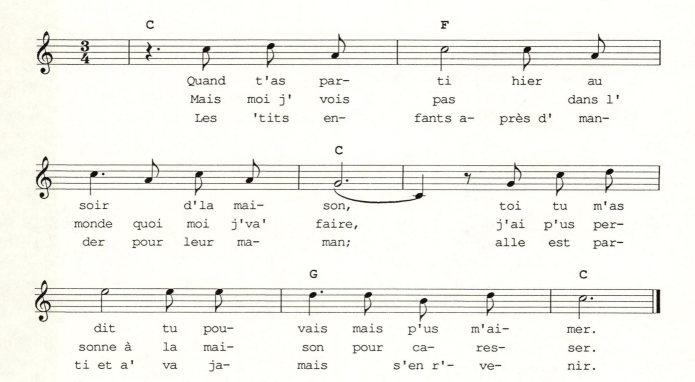

Quand t'as par- ti hier au
Mais moi j' vois pas dans l'
Les 'tits en- fants a- près d' man-

soir d'la mai- son, toi tu m'as
monde quoi moi j'va' faire, j'ai p'us per-
der pour leur ma- man; alle est par-

dit tu pou- vais mais p'us m'ai- mer.
sonne à la mai- son pour ca- res- ser.
ti et a' va ja- mais s'en r'- ve- nir.

Allons Danser Colinda

Key. A
Pattern. Violin: two Tunes and two Turns; Vocal #1;
Violin: two Tunes and two Turns; Vocal #2; Violin: two
Tunes and two Turns.

Version. Oran "Doc" Guidry and Leroy "Happy
Fats" LeBlanc (©Jamil).
Related Song. See: *Madame Young* (Dennis McGee).

Young girls were usually chaperoned by their
mothers and it was considered disgraceful
when the mother wasn't there. This tradition
continued well into the 1940's.

"Doc" and "Happy Fats" recorded this song in
1946. The tune is an old one, but J.D. Miller
gives "Doc" credit for the words.

I'm not sure the tune is the same, but the title
comes from an old dance, the "calinda" known
among the black population in the New
Orleans area many years ago. It consisted of a
line of men and a line of women facing each
other and was, at one time, forbidden to be
danced because of it's sexual style or its
association with voodoo.

Let's Dance Colinda

(1)
Let's dance colinda! Let's dance colinda! Let's dance colinda to make the old women mad!
(2)
Not everyone knows the old time waltzes. While your mother isn't here, let's dance colinda!

Two-Step à Ambrose

Key. A

Version. Ambrose Thibodeaux (©La Lou).

Pattern. Accordion: two Tunes and two Turns; Violin:
two Tunes and two Turns; etc.

Ambrose Thibodeaux, who was one of our
neighbors in L'Anse Chaoui when I was
growing up, made this instrumental two-step.

L'Année de Cinquante-sept

Key. D

Version. Alex Broussard (©La Lou).

Pattern. Violins: introduction (last five measures);
Vocal #1; Violins: one Tune; Vocal #2.

This song recalls Hurricane Audrey in June 25th through 28th, 1957. Then, we did not have the technology to monitor storms so closely and accurately; there was not much advance warning, and many people discounted Audrey's strength and did not evacuate from the costal areas. High water and high winds killed hundreds of people around Cameron Parish, south of Lake Charles, where the storm first struck land.

Hurricanes lose their strength as they travel across land, but, as the eye of the storm traveled near my parent's house, seventy miles from landfall, most of their roof and all of their chicken coops blew into my Uncle Stanislas' field. They believed the house was about to pull loose from the piers and tumble across the field too, so they took refuge inside the car in the garage. As the wind blew, they could see the large posts of the garage moving up and down in the ground. I was attending LSU at the time. All the phone lines to Eunice were out, so as soon as the storm was over, I went to see if my parents were okay. Large oak trees had blown down across the road, and I had to leave the taxi and walk home the rest of the way.

Pecanière (Pecan Island) in this song is located inland south of Kaplan near the Gulf of Mexico. Along the Louisiana coast, "island" means an area that is higher then the surrounding land, such as Avery Island and Jefferson Island.

1- Dans l'an- née de cin- quante sept, dans les
   Tous les bêtes d'la Grand Chê- niere ont 'té no-
2- Tout le reste de la Loui- siane ont pri-
   Au- jour- d'hui, la Pa- ca- nière, les chê-

mèches de la Loui- siane, de dans la mer y a v'nu une
yées de dan les mèches. Les ha- bi- tants d'la Pa- ca-
é pour tous les aut'. La cha- ri- té as é- té do-
nières et Ca- me- ron est l'pa- ra- dise pour les cha-

lame qu' a cou- vert de- su' l'ac- core; tout le
nière on 'té ruin- és par l'eau sal- é, et les
nné pour les ré- si- dants des mèches. Et le
seurs, les pê- cheurs et les piè- geures. Dans les

bien des ré- si- dants a flot- té su' l'herbe d'hi-
ré- si- dants des îles, a- vec tout l'cou- rage du
monde de Ca- me- ron, a- vec des larmes de- dans leurs
mèches de la Loui- siane, les ré- si- dants sont tous con-

ver. On va s'rap- peler de l'ou- ra- gon de- dans l'an-
monde, ont re- tour- né de- su' leur îles de dans l'an-
yeux, ont re- tour- né à Ca- me- ron de- dans l'an-
tents. On va s'rap- peler de l'ou- ra- gon de- dans l'an-

née de cin- quante sept.
née de cin- quante sept.
née de cin- quante sept.
née de cin- qunate sept.

The Year of '57

(1)
In the year of '57, in the marshes of Louisiana, from the sea came a tidal wave that covered the shore.
The residents' goods floated upon the green grass. We'll remember the storm in the year of '57.
All the animals of Grand Chênière were drowned in the marshes.
The inhabitants of Pecanière were ruined by salt water, and the island residents,
with all the courage in the world, returned to their islands in the year of '57.
(2)
All the rest of Louisiana prayed for all of them. Charity was given for all the marsh residents.
And the people of Cameron, with tears in their eyes, returned to Cameron in the year of '57.
Today, Pecanière, the oak groves, and Cameron are a paradise for hunters, fishermen, and trappers.
In the marshes of Louisiana, all the residents are happy. We'll remember the storm in the year of '57.

L'Anse Maigre Two-Step

Key. G
Pattern. Play two Tunes per lead instruments in your band till you think it's enough.

Version. Jamie Berzas, Mark Young, and Cajun Tradition (BEE).

Notice the accidental on the fourth measure. When the band gets to that part, players able to do so usually jump or swing their instruments upwards higher than normal. Simple song, but fun!

L'Anse Maigre is north of Eunice and is known for its poor clay land.

Two-Step d'Arnaudville

Key. G
Pattern. Accordion: two Tunes; Vocal #1; Violin: two Turns; Accordion: two Tunes; Vocal #2; Violin: two Turns; Accordion: two Tunes.

Version. Johnny Richard, vocal; Ray Cormier, violin; "Boy" Frugé, accordion (©La Lou).
Related song. See: *Lake Arthur Stomp* (Varise Connor).

This song is patterned after the instrumental, *Lake Arthur Stomp*. Arnaudville, Louisiana, is a town along the Bayou Teche.

Arnaudville Two-Step

(1)
Oh, it hurts, dear little girl, today you know you're seeing your mistake;
all the advice you listened to.
(2)
Oh, it hurts, today you know that you're seeing your mistake;
all the advice you listened to from your father.

Attention, C'est Mon Coeur Qui Va Casser

Key. G
Pattern. Accordion: one Tune; Vocal #1- one Tune and
one Turn; Steel Guitar: one Tune; Violin: one Tune;
Vocal #2- one Turn; Accordion: one Tune.

Version. Aldus Roger and Phillip Alleman (©Flat
Town).

Be Careful, You're Breaking My Heart

(1)
Be careful, we're separating; be careful, it's my heart that will break.
Every day I'm thinking; be careful, it's my heart that will break.

(Turn)
Every day I'm praying; every night I'm looking for her.
Be careful, we're separating; be careful, it's my heart that will break.

(2 - *Turn*)
Every day I'm praying; every night I'm looking for her.
Be careful, we're separating; be careful, it's my heart that will break.

Une Aut' Chance

Key. C
Pattern. Accordion: one Tune; Vocal #1 (one Tune, one Turn, one Tune); Steel Guitar: one Tune; Violins: one Turn; Accordion: one Tune; Vocal #2 (repeat Vocal #1); Accordion: last half of Tune.

Version. Aldus Roger; Phillip Alleman, vocal (©La Lou).
Author. Johnnie Allan (John A. Guillot).

This song has sixteen measures of tune and nine measures of turn for the instrumental parts. See Ann Allen Savoy's book *Cajun Music: A Reflection Of A People* for the words of this song.

Valse de Balfa

Key. G
Pattern. Violin: two Tunes; Vocal #1; Violin: two Tunes; Vocal #2; Violin: two Tunes; Vocal #3; two Tunes.

Version. Balfa Brothers; Will Balfa, vocal (©Flat Town).

I've included a version of playing "double" on the violin, using two strings together to make a sound.

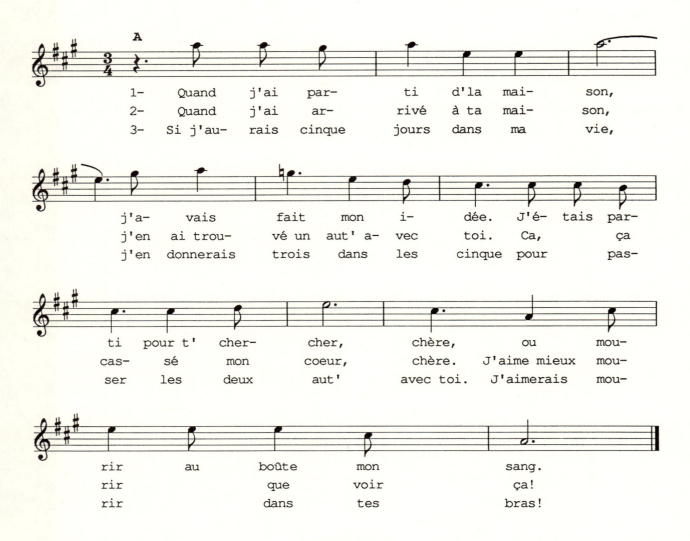

1- Quand j'ai par- ti d'la mai- son,
2- Quand j'ai ar- rivé à ta mai- son,
3- Si j'au- rais cinque jours dans ma vie,

j'a- vais fait mon i- dée. J'é- tais par-
j'en ai trou- vé un aut' a- vec toi. Ca, ça
j'en donnerais trois dans les cinque pour pas-

ti pour t' cher- cher, chère, ou mou-
cas- sé mon coeur, chère. J'aime mieux mou-
ser les deux aut' avec toi. J'aimerais mou-

rir au boûte mon sang.
rir que voir ça!
rir dans tes bras!

Balfa Waltz

(1)
When I left from my house, I had made up my mind.
I was going to get you or die bleeding.
(2)
When I got to your house I found you with another.
That broke my heart, dear. I'd rather die than see that!
(3)
If I had five days left in my life, I'd give away three
so that I could spend two with you. I'd like to die in your arms!

Bayou Noir

Key. G

Version. Felton LeJeune (BEE).

Pattern. Accordion: two Tunes; Vocal #1; Steel Guitar: two Tunes; Violin: two Tunes; Accordion: two Tunes; Vocal #2; Accordion: two Tunes.

This song is named for a bayou west of Hackberry which empties into Sabine Lake.

Black Bayou

(1)
Oh, but dear baby, I'd like for you to come back. I'd like for you to come back to meet me at Black Bayou.
Oh, but dear baby, remember, when you left, the misery you caused me before you came back to Black Bayou.
(2)
Oh, but dear baby, I'd like for you to come back. I'd like for you to come back to meet me at Black Bayou.
Oh, but dear baby, you know I'm lonesome for you. You know I'd like for you to come back to Black Bayou.

1-   Oh, mais chère bé-   bé, moi j'vou-
     Oh, mais chère bé-   bé, rap- pelle
2-   Oh, mais chère bé-   bé, moi j'vou-
     Oh, mais chère ca-   tin, tu con-

drais toi tu t'en r'- viens. Moi j'vou- drais toi tu t'en r'-
toi quand t'as quit- té les mi- sères toi tu m'as
drais toi tu t'en r'- viens. Moi j'vou- drais toi tu t'en r'-
nais j'm'en- nuie de toi. Tu con- nais mais moi j'vou-

viens mais pour me r'- join' au Ba- you Noir.
fait a- vant t'en v'- nir au Ba- you Noir.
viens mais pour me r'- join' au Ba- you Noir.
drais toi tu t'en r'- viens au Ba- you Noir.

Valse à Bélisaire

Key. G
Pattern. Accordion: one Tune; Vocal #1; Violin: one Tune; Accordion: one Tune; Vocal #2; Violin: one Tune; Accordion: one Tune.

Version. Nathan Abshire (©La Lou).
Related songs. Hills Of Roane County; Precious Jewel (Roy Acuff); *Phil's Waltz.*

This song was so popular I decided to include it, but as you see it is definitely not of Cajun origin. I lived four years in Oliver Springs, in Roane County, Tennessee, and heard there *The Hills of Roane County*, about the murder of a Kingston, Tennessee, man and his girlfriend. Many American and English folk songs are about murders. I'm proud to say that we don't have any folk songs about murder and killings in our culture. Later on, Roy Acuff picked up the tune, calling it *Precious Jewel*.

Bélisaire was a dance hall where Nathan played.

Bélisaire's Waltz

(1)
Yes, we're going, oh yes, to see the little blonds.
Yes, to see our friends who come to see us.
Yes, It's we, oh yes, who are so joyful.
Yes, to see us every Saturday at Bélisaire's.
(2)
Yes, it's we, oh yes, who are so joyful.
Yes, to see our friends who come to see us.
Yes, to see us, oh yes, every Saturday.
Yes, to see our friends, our little blonds.

Blues de Soûlard

Key. G   *Version.* Louis Cormier (©Flat Town).
Pattern. Accordion: two Tunes; Vocal #1; Violin: two
Tunes; Accordion: two Tunes; Vocal #2 (repeat vocal
#1); Violin: two Tunes; Accordion: two Tunes.

Drunkard's Blues

(1 & 2)
When I get the blues, I'm gone; I'm gone to get drunk.
When I'm drunk, baby, I'm gone to the house to meet my dear little wife.
When I get to the house, the little wife fusses at me.
I asked her, "Why do you fuss at me?"
She answered, "My lover, it's for you I'm fussing;
I see you leaving all the time."

Quand les "blues" me prend, moi j'su' "gone"; moi j'su' par-ti m' soû-ler. Quand moi j'su' soûl, bé-bé, moi j'su' "gone" à la mai-son pour 'join' ma chère 'tite femme. Quand moi j'ar-rive à la mai-son, la 'tite femme a-près m' querel-ler. Moi j'y ai d' man-dé, "Pour quoi tu m' querelle?" Elle a ré-pond, "Mon nèg', c'est pour toi moi j' te querelle; j'te vois tout l' temps par-ti."

Les Bons Temps

Key. C
Pattern. Accordion: two Tunes; Vocal #1; Steel Guitar:
two Tunes; Vocal #2; Violin: two Tunes; Vocal #3.

Version. Lawrence Walker (©Flat Town).
Related songs. Also: *Laisse les Bons Temps Rouler*;
Valse de Holly Beach.

Holly Beach is a Cajun vacation area along the
Gulf of Mexico. Sometimes we jokingly call
Holly Beach the Cajun Riviera. Hackberry is a
little town near Lake Charles, Louisiana.

The Cajun French word *game* means rooster in
English.

The Good Time

(1)
It's because of your papa and because of your mother,
if I can't love you anymore, but let the good time roll.
I found you in the big marshes; I brought you to Holly Beach;
the mosquitoes are eating me, but let the good time roll.
(2)
Your dad is angry and your mother isn't happy;
the mosquitoes are eating me, but let the good time roll.
I found you in the big marshes; I brought you to Hackberry;
the mosquitoes are eating me, but let the good time roll.
(3)
Your dad is arriving; I hear him on the porch;
your mother is fussing and the children are crying.
The cows aren't milked and the roosters are crowing;
the mosquitoes are eating me, but let the good time roll.

1-   C'est par rap- porte à ton pa-
          J't'ai trou- vé dans les grands
2-   Ton pa- pa il est fâ-
          J't'ai trou- vé dans les grands
3-   Ton pa- pa a- près ar- ri-
          Les vaches sont pas ti-

pa et par rap- porte à ta ma-ly
mèches; j't'ai ame- né aux "Hol- ly
cher et ta ma- man est pas con-
mèches; j't'ai ame- né aux "Hack- ber-
ver; moi l'en- tende su' la gale-
rés et les "games" sont après chan-

man si moi j'peux p'us t'ai- mer, mais laisse le
Beach;" les ma- rin- gouins sont après m'man- ger, mais laisse le
tente; les ma- rin- gouins sont après m'man- ger, mais laisse le
ry;" les ma- rin- gouins sont après m'man- ger, mais laisse le
rie; ta ma- man a- près querel- ler, les en-
ter; les ma- rin- gouins sont après m'man- ger, mais laisse le

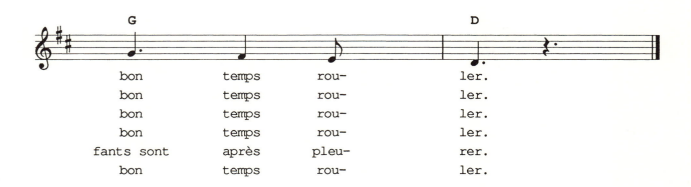

bon temps rou- ler.
bon temps rou- ler.
bon temps rou- ler.
bon temps rou- ler.
fants sont après pleu- rer.
bon temps rou- ler.

Bosco Stomp

Key. G
Pattern. Accordion: two Tunes; Vocal #1; Steel Guitar: two Turns; Violin: two Tunes; Accordion: two Turns; Vocal #2 (repeat vocal #1); Steel Guitar: two Turns; Violin: two Tunes; Accordion: two Turns and two Tunes.

Version. Lawrence Walker (AR).
Related song. Also: *Cajun Stripper* (Doug Kershaw), but it is not played in the Cajun style.

Bosco is a small community north of Scott, Louisiana.

Bosco was named for Bosco Préjean who was my aunt's stepfather. They put up two small stores and the house was for Grandmother Clara. It was named Bosco because of Grandfather Bosco.

Marais Bouleur was just this side of Bosco. When my grandmother, the Boullion generation, came from New Orleans, they settled there. A marais is like a swamp. Wild ducks would come there.

Alban Alleman was my uncle who had married mother's sister. He received a lot of oil money and he built a dance hall called the "Fais Dodo." There was also a place called "The Red Dog" in Bosco, Marais Bouleur... My grandpa fought with some men, some Mèches and some Melançons, at Marais Bouleur. My grandpa stayed the taureau du poteau *("bull of the post"). They took the axel tree from the wagon and hit Grandfather Laval on the head and made a big dent, big enough to hide your finger in the hole and you couldn't see your finger. He died with that mark [many years later], but he had been the bull of the post. He's the only one who stayed on his feet, all*

the others stayed on the ground with the blood. Ha! It was a fight they had there. You talk about a fight at Bosco, at Marais Bouleur! Oh yes, Jack, Grandfather Laval was the best man. They hit him on the head with a single-tree but he never fell.
— Bernice Roger

I couldn't go to school because I had to stay home and work in the field. When I got married I was seventeen and a half years old. I went to live in Bosco near some Americans with whom I started to learn how to speak English. When I started learning how to speak English, I became interested in learning more English. I was a tenant farmer working on halves; half of the crop I'd produce went to the land owner. My father had taken us in after I got married, but he couldn't keep us so I had to find lodging for my wife and myself. While I was farming on halves, that's when I learned how to speak English. I farmed under this arrangement for ten years; then I started working for thirds, two thirds for me and one third for the land owner. That's when I was able to buy myself two horses, a moline, a wagon and some plows. Then I started working for myself.
— Aldus Roger

Bosco Stomp

(1 & 2)
There are some little blonds, there are some little brunettes;
there are some who are so black that the devil doesn't want to see them and that hurts me.
Little one, remember all the misery you caused me;
you made me believe in you and then you turn your back on me and that hurts me.

1- Y en a des 'tites blondes, y en a des 'tites
Pe- tite, rap- pelle toi tous les mi- sères tu m'as

brunes, Y en a qu'est assez noire que l'diable veut
fait; tu m'as fait des ac- croires et là tu m'

pas les voir et ça ce m' fait du mal.
tourne le dos et ça ce m' fait du mal.

Brasse le Couche-couche

Key. G

Version. Leroy Broussard (©La Lou).

Pattern. Accordion: one Tune; Vocal#1; Steel Guitar: one Tune; Violins: two Turns; Saxophone: one Turn; Vocal #2.

Going to Texas was a way to start a new life; Cajuns were especially attracted to east Texas. Orange and Nederland are located in the Port Arthur area. A *couronne* is usually a crown of flowers supporting the wedding veil. See Iry LeJeune's *Country Gentlemen* for an explanation of couche-couche.

Stir the Couche-couche

(1)
I'm going to Texas this morning and I'm taking a young girl with me.
Tell me if you're coming or I leave you here, I'm going to Texas this morning.
(Turn) Stir the couche-couche; milk the cow well; heat the coffee; I'm going to Texas this morning.

(2)
I'm going to Nederland this morning — — my prayer if you're coming.
Tell your dad you're coming and bring your wedding veil; we're getting married in the morning at Orange.
(Turn) Stir the couche-couche; milk the cow well; heat the coffee; I'm going to Texas this morning.

C'est Pas la Peine Tu Brailles

Key. G

Related song. See: *Bébé Créole* (Dennis McGee).

Pattern. Accordion: two Tunes; Vocal #1; Steel Guitar: two Tunes; Violin: two Tunes; Accordion: two Tunes; Vocal #2(repeat Vocal #1); Accordion: two Tunes.

It's No Use for You to Cry

(1 & 2)
Today, pretty doll, I'm tired of you, baby.
You're crying, you watch all the time in front of your father's house.
Today, doll, it's no use for you to cry.
You know I took it hard, what you did, pretty doll.
I'm tired of waiting and today you're not coming back.
You know, doll, it's no use for you to cry.

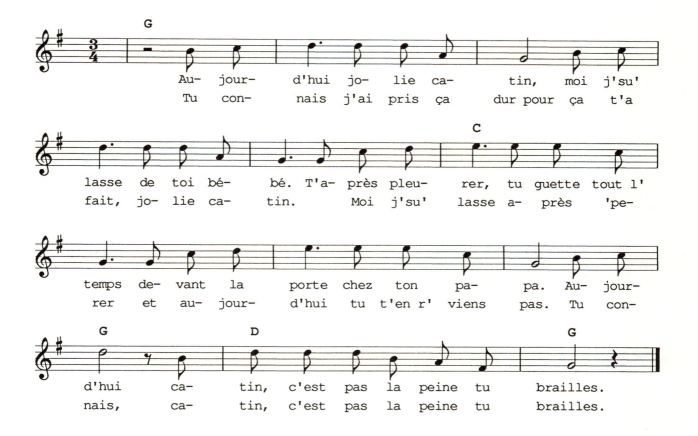

Au- jour- d'hui jo- lie ca- tin, moi j'su'
Tu con- nais j'ai pris ça dur pour ça t'a

lasse de toi bé- bé. T'a- près pleu- rer, tu guette tout l'
fait, jo- lie ca- tin. Moi j'su' lasse a- près 'pe-

temps de- vant la porte chez ton pa- pa. Au- jour-
rer et au- jour- d'hui tu t'en r' viens pas. Tu con-

d'hui ca- tin, c'est pas la peine tu brailles.
nais, ca- tin, c'est pas la peine tu brailles.

Cette-là J'aime

Key. F

Version. Adam Hébert (©Flat Town).

Pattern. Accordion: one Tune; Vocal #1; Steel Guitar:
one Tune; Violin: one Tune; Accordion: one Tune;
Vocal #2; Accordion: one Tune.

The One I Love

(1)
The one I love is like a little bird that flies from one tree to another.
When she's with other men, that's when she flies away from me.
(2)
It was just last night that she told me she'd never take me back.
Oh no, that will never do, even if I'm six feet deep in the ground!

1-   Cette la moi j' aime est comme un 'tit oi- seau
2-   C'est juste hier au soir que a(lle) m'as dit

qui vole à un arbre à l' autre. Quand
que elle, a(lle) m'au- rait ja- mais r'- pris. Oh

elle, alle est a- vec les aut' hommes, c'est
non, ça ça va ja- mais faire, quand

là   a(lle) vient fa- rouche de moi.
même   j'su' six pied fond dans la terre!

Chère Bassette

Key. F
Pattern. Violin: two Tunes and two Turns; Vocal #1;
Violin: two Tunes and two Turns; Vocal #2; Violin: two
Tunes and two Turns.

Version. Balfa Brothers; Dewey Balfa, vocal (©Flat
Town).

This song was originally recorded by J.B. Fusilier.

The first record that I remember making with J.B. Fusilier was The Lake Arthur Waltz, *because we played at a little place in Lake Arthur. Then we played at Pine Island there, so on the other side we made* Pine Island Two-Step. *Then we made* Chère Bassette, Où Toi T'es? *for his wife, who was given this nickname because she was very short. Then we made* Chère Tout-toute. *We were the ones who made that for the first time; that was for his little daughter who had been given the nickname Tout-toute.*

We made four records per session. The man in charge for the recording sessions was Mr. Eli Oberstein. He came from New York and he'd call us; then we'd go to the St. Charles Hotel in New Orleans. We'd make records there; then, at the end of six months, he'd come back and we'd make four more records. I think we made eighteen or nineteen records for R.C.A. We slept in the Monteleon Hotel, then the next day we'd go to the St. Charles Hotel, the third floor I remember, and we'd cut these records there. It wasn't tapes, it was thick wax records.

When we'd make a record the fellow would ask us, "Do you want to hear your voice back and see how it sounds?" I'd say, "I'd be tickled to death to hear that!" So he'd replay it and say, "That's perfect, but you'll have to cut another one because that one is ruined!"
— *Preston Manuel*

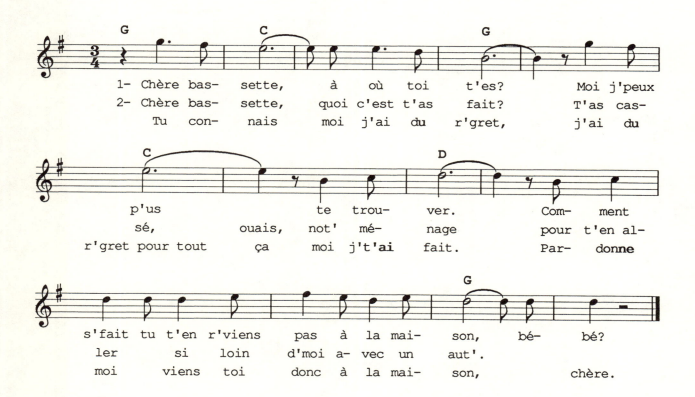

1- Chère bas- sette,   à où toi   t'es?   Moi j'peux
2- Chère bas- sette,   quoi c'est t'as fait?   T'as cas-
   Tu con-   nais   moi j'ai du r'gret,   j'ai du

p'us   te trou- ver.   Com-   ment
sé,   ouais, not' mé- nage   pour t'en al-
r'gret pour tout   ça   moi j't'**ai** fait.   Par- **donne**

s'fait tu t'en r'viens   pas à la mai- son, bé- bé?
ler   si loin d'moi a- vec un aut'.
moi viens toi donc à la mai- son,   chère.

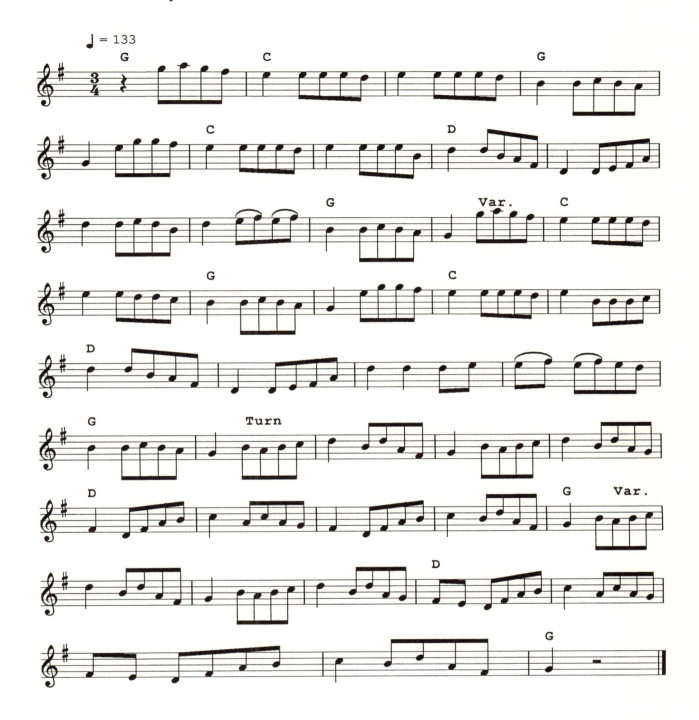

Dear Bassette

(1)
Dear Bassette, where are you? I can't find you. Why don't you come back home, baby?
(2)
Dear Bassette, what have you done? You broke our home to go so far away from me with another.
You know I'm sorry for what I've done to you. Forgive me, come on back home, dear.

Chère Chérie

Key. C   *Version.* Vin (Ervin) Bruce, vocal (©Flat Town).
Pattern. Violin: introduction (last nine measures);
Vocal#1; Steel Guitar: one Tune; Violin: one Tune;
Vocal #2.

Oran "Doc" Guidry and Leroy "Happy Fats"
LeBlanc first made and recorded this tune.

The music staff lyrics (line 1 / line 2 interleaved):

1- Y a per- sonne dans l'pa- ys qu'est plus jo-
2- J'l'ai en- con- tré dans les mèches, j'l'ai ame-

lie qu'ma chère ché- rie. Moi, j'con- nais c'est la plus
né au Ba- you Têche. On s'a ma- rié dans la cha-

belle dans la Loui- siane. Y a un tas qui s'sé-
pelle su' un di- manche. On s'a pro- mi d'l'a- mi-

pare et quand ça 'rrive, il est trop tard. C'est pour
tie pour la ba- lance de la vie. C'est pour

ça moi, j'l'a- ppele ma chère ché- rie.
ça que moi, j'l'a- ppele ma chère ché- rie.

Dear Darling

(1)
There's no one in the world who's prettier than my dear darling.
I know that she's the most beautiful in Louisiana.
There are some hearts who part and, when that happens, it's too late.
That's why I call her my dear darling.
(2)
I met her in the marshlands, I brought her to Bayou Teche.
We got married in the chapel on a Sunday.
We pledged friendship to each other for the rest of our lives.
That's why I call her my dear darling.

Chère Petite

Key. G
Pattern. Accordion: one Tune; Vocal #1; Steel Guitar: one Tune; Violins: one Tune; Accordion: one Tune; Vocal #2; Accordion: one Tune.

Version. Clarence Alleman, vocal; Aldus Roger's band (©La Lou); Preston Manuel, vocal; Ambrose Thibodeaux (*La Valse Que J'aime*, ©La Lou).

Chuck Guillory first made and recorded this song in the middle 1940's. Preston Manuel was a member of Chuck's band and I've included his lyrics.

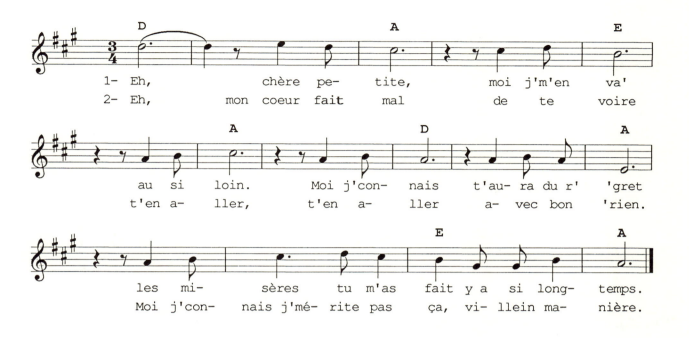

1- Eh, chère pe- tite, moi j'm'en va'
2- Eh, mon coeur fait mal de te voire

au si loin. Moi j'con- nais t'au- ra du r' 'gret
t'en a- ller, t'en a- ller a- vec bon 'rien.

les mi- sères tu m'as fait y a si long- temps.
Moi j'con- nais j'mé- rite pas ça, vi- llein ma- nière.

Dear Little One

(1)
Well, dear little one, I'm going so far away.
I know you'll regret the misery you've caused me for so long.
(2)
Well, my heart hurts to see you leaving, to see you leaving with a good-for-nothing.
I know I don't deserve that, ugly-mannered one.

La Valse Que J'aime

(1)
Oh, mais moi, j' m'en va' aussi loin pour toujours,
(pour) ça t'as fait mais avec moi i'y a pas longtemps, mais chère mignonne.
(2)
Après ma morte, tu vas r'venir t' lamenter pour ça t'as fait
avec moi y a pas longtemps, cher 'tit coeur, mais chère mignonne.

The Waltz I Like

(1)
Oh, but I'm going so far away forever,
because of what you've done to me not long ago, dear beautiful one.
(2)
After my death, you'll come back lamenting for what you've done
to me not long ago, dear little heart, dear beautiful one.

Valse de Coeur Cassé

Key. G

Pattern. Accordion: one Tune; Vocal #1; Violin: one
Tune; Accordion: one Tune; Vocal #2; Steel Guitar: one
Tune; Accordion: one Tune.

Version. Jimmy Thibodeaux (©Flat Town).
Related songs. Also: *Sorrow Waltz.*

Broken-hearted Waltz

(1)
I went to her house to see my dear little girl.
I asked where her mother was. She was in the yard.
I was in Lafayette and I saw in her eyes—
Look, it's too late! I found you with another!
(2)
I turned my back and I started walking
with my hands in my pockets and a broken heart
still thinking of what had happened.
Look, it's too late! I'm dying of grief.

1-   Moi j'ai y   'té à sa mai- son   pour
2-   Moi j'ai tour- né mon dos et j'ai par-

voir ma chère 'tite fille. J'ai d' man- dé à où sa
ti à mar- cher a- vec mes mains dans les

mam'. Alle é- tait dans la cour. J'ai
poches et un coeur aus- si cas- sé tou-

'tais à La- fa- yette et j'ai vu dans ces
jours a- près jon- gler à ça qu'ar- ri-

yeux. 'Garde donc, c'est trop tard! J't'ai trouvé. 'Garde donc, c'est trop tard! J'a- près mou-

vé a- vec un aut'!
rir dans les cha- grins.

Daylight Waltz

Key. F
Version. Sidney Brown (©Tek).
Pattern. Accordion: two Tunes; Vocal #1; Steel Guitar: two Tunes; Violin: two Tunes; Accordion: two Turns; Vocal #2; Accordion: one Tune.
Related songs. Also: *Cankton Waltz; Eunice Waltz.*

Before World War Two, diatonic accordions were ordered from Germany; during the War, we couldn't get them any more. Sidney Brown made the first homemade diatonic accordions in Louisiana. Later, Marc Savoy started an accordion workshop and taught many people how to make quality instruments, the Acadian Accordion. His accordions are so good that he doesn't even have to advertise in order to sell them.

Moi j' connais une belle 'tite
Moi j' l'ai vo- lé, ouais un soir; on a par-
2- Ton pa- pa étais fâ- ché lende- main mat-
I' dit, "Gar- çon, j'veux tu m' dit à où t'as é-

fille, la plus mi- gnonne y a n'a pas une
ti on s'a soûl- er. J'l'ai r'ame- ner
in quand i' m'a vu a- près ar- ri-
té hier au soir, et d' te

aut' dans la Loui sianne, ouais j'con- nais.
donc, lende- main mat- tin su' l'a- vant- jour.
ver a- vec sa fille, ouais si tard.
voir a- près r'ame- ner des- sus l'a- vant- jour.

Daylight Waltz

(1)
I know a beautiful little girl; there is none other more beautiful in Louisiana, I know.
I stole her, yes, one night; we left and we got drunk. I took her back, though, the next day at daybreak.
(2)
Your dad was angry the next morning when he saw me arriving with his daughter, yes, so late.
He said, "Boy, I want you to tell me where you went last night, when I see you returning her at daybreak."

La Dernière Valse

Key. G
Pattern. Accordion: one Tune; Vocal #1; Steel Guitar: one Tune; Violin: one Tune; Accordion: one Tune; Vocal #2; Accordion: one Tune. There is no turn in this song.

Version. Aldus Roger; Phillip Alleman, vocal (©La Lou).

The Last Waltz

(1)
Oh, but miserable one, you're criminal! You told me you couldn't love me anymore.
Oh, little girl, I don't want you to go! Now look indeed, today you turn your back on me.
(2)
Oh, miserable one, you told me you had found another who loves you more than I.
Oh, little girl, I'm lonesome for you! All I ask of you is to stay for the last waltz.

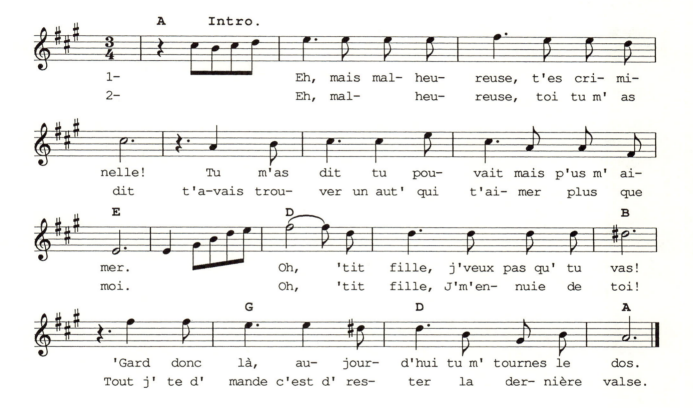

Diga Ding Ding Dong

Key. G
Pattern. Accordion: two Turns; Vocal #1; Steel Guitar:
two Turns; Violin: two Turns; Accordion: two Turns
and two Tunes; Vocal #2; Steel Guitar: two Turns;
Violin: two Turns; Accordion: two Turns.

Version. Aldus Roger; Phillip Alleman, vocal (©La
Lou).

The vocal part is the same as the main tune
and turn; the instrumental parts could be left
out and your own instrumentals inserted. The
instrumental included here is taken from the
accordion part. Improvise!

Diga Ding Ding Dong

(1 & 2)
Diga-ding-ding-dong! Diga-ding-ding-dong! Diga-ding-ding-dong, my girl is gone!
Diga-ding-ding-dong! Diga-ding-ding-dong! Look indeed the bells are ringing!
I'll marry a good friend! I'll marry Mister Gabi! Look indeed, now they know!
Diga-diga-dong! Diga-diga-ding-dong!

Dodge City Waltz

Key. C
Pattern. Accordion: two Tunes; Vocal #1; Steel Guitar: two Tunes; Violin: two Tunes; Accordion: two Tunes; Vocal #2; Accordion: two Tunes.

Version. Joe Bonsall (©Flat Town).
Related song. See: *Valse de Châtaignier* (Austin Pitre).

Austin Pitre's version is practically the same as Joe Bonsall's and was recorded much earlier. Châtaignier is a little settlement near Choupique just about five miles northeast of Eunice, Louisiana. The name came from the wild chestnut trees that once grew there.

1-   Oh,   tous   les   soirs   moi   j'su'
        Quo' faire   donc   que t'es comme   ça?   plus per-
2-   Oh,   tous   **les**   soirs   moi   j'su'
        P'us per- sonne   à   la   mai-   son   pour m' soi-

là   tout l'   temps a- près t'es- pér-   er.
sonne,   'tite   fille,   pour m'ai-   mer.   Iiii!
là   tout l'   temps a- près t'es- pér-   er.
gner.   'Tite   fille,   ça m' fait du   mal.   Iiii!

Dodge City Waltz

(1)
Oh, every night I'm always there waiting for you.
Why are you like that? I have no one, little girl, to love me. Eeeee!
(2)
Oh, every night I'm always there waiting for you.
There's no one anymore at the house to take care of me.
Little girl, that hurts me. Eeeee!

Valse d'Ennui

Key. G
Pattern. Accordion: two Tunes; Vocal #1; Steel Guitar: two Tunes; Violins: two Tunes; Accordion: two Tunes; Vocal #2; Accordion: one Tune. There is no turn in this song.

Version. Aldus Roger; Phillip Alleman, vocal (©La Lou).
Related songs. See: *Drunkard's Waltz* (Chuck Guillory).

I've left this song in its original key with the violin tuned down one step to G. Notice that I've included the violin bass or "second" as we say.

G
1- Oh, yé yaille, jo- lie fille! À où toi
Y a- vait ha- bi- tude tu m' ai- mer mais au- jour-
2- Oh, yé yaille, jo- lie fille! J'ai con- dam-
Y a- vait ha- bi- tude tu m' ai- mer mais au- jour-
C G
t'es? J'm'en- nuie de toi. Pour- quoi donc t'es comme
d'hui tu veux p'us m' voir. Pour- quoi donc t'es comme
né pap' et mam' juste pour toi, et au- jour-
d'hui tu veux p'us m' voir. Pour- quoi donc t'es comme
D G
ça? T'es tout l' temps 'près t'é- loi- gner.
ça? T'es tout l' temps 'près t'é- loi- gner.
d'hui, 'garde donc là, tu veux p'us m' voir.
ça? T'es tout l' temps 'près t'é- loi- gner.

Loneliness Waltz

(1)
Oh, it hurts, pretty girl! Where are you? I'm lonesome for you.
Why indeed are you like that? You're always moving away from me.
You used to love me, but today you don't want to see me anymore.
Why indeed are you like that? You're always moving away from me.
(2)
Oh, it hurts, pretty girl! I've condemned dad and mom just for you,
and today, now look indeed, you don't want to see me.
You used to love me, but today you don't want to see me anymore.
Why indeed are you like that? You're always moving away from me.

Evangeline Special

Key. A
Pattern. Accordion: two Tunes; Vocal #1; Accordion:
one Turn and two Tunes; Vocal #2; Accordion: one
Turn and one Tune; Vocal #3; Accordion: one Turn and
one Tune.

Version. Iry LeJeune (©Tek).
Related song. Also: *Saturday Night Special* (Lesa
Cormier).

This song was named for a night club in Ville
Platte, Louisiana, parish seat of Evangeline
Parish. In Louisiana, parish is the name we use
instead of county.

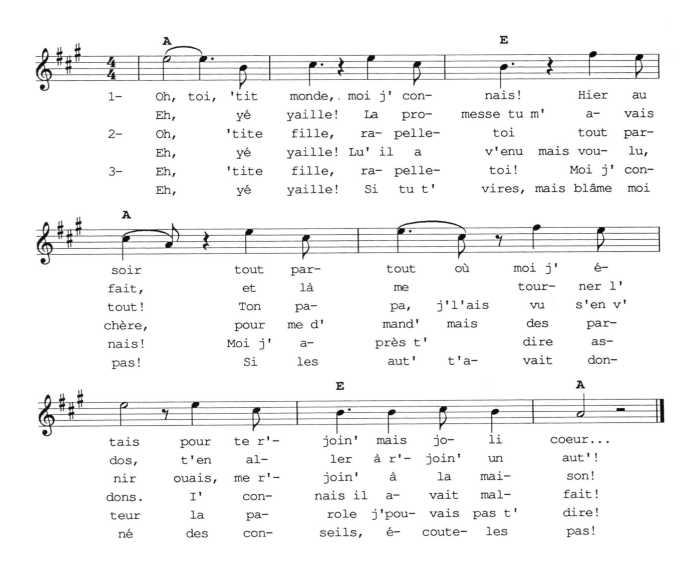

Oh, toi, 'tit monde, moi j' con- nais! Hier au
Eh, yé yaille! La pro- messe tu m' a- vais
Oh, 'tite fille, ra- pelle- toi tout par-
Eh, yé yaille! Lu' il a v'enu mais vou- lu,
Eh, 'tite fille, ra- pelle- toi! Moi j' con-
Eh, yé yaille! Si tu t' vires, mais blâme moi

soir tout par- tout où moi j' é-
fait, et là me tour- ner l'
tout! Ton pa- pa, j'l'ais vu s'en v'
nais! Moi j' a- près t' dire as-
pas! Si les aut' t'a- vait don-

tais pour te r'- join' mais jo- li coeur...
dos, t'en al- ler à r'- join' un aut'!
nir ouais, me r'- join' à la mai- son!
dons. I' con- nais il a- vait mal- fait!
teur la pa- role j'pou- vais pas t' dire!
né des con- seils, é- coute- les pas!

Evangeline Special

(1)
Oh, you, little one! I know! Last night everywhere I went to meet you, pretty heart ...
Well, it hurts! The promise you made to me, and then turning your back on me to go meet another!
(2)
Oh, little girl, remember everywhere! I saw your dad coming to meet me at home!
Ah, it hurts! He came but wanted to ask my forgiveness. He knew he did wrong!
(3)
Well, little girl, remember! I know! I'm telling you now the word I couldn't tell you before.
Well, it hurts! If you backslide, don't blame me! If others have given you some advice, don't listen to them!

Grand Texas

Key. G
Pattern. Accordion: one Tune; Vocal #1(Tune and
Turn); Steel Guitar: one Tune; Violins: one Turn;
Accordion: one Turn; Vocal #2 (Tune only); Accordion:
one Tune.

Version. Clarence Alleman with Aldus Roger's band
(©La Lou).
Related song. Also: *Jambalaya* (Hank Williams).

"Papa Cairo" (Julius Lamperez) made this
song and recorded it with Chuck Guillory's
band. This is an example of musicians
borrowing each other's songs.

Big Texas

(1 & 2)
You left me to go to big Texas, to go so far with another.
Criminal, how do you believe I can make it? You left me to go to big Texas.
(Turn)
You left me to go, to go so far with another.
Criminal, how do you believe I can make it? You left me to go to big Texas.

When Aldus fell sick, I didn't know what was the matter. "Doc" Guidry [the violin player in Aldus' band] told me that Aldus had been "struck." He became sicker and I took him to the Lady of Lourdes Hospital. He stayed there for a good while, then the doctors said they thought he had emphysema. The doctors told me that he'd have to stop smoking or taper off. I said, "Stop smoking or taper off! He has never smoked in his life!" I don't smoke either. The doctor said that I would have to take him back home while he studied the situation further. We went back home and the doctor called us eight days later. We went back to the Lady of Lourdes Hospital. We arrived there and the doctor examined him again. "Oh, I know what he has!" said the doctor. "What does he have?" I asked. "He has some blood clots in his lungs. His lungs have blood clots!" answered the doctor. "No!" I exclaimed. "Oh yes!" he answered. Then I told him, "You don't know what he has, but I know what he has." The doctor didn't ask me what he had. He gave him some medicines. He had to swallow seventeen different kinds of pills during the day!

When I returned from work, Aldus told me that he had almost died because he was short of breath ... I took off from work for three weeks. I started painting the bedrooms. I painted the north room, my little boy's room. While I was painting my bedroom, I heard a voice tell me, "Find out what's wrong with Aldus or he'll die." I climbed down from the ladder with paint on my hands. I went to the phone and called my daughter in Lake Charles. I asked her to find someone for me and Mr. Aldus because we needed some help. She asked me

what was the matter. I said, "I know that it's a gris-gris [hex], but I don't know what kind."

My daughter said that she'd call me back. I told her to find someone in Lake Charles who had been there longer than she had. She called an old woman who had spent her life in Lake Charles. The old woman told my daughter, "I've known an old traiteur [healer], but I don't know if he's still living. I knew him twelve years ago. Tell your mother to come and we'll try to find him."

The next day, Aldus and I left for Lake Charles to meet my daughter. We met the old woman at my daughter's home. We searched till we found the traiteur. When we entered his home and sat down, he told us, "Yes, I see Aldus has been struck." He told me and Aldus, "Someone put some snake poison on your accordion. It smothers you when you hold it." Aldus said, "Yes." The treater said, "Bring it here, I'll put a prayer on it. I'll wash it. I'll help you." But he didn't tell Aldus that he'd heal him. He said he'd help him.

The old man continued to treat Aldus for three weeks. Aldus went back and was treated with a prayer. The old treater looked at me and said, "Don't take out the prayer before he asks you for the accordion." The treater put a prayer in the notes [keys] of his accordion; I pressed on the nine note buttons and he wrote a prayer on a paper and slid the paper between the notes. That paper is still in the box [bellows] of the accordion.

It had been five years and five months that Aldus had not played his accordion. It smothered him each time he'd put his hands on the accordion. I said to myself in my heart, in my head, he'd never play again.

I came back from work one afternoon and he asked me, "Bern, where is my accordion?" He had looked for the accordion but it wasn't in its box. I had put it in the cedar-robe. "It's in the cedar-robe. What do you want to do, sell it?" I asked. "No," he said, "I feel like playing it." It was five years and five months he hadn't touched that accordion. I went and got the accordion and put it in its box in the room where we sleep. I closed it. The next morning, I went to work and when I came back, he had played it. Three weeks afterwards, he was playing at my sister's club in Rayne on a visit.

That's where he started playing again. In my opinion, Aldus plays better now than he ever played. Oh yes! He makes some good music. I guarantee you that!
     — Bernice Roger

Treaters may still be consulted in addition to doctors, particularly when modern medicine doesn't have a complete solution. Recently, my brother was treated for arthritis and my great-niece was treated for warts. (He said it helped and she said it didn't.) Since treating mainly involves prayer, it can even be done over the telephone — you can't beat that for convenience.

Grande Nuit Spécial

Key. C
Pattern. Accordion: one Tune; Vocal #1; Accordion: one Tune, one Turn and two Tunes; Vocal #2; Accordion: one Tune, one Turn and one Tune; Vocal #3; Accordion: one Tune.

Version. Iry LeJeune (©Tek).
Related songs. Also: *Country Playboys' Special* (Adam Hébert); *La Danse du Grand Chevalier* (Merlin Fontenot).

The key of G tuned down or transposed to A for the violin would cause the turn to be more "powerful" than the tune when played in the higher octave; that's why I've chosen the key of C tuned down or D transposed to standard.

Grand Night Special

(1)
Oh, it hurts, darling! I know I'm lonesome for you anyway.
Ah, little heart, you shouldn't forget all you've said to me before you came back.
(2)
Oh, little heart, it's hard to believe that your mom and dad told you I was no good.
Oh, doll, now you have regrets. It's too late! It's no use for you to complain to me.
(3)
Ah, it hurts! Today you complain. You, baby, I can't understand what good it does you.
Oh, my dear, you make yourself miserable. It seems that you deserve — I'm sorry, you don't deserve that.

Hick's Wagon Wheel Special

Key. G   *Version.* Aldus Roger (©La Lou)

Pattern. Accordion: four Tunes; Steel Guitar: two
Tunes; Violins: two Tunes; Accordion: four Tunes;
Steel Guitar: two Tunes; Violins: two Tunes; Accor-
dion: two Tunes. There is no turn in this song.

This instrumental was named for a nightclub
between Opelousas and Ville Platte,
Louisiana.

Homesick Waltz

Key. C

Version. Adam Hébert (©Flat Town).

Pattern. Accordion: two Tunes; Vocal #1; Steel Guitar:
two Tunes; Violin: two Tunes; Accordion: two Tunes;
Vocal #2; Steel Guitar: two Tunes; Violin: two Tunes;
Accordion: two Tunes.

Reggie Matte's vocal, which I've used here, is
almost the same as Adam's original.

Homesick Waltz

(1)
Oh, it hurts! I see myself going away; oh yes, unfortunate one, for the rest of my life.
Oh, it hurts! I don't see how I'll manage; my life is wasted and I'll never see you again.
(2)
Oh, it hurts! There's something I'd want to tell you. The day when I left, I had no choice.
Oh, it hurts! You know I'll be lonesome, but you don't know how much I'll be lonesome.

1-   Oh,   yé   yaille!   J'me   vois   m'en- al-
        Oh,   yé   yaille!   j'vois   pas   com-   ment j'va'
2-   Oh,   yé   yaille! Y a qu'que   chose j'vou-   drais te
        Oh,   yé   yaille! Tu con-   nais   j'va' m'en- nuy-

ler;   oh   oui,   mal-   heu-   reuse, pour la   ba- et
faire;   ma   vie   est   gas-   pi-   llé   et
dire.   Le   jour quand j'ai   par-   ti,   moi j'ai quit-
er,   mais   toi   tu con-   nais   pas   com-

lance   de   ma   vie.
moi   j'va'   jamais   te r'-   voir.
ter   par   o-   bli-   geance.
bien   j'va'   m'en-   nuy-   er.

J'aimerais d' Connaître

Key. C
Pattern. Accordion: one Tune; Vocal #1; Steel Guitar: one Tune; Violin: one Tune; Accordion: one Tune; Vocal #2; Accordion: one Tune.

Version. Adam Hébert (©Flat Town); Elton "Bee" Cormier.

"Bee" Cormier's vocal is very close to Adam Hébert's original version.

I'd Like to Know

(1)
When you left, already it's been a long time, we had to separate by obligation.
There's something happening, I can never see you again. I'd like to know if ever you'll come back.
(2)
The good Lord shouldn't have separated us; we should be together the rest of our days.
Even though you're well taken care of where you are, I'd like to know if ever you'll come back.

1-   Quand t'as quit- té, ça fait dé- jà beau- coup long-
2-   Le Bon Dieu au- rait pas dû nous sé- pa-

temps,   on a eu pour sé- pa- rer par o- bli-
rer;   on dev- rait d'êt' en semb' le reste nos

geance.   I'y a qu'que chose qu'a- près arri-
jours.   Quand même ti t'es bien soi-

ver, j'peux p'us t'r- voir.   J'aime- rais d' con- naît' si ja-
gner à où toi t'es;   j'aime- rais d' con- naît' si ja-

mais tu vas r've- nir.
mais tu vas r've- nir.

J' m'Ennuie Pas d' Toi

Key. G
Pattern. Accordion: two Tunes; Vocal #1 (A,B,C,D, E); Steel Guitar: two Tunes; Violins: one Turn; Accordion: two Tunes; Vocal #2 (repeat Vocal #1); Accordion: one Tune.

Version. Aldus Roger; Phillip Alleman, vocal. (©La Lou).
Author. Johnnie Allan (John A. Guillot).

Not Lonesome Anymore

(1 & 2)
(A) It's a week today that you've been gone. It's strange, but I don't remember you.
(B) My conscience doesn't hurt, that doesn't bother me anymore. Today I've had enough! You, you're no good!
(C - Turn) Oh! Oh! Oh! I'm not lonesome for you! Oh! Oh! Oh! I have no regrets for you!
(D) There's something I wanted to tell you when you left. I didn't have the chance, but I'll tell you now.
(E) Get away from me, ugly-mannered one! I'm so glad you left me! I don't want to see you.

J' su' Pas à Blâmer

Key. G

Pattern. Accordion: two tunes; Vocal #1; Steel Guitar: two tunes; Violin: two tunes; Accordion: two tunes; Vocal #2; Steel Guitar: two tunes; Violin: two tunes; Accordion: two Tunes.

Version. Rodney LeJeune (Cr-Cj).

The vocal to this song is usually sung an octave higher than I've written it and, if the range of the singer is lacking, we say that "it strangles the rooster."

1- Oh,   bé-   bé,   c'est tous les   soirs quand moi   j'me
    Eh,   ca-   tin,   ces 'tits en-   fants sont a- près pleur-
2- Oh,   'tite   fille, c'est ta   fa-   mille qu'est tous cont'
    Eh,   ca-   tin,   si'l vous   plaît re-   viens- toi

couch;   oh,   'tite   fille,   j'm'en- nuie   de
er;   oh,   yé   yaille,i' sont   'près   pleur-
moi;   oh,   'tite   fille,   j'su'   pas à   blâm-
donc;   oh,   'tite   fille,   j'su'   pas à   blâm-

toi   et   tes   par-   ents.
er   pour   leur   ma-   man.
er d'   ça   qu'a   'riv-   é.
er d'   ça   qu'a   'riv-   é.

I'm Not to Blame

(1)
Oh, baby, every night when I go to bed, oh, little girl, I'm lonesome for you and your parents.
Oh, doll, these little kids are crying; oh, it hurts, they are crying for their mother.
(2)
Oh, little girl, all your family is against me; oh, little girl, I'm not to blame for what happened.
Oh, doll, please come back; oh, little girl, I'm not to blame for what happened.

Johnny Can't Dance

Key. A
Pattern. Accordion: two Tunes and two Turns; Steel
Guitar: two Tunes; Violins: two Turns; etc.

Version. Aldus Roger (©La Lou).

Instrumental. I have been reluctant to assign a version or even to attempt writing this song at all, because I certainly can't write how the accordion, steel guitar and even the violin play their parts. Although it has a simple five-measure tune and turn, these are repeated with many variations which complicate this song.

I've tried, as usual, to write this song so that a musician can get an idea of the song. My father says this song entered the Cajun repertoire of songs through an elementary school song book. The song came from *The Rabbit Stole A Pumpkin* and changed over the years.

Jongle à Moi

Key. D

Version. J.B. Fusilier (©Tek).

Pattern. Accordion: two tunes; Vocal #1; Steel Guitar:
two tunes; Violin: two tunes; Accordion: two tunes;
Vocal #2; Steel Guitar: two tunes; Violin: two tunes;
Accordion: two tunes.

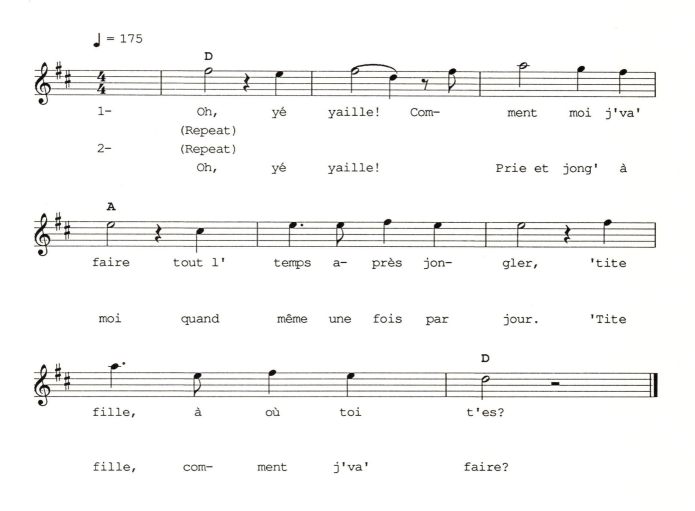

♩ = 175

D

1-   Oh,   yé   yaille!   Com-   ment   moi   j'va'
(Repeat)
2-   (Repeat)
      Oh,   yé   yaille!   Prie   et   jong'   à

A

faire   tout l'   temps   a- près   jon-   gler,   'tite

moi   quand   même   une   fois   par   jour.   'Tite

D

fille,   à   où   toi   t'es?

fille,   com-   ment   j'va'   faire?

Think of Me

(1)
Oh, it hurts! What will I do, always thinking, little girl, where are you?
(Repeat)
(2) *(Repeat first part of first vocal)*
Oh, it hurts! Pray and think of me anyway once a day. Little girl what will I do?

Juste un Rêve

Key. C

Version. Belton Richard (©La Lou).

Pattern. Accordion: one Tune; Vocal #1; Steel Guitar:
one Tune; Violin: one Tune; Accordion: one Tune;
Vocal #2; Steel Guitar: one Tune; Violin: one Tune;
Vocal #3.

Just a Dream

(1)
One day I was walking along the river; I was thinking about what had happened.
I had left the one who will always love me; that's something I should've never done.
(2)
My dear little black eyes started crying when I told her I was leaving.
She asked, "Please don't do that, how do you think I will live?"
(3)
I woke up this morning with a broken heart, tears in my eyes
and I was all discouraged still thinking about what had happened,
when I noticed it was only a dream.

1- Un jour j'tais a- près mar-
2- Mes chers 'tits yeux
3- J'm'ai re- veill- er à ce ma-

cher au long de la ri- vière; j'é-
noirs, ils sont mis à pleu- rer et
tin a- vec un coeur aus- si cas- sé, les

tais a- près jon- gler à ça qu'a- vez ar- ri-
moi, moi j'y ai dit j'su' 'té a- près quit-
larmes de- dans mes yeux et j'é- tais tout dé- cou- ra-

ver. Moi j'a- vais quit- ter cette la qui
ter. Elle a m'a d' man- dé, "S'il vous
gé tou- jours a- près jon- gler à

va tout l' temps m'ai- mer; ça c'est une
plâit fais donc pas ça com- ment
ça qu'av- ez ar- ri- ver; quand j' m'ai a- per-

chose que j'au- rais dû ja- mais faire.
moi tu crois moi j' va' vivre?"
çu ça c'é- tait juste un rêve!

KLFY Waltz

Key. G
Pattern. Accordion: one Tune; Vocal #1; Steel Guitar: one Tune; Violins: one Tune; Accordion: one and a half Tune; Vocal #2; Accordion: one Tune. There is no turn in this song.

Version. Aldus Roger; Phillip Alleman, vocal (©La Lou).
Related songs. Also: *Valse de Lafayette* (Chester "Pee Wee" Broussard).

This song was named in honor of the station in Lafayette, Louisiana, where Aldus played for fifteen years. The version by "Pee Wee" is much like this song but with different lyrics.

I played ten years on television. When KLFY was first opened in Lafayette, I was playing dances at 'Tit Maurice and and at the Midway Club between Lafayette and Breaux Bridge. Ellis Richard and Norris Breaux sponsored our band, The Lafayette Playboys, to advertise their dance halls. I announced the advertisements for the dance hall schedules and Dixie and Blatz beer. We had a full hour on Saturdays from noon till one o'clock to advertise and play. Our band wasn't paid for this. We just announced where we were playing every night. We played dances seven days a week for almost three years. Everyone who had a television set would turn it on and listen. Even those without sets would visit their neighbor and listen to us. Oh, that was something in those days! I was the first Cajun band to play on Channel 10.

I was also the first to play on radio in Lafayette over KLFY. At that time KLFY was only a radio station located near the Joe Huval Bakery. That's when I made the KLFY Waltz.

— Aldus Roger

KLFY Waltz

(1)
You left me, little girl, to go away, to go away so far to meet another.
What will I do, little one? How will I manage? I have no one in Lafayette for me to love anymore.
(2)
Today, little girl, you turn your back on me. I don't see, yes, what in the world
I've done for you to hate me as you do. I have no one in Lafayette to love me anymore.

Lafayette Playboys' Waltz

Key. C
Pattern. Accordion: one Tune; Vocal #1; Steel Guitar: two Tunes; Violin: two Tunes; Accordion: two Tunes; Vocal #2; Accordion: two Tunes.

Version. Aldus Roger; Phillip Alleman, vocal (©La Lou).
Related song. See: *Old Home Waltz* (Shirley Bergeron).

Many, many bands have called themselves the Playboys. One of the best-known of these was Aldus Roger's Lafayette Playboys.

Lafayette Playboy's Waltz

(1)
You told me, baby, that you loved me and today, look at that, you don't want to see me anymore.
I don't see what in the world I've done to make you hate me as much as you do.
(2)
I don't see, little girl, what I'll do. I'm all alone waiting for you to come back.
You told me, little one, that you didn't love me anymore and I thought today you don't want to see me.

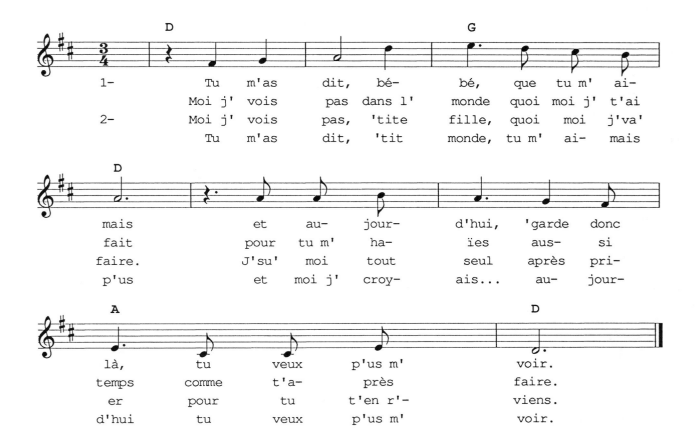

Lafayette Two-Step

Key. G
Pattern. Accordion: two Tunes; Vocal #1; Steel Guitar: two Tunes; Violins: two Tunes; Accordion: two Turns; Vocal #2; Accordion: two Turns.

Version. Aldus Roger, accordion; Fernest "Man" Abshire, vocal (©La Lou).
Related songs. See: *Allons à Lafayette* (Joseph Falcon); *Jeunes Gens de la Campagne* (Dennis McGee).

This song is livelier than Joseph Falcon's older version, although the tempo is indicated as 175. The vocals included here by "Man" Abshire are to be used with Joseph Falcon's vocals as a guide.

Two-Step de Lafayette

(1)
Allons à Lafayette! C'est pour changer ton nom.
On va t'appeler Madame, Madame Canaille Comeaux.
Petite t'es trop mignonne pour faire la criminelle.
Quo' faire tu m' fais tout ça? Oh, ouais, ma si aimable.
(2)
Le monde parle mal de toi, tu danses mais trop collée.
Quo' faire tu m' fais tout ça? C'est pour m' faire fâcher.
Allons à Lafayette, on va changer ton nom.
On va t'appeler Madame, Madame Canaille Comeaux.

Lafayette Two-Step

(1)
Let's go to Lafayette! To change your name.
We'll call you Madam, Madam Rascally Comeaux.
Little one, you're too cute to act like a criminal.
Why do you do all that to me? Oh, yes, my lovable one.
(2)
People speak badly of you, you dance too closely.
Why do you do all that to me? It's to make me angry.
Let's go to Lafayette, we will change your name.
We'll call you Madam, Madam Rascally Comeaux.

Valse de LeBoeuf

Key. C

Pattern. Accordion: two Tunes; Vocal #1; Violin: two Tunes; Accordion: two Tunes; Vocal #2; Violin: two Tunes; Accordion: two Tunes.

Version. Johnny Richard, vocal; "Boy" Frugé, accordion; Ray Cormier, violin (©La Lou).

LeBoeuf is a family name.

1- Hé 'tite fille, jongle donc bien ma mal- heu- reuse;
2- Hé 'tite fille, rap- pelle toi mais cher 'tit monde;

oui, les con- seils, mais les pro- messes que t'as cas- sé.
oui, les pro- messes au- jour- d'hui que t'as cas- sé.

LeBoeuf's Waltz

(1)
Hey, little girl, think seriously, my miserable one; yes, the advice, the promises you broke.
(2)
Hey, little girl, remember, dear little one; yes, the promises you broke today.

Valse de la Louisiane

Key. F
Pattern. Accordion: one Tune; Vocal #1; Steel Guitar: one Tune; Violins: one Tune; Accordion: one Tune; Vocal #2; Accordion: one Tune. There is no turn in this song.

Version. Aldus Roger; Tunice Abshire, vocal (©La Lou).

1- T'a- près m' quit- ter, ma 'tites yeux bleus,
2- Quand j'va' mou- rir, tu vas r' ve- nir

pour t'en al- ler dans la Loui- siane ad- joind' un
te met' à genoux à mon cer- cueil et me d' man-

aut' qu'est pas mieux qu' moi. Pour t'en r' ve-
der de mes par- dons. Tu s'ra trop

nir, s'ra trop tard pour ça t'as fait.
tard, j's'ra p'us là pour t' par- don- er.

Louisiana Waltz

(1)
You're leaving me, my little blue eyes, to go away in Louisiana to meet another who's no better than me.
When you come back, it'll be too late for what you've done.
(2)
When I'll die, you'll come back and get on your knees at my coffin and ask for my forgiveness.
You'll be too late, I won't be there to forgive you.

Lovesick Waltz

Key. C
Pattern. Accordion: one Tune; Vocal #1; Steel Guitar: one Tune; Violin: one Tune; Accordion: two Turns; Vocal #2; Accordion: one Tune.

Version. Aldus Roger; Phillip Alleman, vocal (©La Lou).
Related songs. Also: *Tu Peux t' Blâmer* (Joe Bonsall).

We don't ordinarily use the French title for this song.

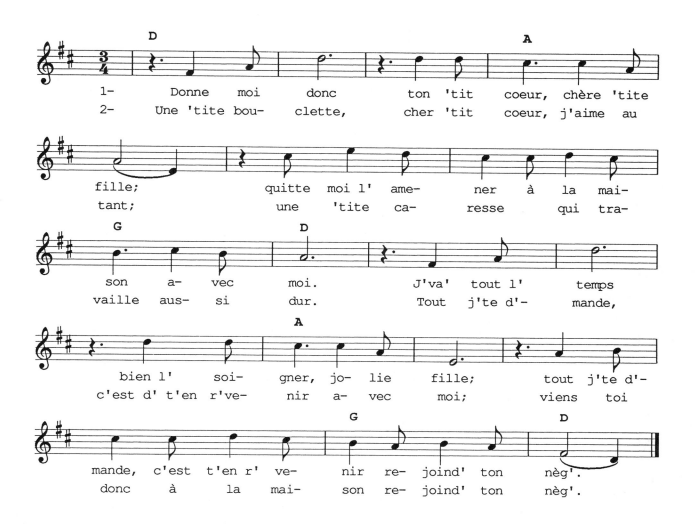

Lovesick Waltz

(1)
Give me your little heart, dear little girl; let me take it back home with me.
I'll always take good care of it, pretty girl; all I ask of you, is to come back and meet your lover.
(2)
A little curl, dear little heart, I like so much; a small caress that works so hard.
All I ask of you, is to come back with me; come home and meet your lover.

Mam', J' su' Toujours Ton 'Tit Garçon

Key. F

Version. Camey Doucet (©Flat Town).

Pattern. Accordion: one Tune; Vocal #1; Steel Guitar: one Tune; Violin: one Tune; Vocal #2; Accordion: one Tune.

This is a modern song.

Mom, I'm Still Your Little Boy

(1)
Hey, Mom, I'm still your little boy.
Hey, Mom, he still thinks of you since you've gone to paradise. Hey, Mom, I'm lonesome a lot for you.
You were there when I fell; you were there when I cut myself, with the best medicine that you could find.
You'd make it with nothing; you'd heal it with your hand. Hey, Mom, I'll never forget that.
(2)
I know I was lucky to have a mother like you. You raised a large family and you always took good care of us.
Now you're not here there's something I want to tell you. Hey, Mom, I'm still your little boy.

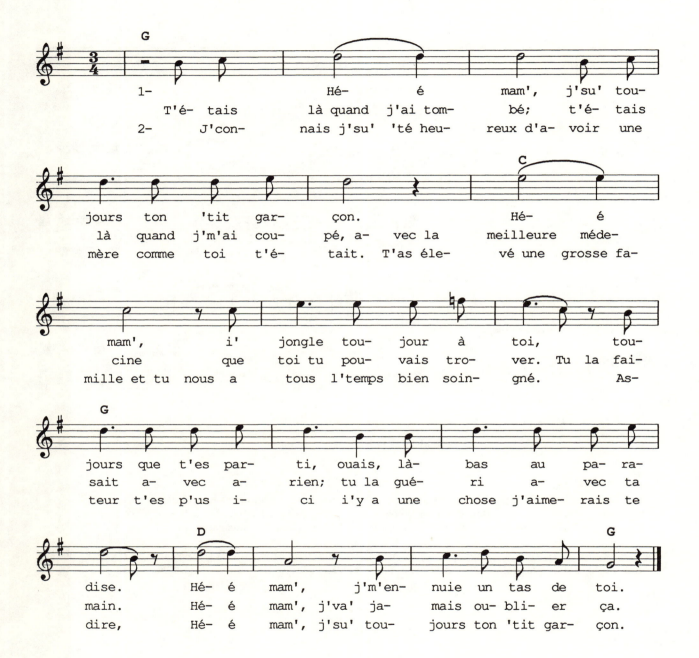

Valse de Malchanceux

Key. C

Version. Lawrence Walker (©La Lou).

Pattern. Accordion: Parts 1 and 2; Vocal #1 (Parts 1
and 2, Turn and Part 3 which is same Tune as part 2);
Steel Guitar: one Turn; Violin: part 2; Accordion: Parts
1 and 2; Vocal #2 (Turn and Part 3). Only the vocals
need to be followed as other arrangements can be done
for different instruments.

For arrangement purposes, part 3 of the vocal
is the same as part 2 of the vocal.

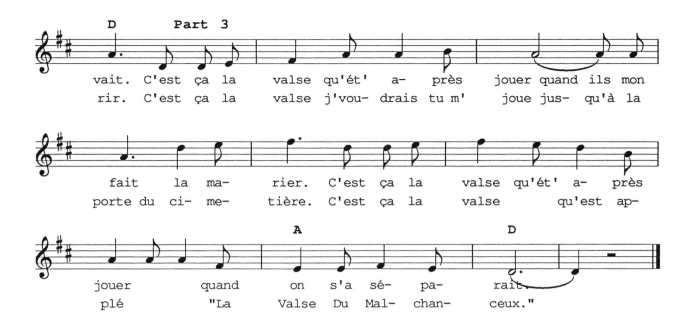

vait. C'est ça la valse qu'ét' a- près jouer quand ils mon
rir. C'est ça la valse j'vou- drais tu m' joue jus- qu'à la

fait la ma- rier. C'est ça la valse qu'ét' a- près
porte du ci- me- tière. C'est ça la valse qu'est ap-

jouer quand on s'a sé- pa- rait.
plé "La Valse Du Mal- chan- ceux."

The Unlucky One's Waltz

(1)
(Part 1) That's the waltz I call "The Unlucky One's Waltz."
That's the waltz that played so much when we courted.
(Part 2) That's the waltz that was playing the night I proposed.
That's the waltz that was playing when her father refused me (her hand in marriage).
(Turn) That's the waltz that was playing the night I stole her (eloped).
That's the waltz that was playing when they found me.
(Part 3) That's the waltz that was playing when they made me marry her.
That's the waltz that was playing when we separated.

(2)
(Turn) That's the waltz I'd want you to play for me on my death bed.
That's the waltz I'd want you to play for me the day I'll die.
(Part 3) That's the waltz I'd want you to play for me till the cemetery gate.
That's the waltz that's called "The Unlucky One's Waltz."

Mamou Two-Step

Key. G
Pattern. Accordion: two Turns and two Tunes; Steel
Guitar: two Turns; Violins: two Turns; Accordion: two
Turns and two Tunes; Steel Guitar: two Turns;
Accordion: two Tunes.

Version. Aldus Roger (©La Lou).
Related Songs. See: *Mamou Two-Step* (Lawrence
Walker).

This instrumental is named for the Mamou
area.

Mamou Two-Step (variation)

Key. G
Pattern. Accordion: two Turns and two Tunes; Violin: two Turns and two Tunes; Accordion: two Turns and two Tunes; Violin: two Turns; Accordion: one Tune.

Version. Lawrence Walker (©La Lou).
Related song. See: *Mamou Two-Step* (Aldus Roger).

Instrumental.

Manuel's Bar Waltz

Key. C
Version. Milton Molitor (Big Mamou).
Pattern. Accordion: two Tunes; Vocal #1; Steel Guitar:
one Tune; Accordion: one Tune; Vocal #2; Accordion:
one Tune and two Turns; Vocal #3; Accordion: one
Tune.

I laughed till I cried when he sang the third
vocal, because I know that feeling.

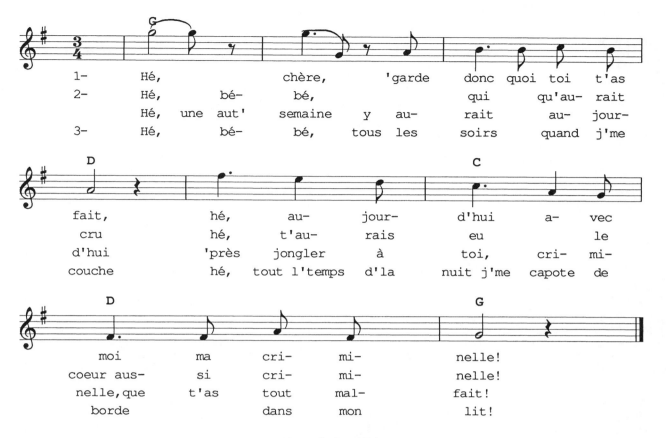

Manuel's Bar Waltz

(1)
Hey, dear, look what you did, hey, today with me, you criminal!
(2)
Hey, baby, who would've believed, hey, you would've had such a criminal heart!
Hey, another week there'd be today, thinking about you, criminal, what you did wrong!
(3)
Hey, baby, every night when I go to bed, hey, all during the night, I flip over in my bed!

Danse de Mardi Gras I

Key. G minor
Pattern. Violin: two Tunes; Vocal #1; Violin: one
Tune; Vocal #2; Violin: one Tune; Vocal #3; Violin:
one Tune.

Version. Balfa Brothers (©Flat Town).
Related song. Sce: *La Chanson de Mardi Gras.*

This song has been revised by the Balfa Brothers for dance hall purposes. Don't let the corncobs baffle you, they can be used in the cook-
stove.

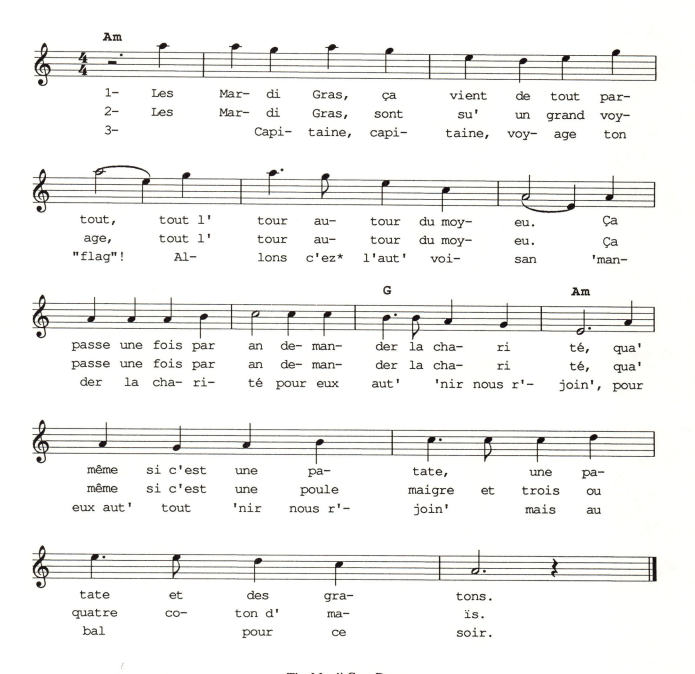

The Mardi Gras Dance

(1)
The Mardi Gras come from everywhere, all around, around the hub.
They pass once a year to ask for charity,
even though it's a (sweet) potato, a potato and some cracklings.
(2)
The Mardi Gras are making a big trip, all around, around the hub.
They pass once a year to ask for charity,
even though it's a skinny chicken and three or four corncobs.
(3)
Captain! Captain! Wave your flag! Let's go to the other neighbor
to ask for charity and invite them to come to the dance tonight.

Danse de Mardi Gras II

Key. F
Pattern. Play parts 1-4 over and over.

Version. Aldus Roger (©La Lou).

This song is played with only G-chords. You are welcome to invent your own lead — mind the rhythm. Various instruments could take any part. The Mardi Gras Dance is played during Mardi Gras season.

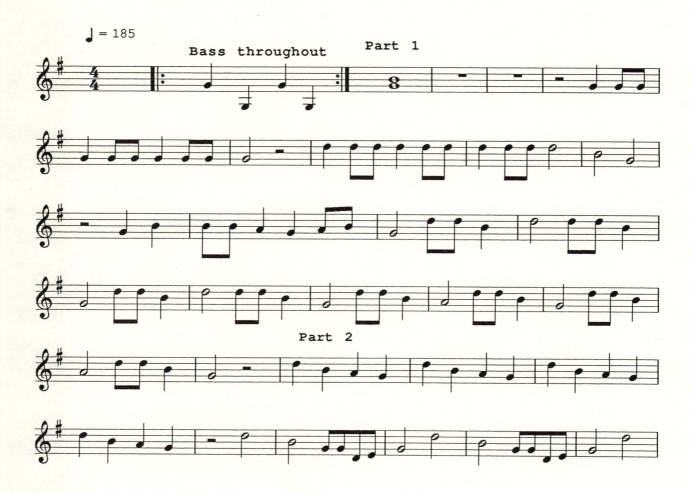

Marie

Key. G
Pattern. Accordion: one Tune; Vocal #1(both stanzas);
Steel Guitar: one Tune; Violins: one Tune; Vocal #2
(both stanzas); Steel Guitar: one Tune; Violins: one
Tune; Accordion: one Tune.

Version. Aldus Roger; Vernon Bergeron, vocal
(©Flat Town).

Marie

(1 & 2)
I can't forget you, baby. You knew that I loved you; you knew that I loved you, doll, since I was fourteen.
Oh, Marie, doll, look what you've done; look at that. You're leaving, leaving your poor old lover, baby.

Mermentau Waltz

Key. G
Pattern. Accordion: two Tunes; Vocal #1; Steel Guitar: two Tunes; Violin: two Tunes; Accordion: two Tunes; Vocal #2; Steel Guitar: two Tunes; Violin: two Tunes; Accordion: two Tunes.

Version. Barry Cormier, vocal. The original recording is by Dunice P. Theriot (©Dunice Theriot).

This is a relatively modern song which shows a unique structure, especially in the vocals. Barry's vocals are close to the original ones by Dunice P. Theriot.

Mermentau is an Indian name. The town of Mermentau, along Highway 90 in southwest Louisiana, is located on the Mermentau River.

♩ = 133

A   E

1- J'ai 'spé- rer   au   boute de mon   chemin;
   C'est juste toi   qui   peut casser mon   couer
2-   Al- lons s'a- mu- ser au- jour- d'hui
   J'peux pas   res- ter décou- ra-   ger

D   E   A

j'ai 'spé- rer à ma   der- nière jour- née.
et j'su' tou- jour   a- près t'es- pé- rer.
tan- dis on peut s'a- voir une belle vie.
et j'su' tou- jours   a- près t'es- pé- rer.

E

2-(cont.) J'su' d'ac- cord   de te par- don- ner

D   E   A

parc'- que   j'peux pas t'ou- bli- er.   C'est juste

E

toi   qui vou- lais sé- pa- rer   et j'su' tou-

jour   a-   près   t'es-   pé-   rer.

Mermentau Waltz

(1)
I waited at the end of my road; I waited till my last day.
It's only you who can break my heart and I'm still waiting for you.
(2)
Let's enjoy ourselves today while we can have a beautiful life.
I can't stay discouraged and I'm still waiting for you.
I'm willing to forgive you because I can't forget you.
It's only you who wanted to part and I'm still waiting for you.

Mon Coeur Fait Mal

Key. F

Version. Rodney LeJeune (Cr-Cj).

Pattern. Accordion: two Tunes; Vocal #1; Steel Guitar: two Tunes; Violin: two Tunes i.e. Part 2; Accordion: two Tunes; Vocal #2; Accordion: one Tune.

My Heart Hurts

(1)
I traveled. I have yet to have you; I couldn't. Dear little girl, what will I do?
The advice you listened to from one and the other, that's why you're like that today.
(2)
I tried to make you like me, little girl; I couldn't. Dear little heart, what will I do?
The advice you listened from your family, that's why, dear little heart, you're like that.

1-   J'ai   rou-   ler,   j'ai   tou-
          Les   con-   seils   toi   t'as é-   cou-
2-   J'ai es- say-   é   de t'faire m'ai-
          Les   con-   seils   toi   'ta é-   cou-

jours pour t'a-   voir;   j'ai   pas   p'us, chère 'tite
té   d'un   et   l'aut'   c'est   pour   ça   q'au- jour-
mé,   'tite fille,   j'ai   pas   p'us, cher   'tit
ter d' ta   fa-   mille,   c'est   pour   ça,   cher   'tit

fille,   com-   ment   j'va'   faire?
d'hui   toi   t'es   comme   ça.
coeur,   com-   ment   j'va'   faire?
coeur,   toi   t'es   comme   ça.

Mother's Day Waltz

Key. C

Pattern. Accordion: one Tune; Vocal #1; Steel Guitar: one Tune; Violin: one Tune; Accordion: one Tune; Vocal #2; Steel Guitar: one Tune; Violin: one Tune; Accordion: one Tune.

Version. Don Guillory, vocal. The original recording was by Joel Sonnier (©Jamil).

This is a modern song.

Mother's Day Waltz

(1)
Today I'm here in prison; no one in the world wants me.
My papa and mama don't have any more money. Just think, it's Mother's Day!
(2)
There's no one in the world who wants me. For a year I've been in this prison.
I don't see what in the world I will do. Just think, it's Mother's Day!

Valse des Musiciens

Key. C

Version. Rodney LeJeune (Cr-Cj).

Pattern. Accordion: two Tunes; Vocal #1; Steel Guitar: two Tunes; Violin: two Tunes; Accordion: two Tunes; Vocal #2; Steel Guitar: two Tunes; Violin: two Tunes; Accordion: two Tunes.

This is a modern song. The vocals are sufficient to make up your own arrangement; each vocal is made up of the two tunes played by each instrument.

1- Oh, 'tite fille, c'est tous les soirs moi j'su'
2- Oh, 'tite fille, quand tu m'a pris, tu sa-

là a- près jon- gler à ça qu'ar- ri- vé. Tu m'as quit-
vez moi j'é- tais un mu- si- cien. Au- jour-

té parce que j'é- tais un mu- si- cien; juste rap-
d'hui t'a- près voir ton er- reur, mais peut-

port à les con- seils toi t'as é- cou- té.
être ça s'ra trop tard pour t' par- don- ner.

Musician's Waltz

(1)
Oh, little girl, every night I'm there, thinking about what happened.
You left me because I was a musician, just on account of the advice you listened to.
(2)
Oh, little girl, when you took me, you knew I was a musician.
Today you're seeing your error, but maybe it'll be too late to pardon you.

Valse de Minuit

Key. G

Version. Lawrence Walker (©Flat Town).
Related song. Also: The turn is very much like
Chuck Guillory's *Drunkard's Waltz.*

For some grand openings, like at Richard's Casino, I'd play one Saturday and Lawrence Walker would play the next. At Midland, I'd play one Saturday and he'd play the next. At Morse, the same. At the River Club, the same. This was years ago, when I was young. These fellows, sometimes they'd baptize a new club. There were three or four that were baptized like that. We would hear over the radio that all the bands were invited to go and the best would get a fifty dollar prize and would play the dance that night. While going to play our dances, we'd hear that and I said, "Y'all hear that, huh? We should go, yes."

Lawrence Walker told me that I was the man who played more like him than any other he had heard among all the musicians who sang and played the accordion. He said, "You make beautiful music." I told him, "I learned your notes. I listened to you when I first started playing again. I caught you over my car radio and I copied what you were doing. Every Saturday that the good Lord made, even though I was at work, I'd sit in my car and listen to you. That's why I am close to you." "Look," he told me, "we're all some copy-cats. I listen to someone else and you listen to me. I want to tell you that you're close to me for not having played longer than you're playing." I told him, "Thank you very much." I liked his music, he played some pretty music, some pretty keys, some pretty notes. He's the one who influenced me most with the accordion, the late Lawrence Walker. For fancy notes, understand? I know all his verses word for word.

— Roy Fusilier

Midnight Waltz

(1)
Oh, baby, it's hard to believe that you and I will never see each other again.
After all I did for you, oh little baby, you shouldn't abandon me.
(2)
Oh, little heart, you know I took it hard when you told me you couldn't love me.

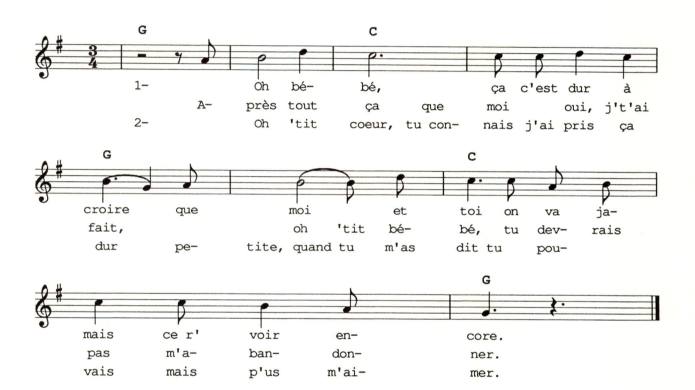

Valse de Newport

Key. C

Version. Dewey Balfa (©Flat Town).

Pattern. Accordion: two Tunes and two Turns; Vocal #1; Violin: two Tunes; Accordion: two Turns; Vocal #2; Violin: two Tunes; Accordion: two Turns.

Dewey made this song about the Jazz Festival at Newport, Rhode Island! Now Cajun music and cooking are known all over the world.

I went to France, Chicago, Birmingham, North and South Carolina, and to Washington D.C. three times. I took Reggie Matte, Preston Manual, Merlin Fontenot, Leland McDaniel, and my daughter, Leola. I made all the arrangements everywhere we went. These weren't small country dances, no! Oh, yé yaille! There were thousands of people!

— Ambrose Thibodeaux

We left from California and came back to New York. It's the first time a Cajun band traveled around the world. We appreciated that very much. Now I am not interested in returning to the same places, surely. I wouldn't be interested in leaving for such a long time, either. It's too long to leave your home, your family, but I'm very happy that I've made that tour. It's an experience that I never thought I'd have.

— Allie Young

Newport Waltz

(1)
If you want a good time, you must go to the festival in Newport.
We went to Newport. We had a barrel of fun.
(2)
To Newport we went. We made ourselves a lot of good friends.
I'd like to tell all the Cajuns, if you want a good time, go to the Festival!

O.S.T. Special

Key. C
Pattern. The tune and turn are each played twice.

Version. Aldus Roger and Phillip Alleman (©Flat Town).
Related song. Also: *Cajun Special.*

Notice that the turn begins and ends with an A-chord, the key of A. The initials O. S. T. stand for Old Spanish Trail (US Highway 90) which runs from east to west in southern Louisiana. This was the name of a nightclub in Rayne, Louisiana.

O. S. T. Special

(1 & 2)
Hey, unfortunate little one, remember, hey, what you did with me not long ago.
Hey, you'd like to come back anyway.
Hey, as for you, look here, I don't want to see you anymore!

Old Fashion Two-Step

Key. G
Pattern. Accordion: two Tunes; Vocal #1; Steel Guitar: two Tunes; Violin: two Tunes; Vocal #2; Accordion: two Tunes.

Version. Willis Touchet, vocal, and Touchet Brothers (©Flat Town).

As you can tell from the lyrics, this is a modern song.

Old Fashion Two-Step

(1)
Your papa and your mama, they don't seem too happy;
when I pass to pick you up, they are right there watching me.
They observe how I'm dressed and, if they don't like how I'm combed,
there's one thing I know, they can forget the old fashion ways.
(2)
I don't see what I've done; it's just that they've too many ideas.
Before they break up our friendship, we'll leave and escape.
They observe how I'm dressed and, if they don't like how I'm combed,
there's one thing I know, they can forget the old fashion ways.

1-   Ton pa-   pa   et   ta   ma-
        Ça ob-   serve comme j'su' ha- bil-
2-   Moi j'vois   pas quoi moi   j'ai
        Ça ob-   serve comme j'su' ha- bil-

man,   ça me r'-   semble pas trop con-   tents; quand moi
lé   et si ça aime   pas comme j'su' pei-   gné,   y a une
fait; c'est juste ça   s'fait trop des i-   dées. A- vant ça
lé   et si ça aime   pas comme j'su' pei-   gné,   y a une

j'passe pour t'ra- mas-   ser, i'   sont   droit
chose que moi j'con-   nais, ça peux ou-   bli-
casse not' a- mi-   tié, on va   par-
chose que moi j'con-   nais, ça peux ou-   bli-

là   a-   près m'guet-   ter.
er l'vieux temps pas-   sé.
tir et s'é- chap-   per.
er l'vieux temps pas-   sé.

Old Home Waltz

Key. D
Pattern. Accordion: one Tune; Vocal #1; Steel Guitar:
two Tunes; Violin: two Tunes; Accordion: two Tunes;
Vocal #2; Accordion: two Tunes.

Version. Shirley Bergeron (©JON).
Related song. See: *Lafayette Playboys' Waltz* (Aldus
Roger).

Reggie Matte's lyrics on the first two vocals
are probably much like Shirley's original ones;
I've also included "Bee" Cormier's lyrics in
vocals three and four.

Old Home Waltz

(1)
My old home is not the same since you're gone; it just looks like an abandoned place.
All I look like is a prisoner who has lost his hope of ever seeing you again.
I've lost track of time, not watching the almanac day by day.
Not ever if one day I'll see you coming down the little crooked road by yourself.
(2)
I'm living in hell today without hope that one day you'll come back.
We could live in paradise all our lives, me and you, so happy in our old home.
(3)
Look, dear baby, what you've done to a little heart which loved you, unfortunate one.
You promised me, baby, to love me; today you're leaving me, what will I do?
(4)
I arrived to get you. There's something that was telling me I'd cry.
They told me, "Yes, your sweetheart is gone!" Seven candles lit at her coffin!
Don't take it so hard, dear baby, I know we'll meet another day.
We'll walk hand in hand, you and I, once more in the blue sky forever.

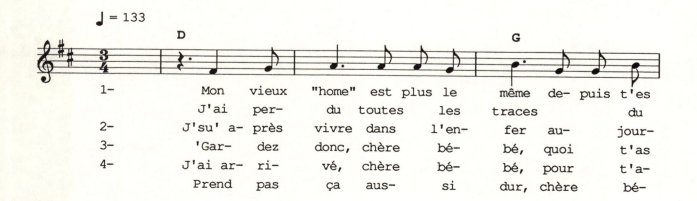

1-   Mon vieux "home" est plus le même de- puis t'es
      J'ai per- du toutes les traces   du
2-   J'su' a- près vivre dans l'en- fer au- jour-
3-   'Gar- dez donc, chère bé- bé, quoi t'as
4-   J'ai ar- ri- vé, chère bé- bé, pour t'a-
      Prend pas ça aus- si dur, chère bé-

"gone,"		ça r'-	semb'	juste	comme	une
temps,		pas	guet-	ter	l'al-	ma-
d'hui		sans	es-	poir	que	un
fait		à un	'tit	coeur	qui	t'ai-
près.		l'y a	que'que	chose	qui m'	di-
bé,		moi j'	con-	nais	on va'	ce r'-

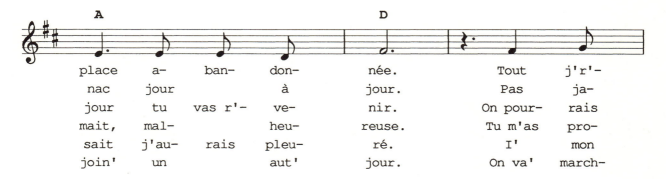

place	a-	ban-	don-	née.	Tout	j'r'-
nac	jour		à	jour.	Pas	ja-
jour	tu vas r'-		ve-	nir.	On pour-	rais
mait,	mal-		heu-	reuse.	Tu m'as	pro-
sait	j'au-	rais	pleu-	ré.	l'	mon
join'	un		aut'	jour.	On va'	march-

semb'	un	pri-	son-	nier qu'a per-	du	son és-
mais	si	un	jour	j'va' te r'-	voir	t'en r'- ve-
vivre dans l' pa-	ra-	dis	tout	not'	vie,	moi et
mis,		bé-	bé, de m'	aim-	er;	au- jour-
dit, "Ouais,		la	belle, elle est	"gone!"	Sept chan-
er	main	en	main moi et	toi	un aut'

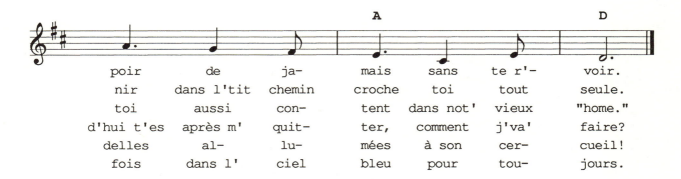

poir	de	ja-	mais sans te r'-	voir.
nir dans l'tit	chemin	croche	toi tout	seule.
toi	aussi	con-	tent dans not' vieux	"home."
d'hui t'es	après m'	quit-	ter, comment j'va'	faire?
delles	al-	lu-	mées à son cer-	cueil!
fois dans l'	ciel	bleu	pour tou-	jours.

Valse des Opelousas

Key. C
Pattern. Accordion: two Tunes; Vocal #1; Steel Guitar: one Tune; Violin: one Tune; Accordion: two Tunes; Vocal #2; Accordion: one Tune.

Version. Austin Pitre; Aubrey "Cabri" Menier, vocal (©Flat Town).

Opelousas, Louisiana, is an old city and was once an Indian trading post. Opelousas is an Indian word for "dark or murky water."

This recording, made in 1959, was among the first records to be made at Floyd Soileau's studio in Ville Platte.

Opelousas Waltz

(1)
Well, little heart, what will I do, yes, all alone, dear little one, at home?
Well, little girl, you know I'm lonesome for you. Why are you gone, dear little one, so far away?
(2)
Well, doll, why are you like that, yes, leaving me all alone in misery?
Well, little one, you know I'm lonesome for you. Yes, dear little heart, come meet me before dying.

Ouvre la Porte

Key. C
Pattern. Accordion: two Tunes; Vocal #1; Steel Guitar: two Tunes; Violin: two Tunes; Accordion: two Tunes; Vocal #2; Steel Guitar: two Tunes; Violin: two Tunes; Accordion: two Tunes.

Version. Adam Hébert (©Flat Town).
Related song. Lay That Pistol Down.

"Bee" Cormier's vocals which I've used here are virtually the same as the original ones. Elsewhere in this book I've already explained where the places mentioned in this song are located.

Grand Ma-mou, au 'Tit Ma-mou, là-bas à l' Anse Cha-

oui! Ouvre cette porte et entre i-ci moi j'

veux t'en poi-so-ner!

Open The Door

(1)
Oh, open the door and come in here. I want to antagonize you.
I saw you last night being caressed behind the door,
together, you and Cousin Lisé.
Oh, open that door and come in here. I want to poison you!
(2)
At Big Mamou, at Little Mamou, over there at Straw Cove,
Everywhere I go, people speak badly of you.
At Big Mamou, at Little Mamou, over there at Raccoon Cove!
Open that door and come in here. I want to poison you!
(Repeat vocal 1.)

Valse du Passé

Key. C
Pattern. Accordion: two Tunes; Vocal #1; Steel Guitar: two Tunes; Accordion: two Tunes; Vocal #2; Accordion: two Tunes.

Version. Shirley Bergeron (©JON).
Related songs. See: *Valse des Vachers* (Dennis McGee). Also: *My Rope and Spurs* (Adam Hébert).

I worked with Alphé and Shirley Bergeron when they made Fais Dodo Dans Les Rangs d' Soybeans, Quelle Étoile, Les Noces Chez Tani, *and* The Old Home Waltz. *Shirley composed the words and his dad was behind the band. Shirley did the M.C.-ing and singing. Alphé played, but Shirley would tell him what to play.*

I also M.C.-ed for him a lot too. You must serve all the people who come up front. They want you to play a particular song and you tell them you're going to play it. You can't satisfy all of them, but you can substitute songs, a song that resembles the one they requested.

The main thing is to pay attention to all who come to the bandstand. You must face them and mention their names on the microphone, that helps a lot. Little things like that don't seem much, but it serves the public when you're hired to play. It's not hard to remember and sing the songs in the order requested. You see, Shirley had left the band for a short period of time and I'd take his place when he'd leave. His father could play anything but didn't like to worry about the people around him. I had to worry about that and M.C. for the band.

— Shelton Manuel

Waltz of the Past

(1)
Let's think of the past when I loved you with all my heart; you'd sit on my knees and we'd kiss.
There were no reprisals, there was no hatred; everything was beautiful with you here.
(2)
Today we're separated, we've started to regret it; our grief will remain all our lives.
Let's get back together, forget, take courage and help one another; our past is gone forever.

Pine Grove Blues

Key. D
Pattern. Accordion: play first nine measures; Vocal #1;
Violin: bass vocal part; Accordion: play "Inst. between
vocals;" Vocal #2; Violin: improvise vocal part; Accordion: play instrumental between vocals.
Rhythm. The rhythm guitar usually plays four quarter-note beats per measure.

Version. Nathan Abshire (©Flat Town).

The violin bass chords are included here at the end of the song and should be used throughout except when taking the lead part which comes from the vocal part. During the vocals a band member may jokingly make comments such as *Quoi tu veux, nèg'?* (What you want, black man?), *J'ai été m'soûler.* (I went and got drunk.) *Dans la barrière* (In the fence.)

Pine Grove Blues

(1) Hey, black woman! (What you want, black man?)
Where did you go last night, my black woman?
You came back this morning; the sun was coming up. I feel sorry for you!
(2)
Hey, black woman! (What you want, black man?)
Where did you go last night, my black woman? (I went and got drunk.)
Hey, black woman! (What you want, black man?)
Where did you pass last night, my black woman? (In the fence.)
You came back this morning, your dress was all torn up!

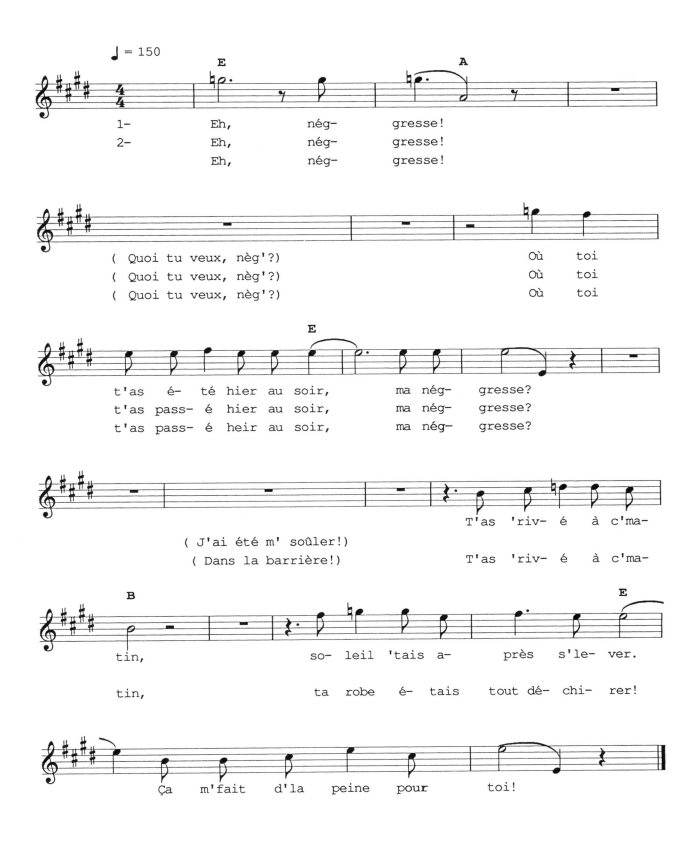

La Porte d'en Arrière

Key. G
Pattern. Accordion: one Tune; Vocal #1; Steel Guitar: two Tunes; Violin: two Tunes; Accordion: two Tunes; Vocal #2; Accordion: one Tune.

Version. Doris Leon ("D.L.") Menard, vocal, and the Louisiana Aces (©Flat Town).

This song is considered by most Cajun music fans as the most famous Cajun song of all!

The Back Door

(1)
My sweetheart and I went to the dance. We went to all the honky-tonks.
We came back the next morning at daybreak. I passed through the back door!
This afternoon I went to town and got so drunk that I couldn't walk. They took me back home.
There was some company; they were strangers. I passed through the back door!
(2)
When I arrived, my old dad tried to change my ways. I didn't listen to him, I was too hard-headed.
"Some day, my son, you'll regret having passed through the back door!"
I had a lot of friends when I had money; but now I'm broke, they don't want to see me.
I went to town and got into trouble. The law picked me up and we're going to jail.
They will take me through the back door!

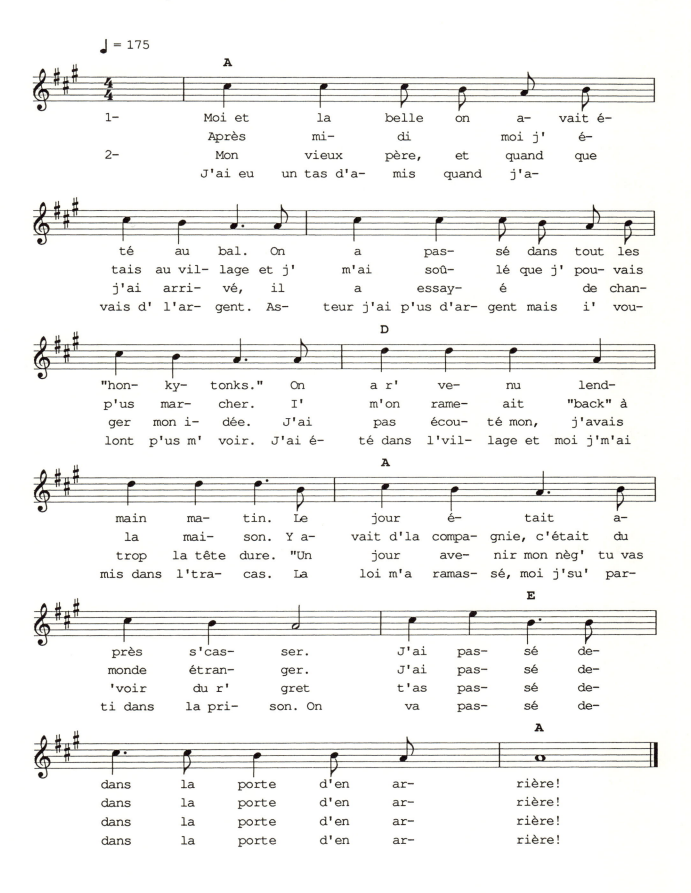

Valse de Port Arthur

Key. C
Pattern. Accordion: two Tunes; Vocal #1; Steel Guitar: two Tunes; Violins: two Tunes; Accordion: two Tunes; Vocal #2; Accordion: two Tunes. There is no turn in this song.

Version. Aldus Roger and Phillip Alleman, vocal (©La Lou).
Related songs. Also: *Lake Arthur Waltz*.

This song is named for Port Arthur, Texas; it's a place to make a new start and a place where other Cajuns have migrated.

Port Arthur Waltz

(1)
Oh, little girl, I'll go to Port Arthur! Oh, little one, today you don't want to see me anymore!
Oh, it hurts! You said that you love me! Oh, little one, today you turn your back on me!
(2)
Oh, little girl, you decided that you no longer loved me! Oh, little one, today you don't want to see me anymore!
Oh, it hurts! It's sad to see you, yes, all the time! I'll go to Port Arthur!

Pour la Dernière Fois

Key. G

Version. Adam Hébert (©Flat Town).

Pattern. Accordion: one Tune; Vocal #1; Steel Guitar:
one Tune; Violin: one Tune; Accordion: one Tune;
Vocal #2; Accordion: one Tune.

For the Last Time

(1)
Let me hold you in my arms one more time before I die.
Put your rosy cheek against mine, your pretty curls upon my shoulder,
and let me see your beautiful blue eyes.
After tonight, this will be the last time.
(2)
Tomorrow morning you'll receive the news that I'll be gone.
You can blame yourself for all that will happen.
Don't come cry at my coffin to try and forgive yourself.
You'll be too late; I'll be gone for the last time.

1- Laisse moi t'nir dans mes bras une aut'
2- Demain ma- tin tu vas con- naît' la nou-

fois a- vant d' mou- rir; met ta chère joue
velle que j' sera "gone." Tu peu't' blâ- mer pour tout

rose cont' la meinne, tes belles bouc- lettes su' mon é-
ça qui va 'rri- vé. Viens pas braill- er à mon cer-

paule, et quitte moi r'- voir tes beaux yeux bleus, a- près à
cueil pour es- say- er de t' par- don- né. Tu sera trop

soir, ça se- ra la der- nière fois.
tard, moi j' s'ra "gone" pour la der- nière fois.

La Promesse J'ai Fait

Key. C   *Version.* Phil Menard (©Whitewing).

Pattern. Accordion: one Tune; Vocal #1(do all of vocal
#1 then do Part B of 2nd stanza); Steel Guitar: one
Tune; Violin: one Chorus; Accordion: one Tune; Vocal
#2 (do all of vocal #2 then do Part B of 2nd stanza);
Accordion: one Tune.

The Promise I Made

(1)
The last time you and I were together —
With tears in our eyes we kissed. Today I'm doing what I said.
Even though we can't see each other, the truth is you'll be in my memory.
Even though we'll never see each other again, this song I'm singing is just for you.
(2)
All my life you'll be there with me. In my mind you'll be there always.
Even though we'll never see each other again, this song I'm singing is just for you.
Even though we can't see each other, the truth is you'll be in my memory.
Even though we'll never see each other again, this song I'm singing is just for you.

Valse de Prison

Key. C
Pattern. Accordion: two Tunes; Vocal #1; Steel Guitar: two Tunes; Violin: two Tunes; Accordion: two Turns; Vocal #2; Accordion: two Tunes.

Version. Marc Savoy and Dallas Roy (Cr-Cj); Leroy Broussard made the original recording (©Tek).
Related song. See: *Manuel's Bar Waltz* for the turn.

Prison Waltz

(1)
In prison sitting on my bed thinking of you. Little girl, what will I do?
Oh, it hurts, my heart is all broken thinking of you; doll, I'm gone.
(2)
Oh, little girl, why are you like that? Today you're leaving me.
Little girl, you don't want to see me anymore.
Oh it hurts, my heart is all broken in prison. What will I do?

1-   De-   dans   la   pri-   son   as-
                       Oh   yé   yaille,   mon
2-   Aïe,   'tite   fille,   quo'
                       Oh   yé   yaille,   mon

sis   de- sus   mon   lit   a-   près   jon-   gler   à
coeur est tout bri-   sé   a-   près   jon-   gler   à
faire t'es comme ça?   'Jour- d'hui t'a-   près m' quit-
coeur est tout cas-   sé   de-   dans   mais   la   pri-

toi;   'tite   fille,   com-   ment   j'va'   faire?
toi;   ca-   tin,   mais   moi j'   m'en   va'.
ter;   'tite   fille,   tu   veux   plus m' voir.
son;   'tite   fille,   com-   ment   j'va'   faire?

Rainbow Waltz

Key. G
Pattern. Accordion: two Tunes; Vocal #1; Steel Guitar: two Tunes; Violin: one Tune; Accordion: one Tune; Vocal #2; Accordion: one Tune. (No Turn)

Version. Austin Pitre (©Flat Town).
Related songs. See: *'Tits Yeux Noirs* (Lawrence Walker). Also: *Country Waltz* (Lawrence Walker); *Valse à 'Tit 'Dam Hanks* (original).

This song is named for a nightclub. Create your own instrumentals from the first eight bars.

1-   Eh, bé- bé, tu m'as dit hier au soir,
     Eh, bé- bé, par rap- port à tes ma- nières,
2-   Eh, bé- bé, tu m'as dit, chère ca- tin,
     Eh, 'tite fille, par rap- port à tes pa- rents,

oui, chère ca- tin, tu pou- vais p'us ai- mer ton
oui, t'au- rais 'cou- té ton pa- pa plu- tôt à
ton a- mi- tié bien soi- gné tu la per-
oui, t'es là seule, oui, c'est de voir j'peux pas al-

nèg'.   Ouais, tu con- nais pas   comme
toi!   Ouais, j'l'ai bien fait pour t'a- vais
du.   Ouais, moi j' con- nais si tu la soignes
ler,   oui, te cher- cher et r'me-

moi j'ai pris ça dur.
fait, mon chère bé- bé.
pas, a' va s'en al- ler.
ner à la mai- son.

Rainbow Waltz

(1)
Well, baby, you told me last night, yes, doll, you couldn't love me anymore.
Yes, you don't know how hard I took it. Well, baby, it's because of your ways!
Yes, if you would've listened to me rather than to yourself!
Yes, I did well, despite what you've done, my dear.
(2)
Well, baby, you told me, dear doll, you lost your remarkable friendship for me.
Yes, I know, if you don't take care of it, she will go away.
Well, little girl, it's because of your parents, yes, that you're there alone.
Yes, I see that I can't go, yes, to get you and take you home.

When I first started playing, I was about eighteen or nineteen years old. My first dance was in Iota, Louisiana. I started playing with J.B. Fusilier and The Merrymakers, just a little group. The first record I made for R.C.A. Bluebird was in 1936 in New Orleans. We made, I think, about nineteen records there. I played about twenty-five years with J.B. and the Merrymakers. That's when I played with Chuck Guillory, in between that time. I had quit playing with J.B. for a few years, right after World War II, and we organized a band, me and Chuck, The Rhythm Boys. Then Chuck quit playing, so I rejoined with J.B. and the Merrymakers again.

Chuck went in business on his own. He had opened up that big Superette store in Mamou and then he stopped playing; then he sold his store and he started playing again. He calls that a "re-comeback" now. Yeah, we got a good little four-piece band, sometimes five pieces. There's me, Chuck, Sylvian Fontenot on the drums and an electric guitar man from Erath by the name of Dave Baudoin. When we need an accordion, we usually pick up a good accordion man from Mamou, like Jimmy Berzas.

Then I played a good while with Eddie Bearb and the Bristol Ramblers. Then I played with Nathan Abshire, Will Kegley at the old Avalon Club in Basile. And I play with Revon Reed on the Mamou Hour. I've been playing there about twenty-one years. Yeah, we started in 1961. I played every Saturday morning with Sady Courville and Revon Reed. Charles Kuralt took our pictures for "On The Road." I heard that I was seen all over the United States, in France and all over.

I had a wonderful time, in fact. About all I've ever done was play music. I worked a few years back in furniture stores, until my eyes gave out. All I can do now for a pastime is play music. On the Mamou Hour, we've got two violins, Roy Fontenot and Sady. For the accordion, we substitute. Sometimes Nonc' Allie Young comes and plays; sometimes it's Jason Fry, a young boy. He's a good little accordion man. He also make accordions. I like to play with him, he's a nice guy and plays peppy.

My main man is Chuck. I like to play with him and he's such a nice guy. He's a good fiddler too! I also played with Merlin Fontenot and Ambrose Thibodeaux. We made two good albums together. I enjoyed playing with Merlin very much; he's such a good musician. Then another group I played with a long time ago was our late Austin Pitre. Yes, we played many dances — me, and Austin, his son, Jimmy, J.W. Pelsia, the steel player, and our late Roy Tate. About nine years ago we went to Washington, D.C. for nine days. We played in Arlington, Virginia, for that big fair. We played a lot of dances all over, at the Blue Goose, Lake View and all over.

— Preston Manuel

René's Special

Key. G
Pattern. Accordion: two Tunes, one Turn, one Tune, one Turn and one Tune; Steel Guitar: one Turn, Accordion: one Tune, one Turn, two Tunes, one Turn and one Tune; Steel Guitar: one Turn; Accordion: two Tunes.

Version. Austin Pitre (©Flat Town).

Many variations are possible! This instrumental was probably named for one of his daughters. As disk jockey on radio station KEUN, Eunice, Louisiana, I used this tune for my theme song during the early sixties on a one-hour program on Saturdays called the Church Point Hour.

Reno Waltz

Key. C
Pattern. Accordion: one Tune; Vocal #1; Violins: one
Tune; Accordion: one Tune; Vocal #2; Violins: one
Tune; Accordion: one Tune; Vocal #3.

Version. Lawrence Walker (©La Lou).

No turn. Named for a nightclub between Kaplan and Abbeville, Louisiana.

*Lawrence Walker was a very good musician,
He was precise in his music, especially on his
tune-ups. He made sure everything was tuned
right, and we wore uniforms back then. We
wore white shirts with ties. We'd travel around
in a station wagon. We had a local broadcast*

*at KPLC in Lake Charles once a week. We'd
do the broadcast at the same time that we had
a dance in the vicinity. The broadcast was on
the route to the dance. He was working pretty
much back then. He had two dances at the
O.S.T. in Rayne, one in Lake Charles at the
South Street Club. I spent about a year doing
that.*

— Shelton Manuel

Reno Waltz

(1)
Yes, the place I'd want to die is in the arms of my little baby,
asking forgiveness for what I've done. I'd be willing to go away to big Gueydan.
(2)
When I die, I'd like you to come close my eyes, little baby, for me to go,
for me to go in the ground for always. As you know, it hurts just to think about it.
(3)
You're so petite and also cute. You're a rascal, little baby, but I love you all the same.
I don't see what in the world I'll do, I've nobody in the world who wants to love me.

Rêve de Soûlard

Key. G

Pattern. Accordion: one Tune; Vocal #1; Steel Guitar: one Tune; Violin: one Tune; Accordion: one Tune; Vocal #2.

Version. Cleveland Crochet's band with Vorris "Shorty" LeBlanc, accordion (©Tek).

Drunkard's Dream

(1)
I arrived last night at the house; I knocked, I called, there was no answer.
Suddenly, I knew you weren't there! What hope and what future can I have?
(2)
Drinker, rambler and big gambler, that's all I was all my days till I met you.
I promised, dear little girl, never to do that. It's so hard to know you're not there.

1- J'ai ar- ri- vé hier au soir à la mai- son; j'ai co- gner, j'ai cri- é, j'ai pas d' ré- ponse. J'ai con- nu au mo- ment t'é- taits pas là! Quel es- poir, quel a- venir mais moi j' peux a- voir?

2- Bam bo- cheur, traî- nai- eur et un grand "gam- bleur", c'est tout j'ai 'té tous mes jours jus- qu'à j't'ai r' join'. J'ai pro- mit, chère 'tite fille, de p'us faire ça. C'est si dur, c'est d' con- nêt' mais t'es pas là.

Valse de Samedi Soir

Key. G
Pattern. Accordion: one Tune; Vocal #1; Steel Guitar: two Tunes; Violin: one Tune; Accordion: two Tunes; Vocal #2; Accordion: one Tune.

Version. Dallas Roy (Cr-Cj); Joe Falcon made the original recording.

This is a modern version with no turn.

Saturday Night Waltz

(1 & 2)
You took me from home on a Saturday night, baby.
You told me, doll, that you loved me; today you're leaving.
Remember all the promises you made to me, darling.
You told me, doll, that you loved me; today you turn your back on me.

A

Tu   m'as   pris, d'la mai-   son   un same- di au
R'ap- pelle   toi   les pro-   messes que tu   m'as

soir,   bé-   bé. Tu m'as   dit,   ca-   tin, que tu m'ai-
fait,   mi-   gnonne. Tu m'as dit,   ca-   tin, que tu m'ai-

mais;   aujour   d'hui   toi   t'es
mais;   aujour   d'hui   toi   t'es

là   a-   près   m'quit-   ter.
là   a-   près m'tour-   ner l'   dos.

Sauvage su' l' Chicot

Key. G

Pattern. Violin: Part 1, Part 2 and Part 1; Vocal #1;
Violin: Part 1, Part 3 and Part 1; Vocal #2; Violin: Part
1, Part 3 and Part 1; Vocal #3; Violin: Part 1, Part 3.

Version. Dewey Balfa (©Flat Town).

Dewey recorded this song in what we call
"Indian tuning" — C-A-G-A; the lowest string
is C. I've used standard tuning.

Many Cajun families can claim Indian as well
as European ancestry. I don't know of any
Indian ancestors of my own, but my maternal

step-grandfather *Pépère* John was half Indian.
When he was pleased about something, he
would say *wash*-tah, which I've recently dis-
covered is an Indian word meaning "good"
which was also used by the northern Plains
Indians.

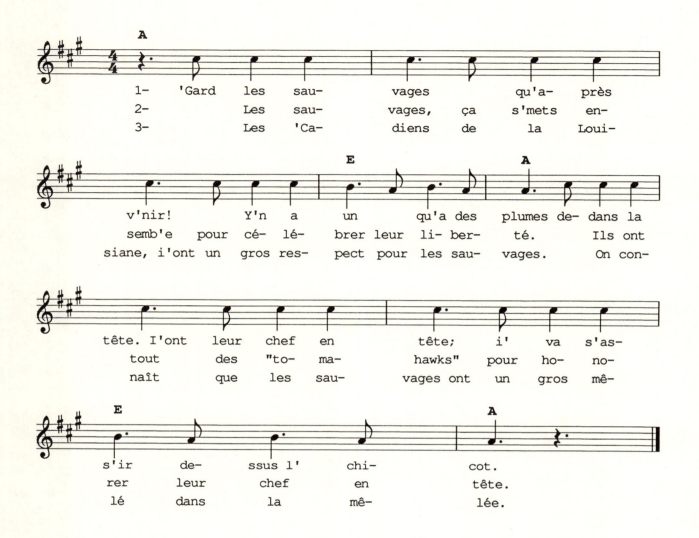

1- 'Gard les sauvages qu'a-près v'nir! Y'n a un qu'a des plumes de-dans la tête. I'ont leur chef en tête; i' va s'as-s'ir de-ssus l' chi-cot.

2- Les sauvages, ça s'mets en-semb'e pour cé-lé-brer leur li-ber-té. Ils ont tout des "to-ma-hawks" pour ho-no-rer leur chef en tête.

3- Les 'Ca-diens de la Loui-siane, i'ont un gros res-pect pour les sau-vages. On con-naît que les sau-vages ont un gros mê-lé dans la mê-lée.

Indian on a Stump

(1)
Look at the Indians coming! There's one wearing feathers.
They have their chief, who goes and sits on the stump.
(2)
The Indians get together to celebrate their freedom.
They all have tomahawks to honor their chief.
(3)
The Cajuns of Louisiana have a great respect for the Indians.
We all know that the Indians have a big mixture in our population.

Shamrock Two-Step

Key. F
Pattern. Each instrument plays two tunes. There is no turn in this song.

Version. Aldus Roger (©La Lou).

This instrumental is named for a night club in Lake Charles, Louisiana, and probably has Mexican influence.

There was a church fair here and every year they pick me to play. I said I'd play three or four tunes, if there were some musicians. I listened to these musicians from everywhere. That's how they played for these young people. When they played, they wanted to kill themselves. And me? When I got up there, I played as fancy as I could, and pretty. They didn't see me, these outsiders. The local people would jump, though. They would jump! But these strangers? Humph! No, I didn't play right at all, me. When the others would get up and play something slow, then they'd jump. Slow, simple notes, nothing fancy at all, you see. That's how they are, overseas. I don't want to put them down, but they're not accustomed to Cajun music. They're not used to something fast; they're slow.

Now there are many musicians in Canada and France who play Cajun. They came over here and learned our music. Taped, taped and taped! They copy-cat the music and some of them play it. I heard some play; we never play like that. They play reels and contredances. *I wanted to see, to understand something. I took this fellow's accordion and started sounding it note by note and I noticed that it wasn't tuned like ours. Uh uh, it sounded as far off as could be. I couldn't play anything on it, but they would take it and you don't imagine how fast they'd play their jigs and things like that. They would play these so easily, it didn't strain them at all. It's the way the instruments were tuned, and they were born and raised listening to that kind of music and they'd practice that way. They beat us for that.*

We're better than they are with our music. They like our tunes very much too. If we tried to play their tunes, it would be difficult, too. We'd have to have been born and raised with them over there and practice, practice to come to play like that. I couldn't play our dances right away; I had to practice a lot. And over there, it's the same thing, you must practice a lot until it comes easy, if you want to learn what they play.

— Roy Fusilier

Valse à Tante Adèle

Key. A

Version. Louis Cormier (©La Lou).

Pattern. Accordion: two Tunes; Vocal #1; Steel Guitar: two Tunes; Violin: two Tunes; Accordion: one Tune; Vocal #2 (repeat vocal #1); Accordion: two Tunes.

Ouain-ouain is Cajun slang for baby and is taken from the sound of a baby crying.

1- Quand tu dis, "tante A- dèle," tante A-
    Quand tu dis, "tante A- dèle," tante A-

dèle est dans la chamb'. Mais quoi alle a- près
dèle est dans l'aut' chamb'. Mais quoi tu crois alle a- près

faire? 'Près faire té- ter ces 'tits "wan- wans."
faire? 'Près faire man- ger ces 'tits bé- bés.

Aunt Adèle's Waltz

(1 & 2)
When you say "Aunt Adèle," Aunt Adèle is in the room.
But what is she doing? She's breast-feeding her little babies.
When you say "Aunt Adèle," Aunt Adèle is in the other room.
But what you think she doing? She's feeding her little babies.

'Tit Maurice

Key. C
Pattern. Accordion: one Tune; Vocal #1; Steel Guitar: one Tune; Violin: one Turn; Accordion: one Tune; Vocal #2; Accordion: one Tune.

Version. Felton LeJeune (BEE); Oran "Doc" Guidry and Leroy "Happy Fats" LeBlanc.
Related Songs. See: *Valse d'Amour* (Dennis McGee). Also: *Valse du Coteau Magnolia* (Dennis McGee); *Chinaball Blues* (Austin Pitre); *Basile Waltz* (Rufus Thibodeaux); *Valse de Grand Basile* (Jimmy Newman).

I have used Felton LeJeune's lyrics, but I think they are very close to the original by "Happy Fats". This song was named for a nightclub in Vatican, about twelve miles northeast of Rayne near Bosco, Louisiana.

1- C'est s'en al- ler, ouais, chez 'tit Mau- rice!
2- C'est nous aut', ouais, q'est si joy- eux!

C'est pour voir et cour- ti- ser toutes les 'tites filles!
C'est nous aut', mais q'aimes au- tant mais la mu- sique!

Et viens nous r'- join', ouais, pour un bon temps!
Pour un bon temps, ouais, viens donc nous r'- join'!

C'est là- bas chez 'tit Mau- rice le same- dis soirs!
C'est là- bas chez 'tit Mau- rice tout les same- dis!

Little Maurice

(1)
We're going to Little Maurice's! To see and court all the little girls!
Come meet us for a good time over there at Little Maurice's on Saturday nights.
(2)
We're so joyful! We like music so much! For a good time, yes, come meet us!
Over there at Little Maurice's on Saturday nights.

'Tits Yeux Bleus

Key. C
Pattern. Accordion: one Tune; Vocal #1; Steel Guitar: one Tune; Violin: one Tune; Vocal #2; Accordion: one Tune.

Version. Duson Playboys; Joel Sonnier, vocal (©Jamil). This was recorded when Joel was about twelve years old.

Little Blue Eyes

(1)
Oh, my little blue eyes, you've left me for another.
Look at this, what will I do? I'm all alone at home in misery.
(2)
Oh, my little blue eyes, you'll cry for me.
Look at this, what will I do? I'm all alone at home in misery.

1- Aïe,   mes 'tits yeux bleus   tu m'as quit-   té
2- Aïe,   mes 'tits yeux bleus   tu vas bra-   iller,

pour un aut'.   Re- gard- ez donc,   com- ment j'va'
brailler pour moi.   Re- gard- ez donc,   com- ment j'va'

faire?   J'su' moi tout seul à la mai- son dans les mi- sères.
faire?   J'su' moi tout seul à la mai- son dans les mi- sères.

'Tits Yeux Noirs

Key. C

Version. Lawrence Walker (©La Lou).

Pattern. Accordion: one Tune; Vocal #1; Steel Guitar:
one Tune; Violin: one Tune; Accordion: one Tune;
Vocal #2.

Lawrence Walker, accordion player and vocalist, recorded this song during the 1960's.

Little Black Eyes

(1)
This morning, I found myself sitting on my bed crying with a broken heart,
because I had dreamed of my little black-eyed darling, who is gone and will never come back.
(2)
This evening, I'm sitting upon my porch watching the sun going down.
I'm lonesome and I'm sleepy for my dear black-eyed darling, that's why my heart is so broken.

Touche Pas Ça Tu Vois

Key. C

Pattern. Accordion: four Tunes; Vocal #1; Violin: two
Tunes; Vocal #2; Accordion: two Tunes.

Version. Moïse Robin (©Tek).

Moïse made this song after he was tricked out
of all the money he was carrying during a visit
to Port Arthur, Texas.

*They [the police] were cruising slowly and I
flagged them. Then I told them about my
problem. So, they asked me where I was from.
I told them that I was from Louisiana. They
said, "Did they take all your money?" "Aw," I
said, "everything!" The policeman started his*

*lecture. He said, "Do you need a few pennies
to go back?" "No," I said, "my tank is full.
I'll go back like that."*

*So then, when I returned home, it was several
days, I started figuring that I would make a
record. I practiced on a song and a tune.
That's when I made* Don't Touch What You
See.

— *Moïse Robin*

Don't Touch What You See

(1)
Oh, I went to Port Arthur. I met a dear little blond on Crocket Street.
She took me and brought me to her house. She took off my shirt and shoes.
(2)
I was robbed, I was robbed in Port Arthur! I was robbed by a pretty little blond!
I was robbed, I was robbed in Port Arthur! I was robbed over there at Crocket Street!

Toujours Après Espérer

Key. C
Pattern. Accordion: one Tune; Vocal #1; Steel Guitar: one Tune; Violin: one Tune; Vocal #2; Accordion: one Tune.

Version. Robert Bertrand (*All Through the Night,* ©Tek).

Still Waiting

(1)
It's a week since you left; I'm still waiting. The kids are crying, little girl, and I'm lonesome.
You had promised to come back, look what you're doing! Today I'm thinking, little one, I'm still waiting.
(2)
Christmas is coming, little heart, and I'm broke; no presents for the kids, little one, they're always crying.
They'd want their dear mother and she doesn't want to come back. I'm still thinking, little girl, I'm still waiting.

1- Y a une s'main toi t'as quit- té;
2- "Christ- mas" est a- près ar- ri- ver, 'tit

j'su' tou- jours a- près 'pé- rer. Les en-
coeur, et moi j' su' aussi cas- sé; pas d' pre-

fants sont a- près braill- er, 'tite fille, et
sents pour les en- fants, 'tit monde, i'sont tou-

moi a- près m'en- nuy- er. T'avez pro- mis t'en r'- ve-
jours a- près braill- er. Ça vou- drait leur chère mam-

nir, 'garde donc quoi toi t'a- près faire!
man et elle a(lle) vou- drait pas r'- ve- nir.

Au- jour- d'hui j'su' a- près jon- gler, 'tit
J'su' tou- jours a- près jon- gler, 'tite

monde, j'su' tou- jours a- près es- pé- rer.
fille, j'su' tou- jours a- près es- pé- rer.

Tous les Soirs

Key. C
Pattern. Accordion: one Tune; Vocal #1; Steel Guitar: one Tune; Violin: one Tune; Vocal #2 (repeat Vocal #1); Accordion: one Tune.

Version. Joe Bonsall (©Flat Town). The original recording was by Dee Landry, ©Jamil.

This is a modern song.

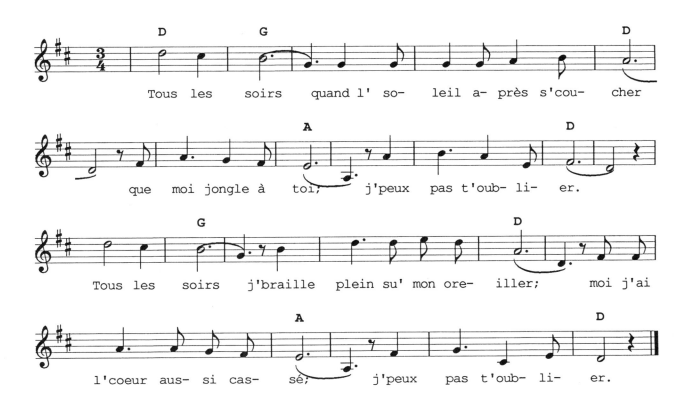

Tous les soirs quand l' so- leil a- près s'cou- cher

que moi jongle à toi; j'peux pas t'oub- li- er.

Tous les soirs j'braille plein su' mon ore- iller; moi j'ai

l'coeur aus- si cas- sé; j'peux pas t'oub- li- er.

Every Night

(1 & 2)
Every night, when the sun is setting, I think of you; I can't forget you.
Every night I cry on my pillow. I have a broken heart; I can't forget you.

Valse de Tout l' Monde

Key. F
Pattern. Accordion: two Tunes; Vocal #1; Steel Guitar: two Tunes; Violin: two Tunes; Vocal #2; Accordion: two Tunes.

Version. Chester "Pee Wee" Broussard (©Flat Town).

Try playing this song an octave lower for variety.

T'a- près quit- ter   de ma mai-   son
Quoi toi tu crois   que moi j'va'   faire;

pour t'en al-   ler, 'tite fille, a- vec un aut'.
j'ai p'us per-   sonne, 'tite fille, qui veut m'ai- mer.

Everybody's Waltz

(1 & 2)
You're leaving from my home to go away, little girl, with another.
What do you think I'll do? I have no one any more, little girl, who wants to love me.

Traces de Mon Boghei

Key. G

Pattern. Accordion: one Tune; Vocal #1; Steel Guitar: one Tune; Violin: one Turn; Accordion: one Tune; Vocal #2; Accordion: one Tune and one Turn.

Version. Doris Matte (©Flat Town).

Related song. Also: *Before I Met You* (Carl Smith).

My Buggy Tracks

(1)
I used to ramble every night in my buggy and had no idea of quitting.
There's something that happened that changed my mind. I sold my horse and buggy.
(Turn 1)
They followed my buggy tracks all night long. They found me doing wrong.
That's why I'm divorced today. I lay the blame on my buggy tracks.
(Turn 2)
She followed my buggy tracks all night long and she told me we were finished.
That's why today my family is all broken up. I put the blame on my buggy tracks.

Trop Jeune Pour s' Marier

Key. C

Pattern. Accordion: two Tunes; Vocal #1; Steel Guitar: two Tunes; Violin: two Tunes; Accordion: two Tunes; Vocal #2; Accordion: two Tunes.

Version. Jimmy Venable, vocal (BEE). The original recording is by Doris Matte (©Flat Town).

Too Young to Marry

(1)
The night I met her, she seemed to listen well.
We left together once; I've known her friendship.
I asked her family for her hand in marriage.
"Too young to get married! She's too young to court!"

(2)
I promised to always love her and always keep her cared for,
but they always told me, "She's too young to get married!"
I'll go back again once more, get on my knees and ask them.
"She's too young to get married! She's too young to court!"

1-   Le   soir   j'l'ai   ren-   con-
         Moi   j'ai   d'man-   dé   à   sa   fa-
2-   J'ai   pro-   mi   tout l'   temps   l'aim-
      J'va' r'-   tourn-   er   en-   core   une

tré,   elle   me r'-   sem-   blé   d'bien   é-   cou-
mille   pour   sa   main   au   marier   et   tout l'   temps   la   garder   soi-

ter.   On   a   par-   ti   un   fois   en-   semb';   j'ai   con-
age.   "Elle   est   trop   jeune   pour   se   ma-   rier!   Elle   est   trop
gné,   mais   tou-   jours   ils   mon   dit,   "Elle   est   trop
er.   "Elle   est   trop   jeune   pour   se   ma-   rier!   Elle   est   trop

nu   son   a-   mi-   tié.
jeune   pour   cour-   ti-   ser!"
jeune   pour   se   ma-   rier!"
jeune   pour   cour-   ti-   ser!"

Tu Peux Pas Casser Mon Coeur

Key. C
Pattern. Accordion: two Tunes; Vocal #1; Steel Guitar: two Tunes; Violin: two Tunes; Accordion: two Tunes; Vocal #2; Steel Guitar: two Tunes; Violin: two Tunes; Accordion: two Tunes.

Version. Chester "Pee Wee" Broussard (©Flat Town).

Like some other songs I've written in this book, this song was recorded live while I was playing at Manuel's Truck Stop near Crowley, Louisiana, with Leeman Prejean, "Pee Wee" Broussard, Mike Barth, and Kenneth Prejean.

Oh   rap-   pelle   toi   les   mi-
Quo'faire toi   t'es   comme   ça,   tout l'   temps

sères   toi   tu   m'as   fait   'tit   monde,   quand   t'as
dans   un   tas d'   cha-   grins?   Eh,   rap-   pelle

dit   t'a-   près   pen-   ser   pour   t'en   al-   ler.
toi,   tu   vas   ja-   mais   cas-   ser   mon   coeur.

You Can't Break My Heart

(1 & 2)
Oh, remember all the miseries you caused me, little one,
when you said you were thinking of going away.
Why are you like that, all the time regretful?
Well, remember, you'll will never break my heart.

La Vie d'un Musicien
Key. C
Version. Nathan Abshire (©Flat Town).

Pattern. Accordion: two tunes; Vocal #1; Violin: one
Tune; Accordion: one Tune; Vocal #2; Violin: one
Tune; Accordion: one Tune.

In the late 70's I took some friends who were interested in Cajun music to meet Nathan at his home in Basile. His wife was cooking a pot roast and we all sat in the kitchen and Nathan played this song for us. Nathan said he missed the drums and was stomping on the floor with his bare feet to keep time. This shook the little house so much that the pot fell off the stove and we left soon afterwards.

The Life of a Musician

(1)
The life of a musician, that's something very beautiful and, when he's not married, there's no one waiting for him.
The musicians listening to me, take some good advice: don't get married now. The amusement is too pretty.
The little girls are so beautiful and the old women are mortifying. It's hard to see myself today in misery.
(2)
My dear son is so beautiful and handsome. He's the only one I love in the whole wide world.
See me today in misery and grief! I don't see what I'll do by myself at home.

1- C'est la vie d'un mu- si- cien, c'est la
Les mu- si ciens qu'a- près m'en- tend' pre- nez
Les 'tites filles sont si mi- gnonne, et les
2- C'est mon cher 'tit gar- çon qu'est mi-
C'est me voir au jour- d'hui dans les mi-

chose qu'est bien jo- lie et quand il est pas ma-
donc un bon con- seils mar- iez vous aut' pas as-
femmes sont mor- ti- fiantes. C'est dur de me
gnon et jo- lie. C'est le seul que moi j'ai-
sères et les cha- grins. Moi j'vois pas quoi moi j'va'

rié, y a per- sonne pour l'és- per- er.
teur, l'a- mu- sette est trop jo- lie.
voir au jour- d'hui dans les mi- sères.
mais, c'est tout l' tour du grand pa- ys.
faire moi tout seul à la mai- son.

La Vie J' croyais J' voulais

Key. C
Pattern. Accordion: two Tunes; Vocal #1; Steel Guitar: two Tunes; Violin: two Tunes; Accordion: two tunes; Vocal #2; Accordion: two Tunes.

Version. Touchet Brothers (©Flat Town); Reggie Matte, vocal (BEE).

The Life I Thought I Wanted

(1)
I don't like to think of long ago when I and my girlfriend got married.
I've done some things I shouldn't have; today I have a broken heart.
To get dressed and decked out, that's all I wanted to amuse myself.
Never in my life I would've thought that my old wife would leave me.
(2)
Every Saturday I wanted to go to the dance to amuse myself.
Never in my life I would've thought that my old wife would leave me.
And now that we're married, it's a bit too late for me to change.
That's the life I thought I wanted; today I have a broken heart.

Wafus Two-Step

Key. C
Pattern. Accordion: two Tunes; Vocal #1; Steel Guitar: two Tunes; Violins: two Tunes; Accordion: two Turns; Vocal #2; Accordion: one Turn and one Tune.

Version. Aldus Roger and Phillip Alleman, vocal (©La Lou).
Related Songs. Also: *Midway Two-Step* (Austin Pitre, Milton Molitor).

I have never been able to find an explanation of the name Wafus. Aldus also calls this the *Waffle Two-Step* and "Pee Wee" Broussard calls it the *Pancake Two-Step*.

Wafus Two-Step

(1)
Oh, little girl, it's the first time! Oh, it hurts! You told me that you loved me!
Oh, little one, today you treat me like that! Oh, It hurts! It seems that you left me!
(2)
Oh, little girl, it's the first time! Oh, it hurts! You said you wanted to leave me!
Oh, little one, today you turn your back on me! Oh, it hurts! I don't see what I've done to you!

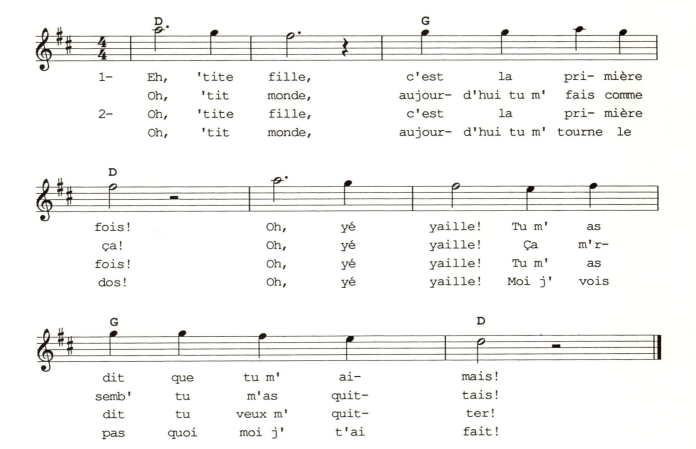

1- Eh, 'tite fille, c'est la pri- mière
Oh, 'tit monde, aujour- d'hui tu m' fais comme
2- Oh, 'tite fille, c'est la pri- mière
Oh, 'tit monde, aujour- d'hui tu m' tourne le

fois! Oh, yé yaille! Tu m' as
ça! Oh, yé yaille! Ça m'r-
fois! Oh, yé yaille! Tu m' as
dos! Oh, yé yaille! Moi j' vois

dit que tu m' ai- mais!
semb' tu m'as quit- tais!
dit tu veux m' quit- ter!
pas quoi moi j' t'ai fait!

Southwest Louisiana

This map shows the Acadian parishes of southwestern Louisiana. It is based on the official State highway map of 1924. I have added locations of many of the places I've mentioned in this book. Notice that our major improved highways were the Old Spanish Trail, now U.S. 90, running east and west from Breaux Bridge through Lake Charles; and the road connecting Port Barré and Jeanerette, roughly following the course of the Bayou Teche. Other roads were mostly gravel and dirt.

Out in the country, there were only trails of dirt roads. When it rained, everybody stayed home; the roads changed from dust to sticky mud and there were no bridges over the gullies and bayous. It was a major undertaking to travel more than fifteen miles from home. My father still likes to tell about his trip from Eunice to Crowley to get his driver's license in 1921. It took two and a half hours by horse and buggy and to pass the time he counted all the houses he could see from the road: there were seven. (Now the trip takes twenty minutes and there are too many houses to count.) Even in 1935, when I was a child, it was a big thrill to see a caterpillar tractor plowing drainage ditches once a year on each side of the road. To see a car pass was also exciting.

A network of railroad lines also connected many of these small towns; these provided the most reliable transportation, but even these were threatened with floods from year to year. Few people traveled very far, because they had no reason or money to do so. The first time I rode a train was during a first grade class outing. My teacher made us each save a dime and we rode from Crowley to Rayne.

Cajun music, as we know it today, developed in the areas of Church Point, Eunice, Crowley, Ville Platte, along the Bayou Teche and the Old Spanish Trail towards Texas.

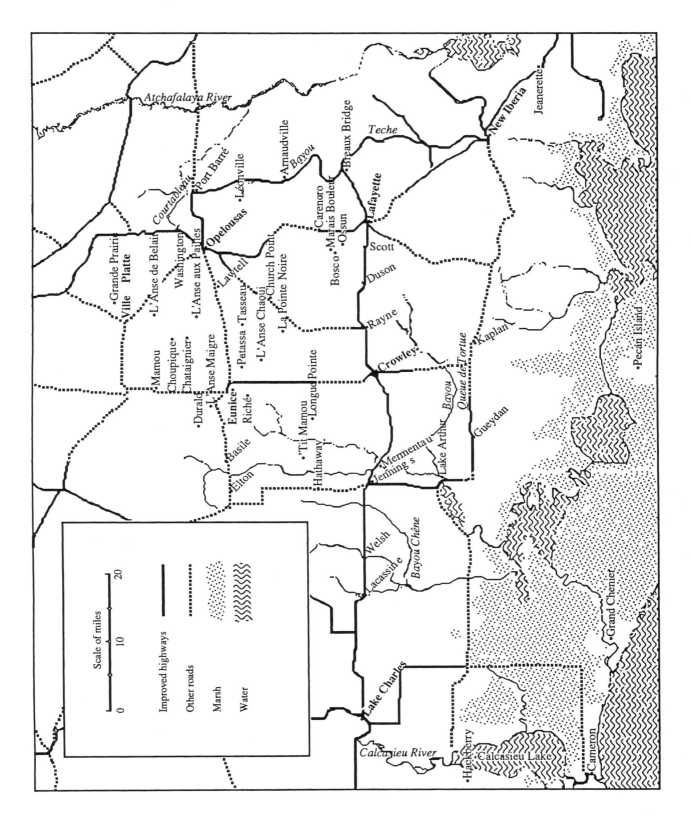

Afterwards

Blessed is he who was Cajun before it became vogue.
— *sign in Marc Savoy's music store*

Everybody is proud to be a Cajun today and I'm glad of it, but I think musicians are too eager to use this label. Every band that knows the tune for *Jolie Blonde* wants to claim they play Cajun music. I would be more comfortable, if they would call it something else, like Cajun jazz or Cajun rock 'n roll. Their music makes me think of Chef Paul Prudhomme's cooking style: imaginative, interesting, uses local ingredients, but nothing like what I grew up with.

I have tried very hard to explain Cajun music as I understand it in this book. You must keep the tune and the beat and the stress and the chord changes, if you want to say you play Cajun music. I think these are more important than whether or not you sing in French or play with the traditional Cajun instruments. Although I have omitted many songs from this book because I knew they were borrowed from another musical tradition, I am not really against borrowing. It's inevitable. But I think what you borrow should be adapted into the Cajun musical structure. And what I feel is happening is that Cajun music is being raided for ideas that are being adapted to other traditions. The musicians who do this should not claim that they are playing or preserving Cajun music.

Labeling too many different styles as Cajun confuses people about what Cajun really is. As I was finishing this book, a good example of this kind of confusion occurred in Lafayette. The City proudly announced its sponsorship of Cajun bands to go on tour to promote Acadiana. Since not one of the bands selected actually played traditional Cajun music, this produced some lively letters to the editors of the local papers.

What a shame! How can the Mayor of Lafayette go on national television and announce the proposed national tour of the U.S. of five Cajun bands when, in fact, these five bands no longer play Cajun music? ... Two of these bands play Zydeco, one is progressive country/rock type, and the other two are country. I am a fan of all of this type of music, but it seems to me that there is misrepresentation here. Who selected these bands? Are they talking about musicians who are of Cajun ancestry, or do they mean musicians who play Cajun music? True, these musicians are Cajun-born, but they no longer play Cajun music.
— *Louella B. Latiolais*

The Mayor's response defended the choice based on the musician's backgrounds, the fact that they played Cajun tunes, or that they sang in French. I don't believe that he even understood the objections that were raised.

In the smaller towns west of Lafayette, where the largest number of traditional Cajun musicians live and play, Cajun music is better understood, but I don't feel confident about what it's future is. At many dances, the people on the dance floor are getting older and older, just like the musicians are. Many younger Cajuns prefer music that is more mainstream American. I hope that *their* children will develop an interest in the past and find my book useful.

It's nice to live long enough to see one of the little kids become a member of the older generation.
— *Dennis McGee*

References

HOW TO FIND OUT MORE
To learn about local musicians, musical styles, and musical instruments, see Ann Savoy's book *Cajun Music: A Reflection of a People, Volume 1*, Bluebird Press, 1984. Bluebird Press' address is P.O. Box 941, Eunice, LA 70535. This is my favorite book on Cajun music. It includes photographs, interviews, a detailed discography, and musical transcriptions of the vocal parts of songs.

The earliest study of Louisiana French music was done by Irène Thérèse Whitfield in *Louisiana French Folk Songs,* Louisiana State University Press, 1939.

Interesting interviews with Cajun musicians are found in both French and English in Barry Jean Ancelet's *The Makers of Cajun Music,* University of Texas Press, Austin, 1984. This book may be a good introduction to Cajun French, if you are already familiar with standard French, and it includes a discography and some handsome photographs by Elemore Morgan, Jr.

Contemporary photographs of local musicians have been collected and edited by Johnnie Allen in *Memories: A Pictorial History of South Louisiana Music, 1920s-1980s,* JADFEL Publishing Company, 1988. The address of JADFEL is 204 Kevin Drive, Lafayette, LA 70507.

John Broven's book *South to Louisiana,* Pelican Publishing Company, Gretna, LA, 1983, gives a good overview of several Louisiana music styles.

If you are not familiar with standard French, you might find James Donald Faulk's *Cajun French I* helpful. He explains a lot of the vocabulary and grammar, but he uses a phonetic spelling that could be very confusing, if you already know standard French. This was printed by the Cajun Press, Crowley, LA, 1977.

Conversational Cajun French I by Randall P. Whatley and Harry Janise, The Chicot Press, P.O. Box 21988, Baton Rouge, LA 70893, provides basic vocabulary, useful phrases, and some information on the history of Cajun French. It uses standard French spelling.

For interesting information about some of the Cajun French vocabulary, see William A. Read's *Louisiana-French,* Louisiana State University Press, 1963.

WHERE TO GET RECORDS
These are the major publishers and distributors of traditional Cajun recordings:

Arhoolie Records (Arhoolie and Old Timey labels), 10341 San Pablo Avenue, El Cerrito, CA 94530. For a 78 page catalog listing of CD's, cassettes, LP's, and video cassettes and a recent issue of Down Home Music Newsletter, send $2.00 for postage to Arhoolie Catalog at the address above.

Swallow Records, P.O. Drawer 10, Ville Platte, LA 70586.

La Louisianne Records, 711 Stevenson Street, Lafayette, LA 70501.

Sources for other recording labels are:

Bee Records Production, Elton "Bee" Cormier, Route 3, Box 0, Church Point, LA 70525.

Goldband Recording Corporation, P.O. Box 1485, Lake Charles, LA 70602.

Lanor, P.O. Box 233, Church Point, LA 70525.

Master-Trak Enterprises (Kajun, Cajun Classic, Flyright, Modern and Bayou Classic labels), 413 North Parkerson Avenue, P.O. Box 1345, Crowley, LA 70526.

Sugarhill Studios (Crazy Cajun label), 5626 Brock Street, Houston, TX 77023.

Musicians and Song Credits

It has been hard, after knowing and playing most of these songs for so many years, to provide information on exactly where I learned all of them. Sometimes I have written these songs based on the way I play them, sometimes from material that I got from other musicians, or from records. In listing records or other sources, if I have made errors or omissions, I will correct them in future printings, if notification is sent to the publisher.

Some of these records are listed just for your information; the records which I have listened to while writing this book and which influenced the way I wrote the music are in bold type.

If you plan to make any commercial use of material in this book, note that some of the songs in this book are copyrighted and are used by permission of the publisher.

Arhoolie recordings ©Tradition Music BMI.

Goldband recordings ©Tek Publishing.

Master-trak recordings (Kajun, Flyright, Modern, and Bayou Classics labels) ©Jamil or ©Whitewing.

La Louisiane recordings ©La Lou Music.

Lanor recordings ©JON Music BMI.

Swallow and Khoury recordings ©Flat Town Music.

Abbreviations Used for Recording Labels

AR: Arhoolie
BC: Bayou Classics
BEE: Bee Records
CC: Cajun Classics
Co: Columbia
Cr-Cj: Crazy Cajun
FLY: Flyright
GB: Goldband
Kj: Kajun
LL: La Louisiane
Lnr: Lanor
Mod: Modern
MS: Morningstar
OT: Old Timey
SW: Swallow
Vi: Victor

Abshire.
Fernice "Man" Abshire was a vocalist with Aldus Roger and the Lafayette Playboys. (See Aldus Roger.)

Nathan Abshire was an outstanding accordion player. He lived in Basile, Louisiana, and his band was the Pine Grove Boys. I obtained La Vie d'un Musicien live, but it is also on SW-LP6014. Recording of his songs mentioned in this book are: **LL-139:** Valse de Bélisaire; Valse des Mèches,©La Lou; OT-128: Blues Français; **SW-LP6014:** Chanson de Limonade (Leroy Broussard, ©Tek); Pine Grove Blues, La Vie d'un Musicien; Sur le Courtableau; Valse du Bayou Teche, ©Flat Town; **SW-LP6023:** Choupique Two-Step; Valse de Kaplan I, ©Flat Town.

Tunice Abshire was a vocalist with Aldus Roger and the Lafayette Playboys. (See Aldus Roger.)

Aguillard.
Lawrence Aguillard made no records. He played house-dances near Eunice, Louisiana. My father learned some songs from him. Ambrose Thibodeaux, Lawrence's cousin, recorded some of his songs.

Alleman.
Clarence Alleman and Phillip Alleman were both vocalists with Aldus Roger and the Lafayette Playboys. (See Aldus Roger.)

Allen.
Johnnie Allan's (John A. Guillot's) songs Une Aut' Chance and J' m'ennuie Pas d' Toi were recorded by Aldus Roger and are included on **LL-LP114.**

Ardoin.
Amédé Ardoin was an outstanding accordion player and vocalist from near Eunice, Louisiana. A great deal has been written about him; see John Broven's and Ann Savoy's books. Many of his early recordings have been reissued on the Old Timey label. **OT-114:** La Turtape de Saroid (Là Tu Attrapes du Sirop); **OT-108:** One-Step des Chameaux (with Dennis McGee). Also see OT-124.

Balfa.
Dewey Balfa and his brothers played together as the Balfa Brothers until the tragic deaths of Rodney and Will Balfa in 1979. Ann Savoy has written about this talented family in her book. Songs mentioned in this book can be found on: **SW-LP6011:** Sauvage su' l' Chicot, Valse de Newport, My True Love, Parlez-nous à Boire, Valse de Balfa, ©Flat Town; **SW-LP6019:** 'Tit Galop Pour Mamou, Je Suis Orphelin, Two-Step de l'Anse aux Pailles, Chère Bassette, Madeleine, Danse de Mardi Gras, ©Flat Town. **SW-LP6020:** Casse Pas ma Tête, ©Flat Town.

Bergeron.
Shirley and his father, Alphée Bergeron, played with the Veteran Playboys in the 1940's and 50's. Songs mentioned in this book can be found on Lnr-502: Fais Do-Do (Les Rangs de "Soybean"), ©JON BMI. Lnr-505: Valse du Passé, ©JON BMI. Lnr-LP1000/505: Madame Bosco, ©JON BMI. Lnr-LP1000/510: Old Home Waltz, ©JON BMI.

Vernon Bergeron was a vocalist with Aldus Roger's band. (See record list under Roger.)

Bertrand.
"Hobo" Bertrand's version of La Valse de Crève de Faim is on GB-1136, ©Tek.

Robert Bertrand was a vocalist and drummer in the Lake Charles area. Musicians he played with included Iry LeJeune, Phil Menard, and Joel Sonnier. GB-1205: All Through the Night (Toujours Après Espérer), ©Tek.

Berzas.
Maurice Berzas was an accordion player and bandleader from Ville Platte. His son, Vorance was drummer and vocalist in the same band, the Louisiana Rhythmaires. SW-10141: Eunice Two-Step, ©Flat Town; his Valse des Mèches is on the Swallow label, ©Flat Town. Jamie Berzas also plays accordion. BEE-155: L'Anse Maigre Two-Step (Jamie Berzas, Mark Young, and Cajun Tradition).

Bonsall.
Joe Bonsall's recordings mentioned in this book can be found on SW-LP6049: Hippy Ti Yo (Les Huppés Taïauts), Dodge City Waltz (Clifton Newman); Le Hack à Moreau; Valse de Grande Prairie, ©Flat Town; Tous les Soirs (Dee Landry, ©Jamil).

Breaux.
Amédé, Ophy and Cleoma Breaux's recordings of Vas Y Carrément and Ma Blonde Est Parti can be found on **OT-114.** The Breaux Frères' (Amédé, Ophy and Clifford Breaux) recording of One-Step à Marie is also on **OT-114.**

Broussard.
Alex Broussard's L'Année de Cinquante-sept is on **LL-103** and LL-8020, ©La Lou.

Chester "Pee Wee" Broussard's versions of Tu Peux Pas Casser Mon Coeur and La Valse de Tout l' Monde (also on SW-LP6045, ©Flat Town) were obtained from tape recordings that I made when I was playing with him and Leeman Prejean.

Leroy Broussard's Brasse le Couche-couche is on **LL-8032**, ©La Lou; his Chanson de Limonade and Valse de Prison are on GB-1048, ©Tek. His son Gerald is also a vocalist; his recording of Valse de Prairie Ronde is on Cr-Cj-536.

Brown.
Sidney Brown's songs mentioned are on GB-1061: La Pistache à Tante Nana, ©Tek. GB-1099: Daylight Waltz, Two-Step de Criminelle, ©Tek. SW-LP6001: Fond d' Culotte Two-Step, ©Flat Town.

Bruce.
Vin (Ervin) Bruce's version of Chère Chérie is included on SW-LP6002, ©Flat Town. (The original recording of this song was made by "Happy Fats" LeBlanc and "Doc" Guidry, ©Jamil.)

Connor.
Varise Connor is a very fine violin player. For additional information about him, see Barry Ancelet's book. Unfortunately, he made no records. The songs I obtained from him when I visited him in Lake Arthur were from tape recordings that he had made himself.

Cormier.
I obtained Barry Cormier's version of Dunice Theriot's Mermentau Waltz live.

Elton"Bee" Cormier's version of the songs mentioned in this book were also obtained live; his version of J'ai Passé Devant Ta Porte is also recorded on **BEE-104.**

Lionel Cormier is credited with making the original recording of Bayou Noir, but I have not been able to locate the record.

Louis Cormier's version of Valse à Tante Adèle is on LL-110 and LL-8064, ©La Lou; Blues de Soûlard is included on SW-LP6001, ©Flat Town.

Ray Cormier played the violin with "Boy" Frugé. (See Frugé.)

Courville.
Sady Courville played violin with his brother-in-law, Dennis McGee. See Ann Savoy's and Barry Ancelet's books for more information about them. See Dennis McGee's entry for a list of records.

Crochet.
Cleveland Crochet was a violin player and bandleader of the Sugar Bees. Their recording of Drunkard's Dream (Rêve de Soûlard) is on GB-1106 and GB-7749, ©Tek.

Deshotels.
Bee Deshotels' Chanson de Mardi Gras is available on **AR-5009**. (My transcription of this song is based on a tape recording that I had made and differs slightly from this record.)

Doucet.
Camey Doucet's recording of Mam', J' su' Toujours Ton 'Tit Garçon is on **SW-10251**, ©Flat Town. (Also see Jimmy Thibodeaux.)

Falcon.
Joseph Falcon's early recordings of Aimer et Perdre and Allons à Lafayette are on **OT-108**; the Ossun One-Step is on OT-100. Fi Fi Poncho was recorded on Co-15301.

Favor.
Dudley and James Favor's recordings of Mazurka de la Louisiane and T'es Petite et T'es Mignonne are available on **OT-114**.

Fontenot.
Canray Fontenot's Les Barres d' la Prison is available on AR-1070, ©Tradition Music.

Hadley Fontenot, vocalist and accordion player with the Balfa Brothers. (See Balfa.)

Isom J. Fontenot played harmonica. His version of Saute, Crapaud is available on **AR-5009**.

Forestier
"Blackie" Forestier is an accordion player and band leader; his recording of La Valse des Grands Pins is on LL-128, ©La Lou.

François.
Leopold François, my father, has not made any records. He appears in the film Cajun Visits, playing accordion with Dewey Balfa and myself on violin. His songs which I have used in this book were obtained live.

Frugé.
"Boy" Frugé was a well-known accordion player from around Arnaudville. His records are no longer available. His versions of Two-Step d'Arnaudville and Valse de LeBoeuf were recorded on the La Louisiane label.

Columbus Frugé's version of Valse de Bayou Teche is available on **OT-108**.

Ernest Frugé was one of Dennis McGee's violin partners. (See McGee.)

Gerald Frugé and the 'Tit Mamou Mardi Gras' Chant de Mardi Gras was obtained live.

Fusilier.
J.B. Fusilier's recordings of Chère Tout-Toute and Chère Bassette are available on OT-110. Jongle à Moi is on GB-LP7738, ©Tek.

Roy Fusilier played accordion with a number of different bands.

Gaspard.
Blind Uncle Gaspard's recording of Baoille (Baieonne) is available on **OT-114**.

Granger.
Wilson Granger played violin with Iry LeJeune's band.

Guidry.
Oran "Doc" Guidry played violin with both Aldus Roger and Leroy "Happy Fats" LeBlanc. (See their entries for recordings.)

Guillory.
Murphy "Chuck" Guillory made a number of records, but they are no longer easily available. He reissued his Valse à Tolan on his own label CG-101.

Don Guillory was the vocalist and drummer for Aldus Roger's Lafayette Playboys during the mid 80's when I also played with Aldus. I have obtained his versions of the songs I have mentioned from tape recordings which I made when we played together.

Hébert.
Adam Hébert's songs mentioned in this book are on: SW-LP6003: La Porte du Nord, ©Flat Town; **SW-LP6065**: Madeleine, Cette-là J'aime, Homesick Waltz, J'aimerais d' Connaître, Ouvre la Porte, Pour la Dernière Fois, ©Flat Town.

Lachney.
Dela Lachney played violin with Blind Uncle Gaspard. (See Gaspard.)

LaFleur.
Mayuse LaFleur sang and played accordion with Leo Soileau during the late 1920's. Valse Criminelle and Tu M'a Jeté Dehors were recorded in 1928 on Vi-21770.

Lamperez.
"Papa Cairo" (Julius Lamperez) made his recording of Big Texas on Mod-20-612, ©Jamil.

Langly.
Thomas Langly, vocalist with Nathan Abshire and the Pine Grove Boys. (See Abshire.)

LeBlanc.
Leroy "Happy Fats" LeBlanc's Veuves de la Coulée is on LL-103, ©La Lou. Gabriel was recorded on the Kajun label, ©Jamil. Allons Danser Colinda and the Crowley Two-Step have been reissued on FLY-609. 'Tit Maurice is on LL-8083, ©La Lou.

Vorris "Shorty" LeBlanc played accordion with the Sugar Bees. (See Cleveland Crochet.)

LeJeune.
Angélas LeJeune made recordings in the 1920's. His Bayou Pompon and Valse de Pointe Noire were are available on OT-114.

Felton LeJeune's versions of 'Tit Maurice and Bayou Noir were recorded by Bee Records, on BEE-104. This album was made at the time I was a member of the Church Point Playboys and was part of a project to develop and encourage young accordion players. I later played for several years with Felton's band.

Iry LeJeune's songs have been collected and reissued on GB-LP7740 and GB-LP7741. GB-LP7740: Donnez-moi Mon Chapeau (Catch My Hat), Church Point Breakdown, Country Gentlemen (Don't Get Married), J'étais au Bal, Lacassine Special, Valse de Quatre-vingt-dix-neuf Ans (Convict Waltz), Valse de Séparation (Parting Waltz), Valse des Grands Chemins, Viens m' Chercher, ©Tek. GB-LP7741: 'Tit Monde, Evangeline Special, Grande Nuit Spécial, Jolie Catin, La Branche du Mûrier, Love Bridge Waltz, Teche Special, Valse de 'Cadien, Valse de Bayou Chêne, Valse de Calcasieu, Valse de Durald, ©Tek.

Rodney LeJeune is from La Pointe Noire; his songs J'su' Pas à Blâmer, Mon Coeur Fait Mal, Seventy-three Special, and Valse des Musiciens were recorded on the Crazy Cajun label. (Also see under Roy.)

Manuel.
Abe Manuel was an accordion player from Eunice.

Preston Manuel is a guitar player and vocalist from Eunice who has played with a great many Cajun musicians, including J.B. Fusilier and Ambrose Thibodeaux. La Pointe aux Pins was obtained live. The other songs I've mentioned are on LL-112, ©La Lou.

Shelton Manuel, from near Eunice, has played violin with a number of Cajun bands.

Matte.
Doris Matte's Traces de Mon Boghei is available on SW-LP6003, ©Flat Town. Trop Jeune Pour s' Marier is on SW-LP6007, ©Flat Town.

Reggie Matte's versions of songs mentioned in this book were obtained live when I played with him, as a member of The Church Point Playboys. La Vie J' croyais J' voulais is also on BEE-137.

McGee.
Dennis McGee made many records. Many have been reissued on MS-45002: Blues de Texas, Happy One-Step, Jeunes Gens de la Campagne, L'Anse de Belair, One-Step de Choupique, Valse à Pap', Valse des Vachers, Ville Platte Two-Step, Valse de Courville et McGee. Others are available on: OT-108: Bébé Créole, One-Step des Chameaux; OT-114: Madame Young; SW-6030: Devillier Two-Step, Rosa, Demain C'est Pas Dimanche, Valse à Kathleen, Valse à Napoléon, Valse à Tante Aleen, Valse des Frugés, Valse des Vachers. Valse Qu'a Fini Dans l' Coin, Valse d'Amour, ©Flat Town. I obtained Valse à Guilbeau and Valse à Macareau live when I visited him, and Crapaud is a tune which he taught to Jeanie McLerie.

Menard.
Doris Leon ("D.L.") Menard is the vocalist and guitar player with the Louisiana Aces. His song La Porte en Arrière appears on Rounder 6003 and SW-LP6038, ©Flat Town.

Phil Menard's La Promesse J'ai Fait is on Kj-1011, ©Whitewing

Menier.
Aubrey "Cabri" Menier was a vocalist with Austin Pitre in the late 50's. (See Pitre.)

Molitor.
Milton Molitor's Manuel's Bar Waltz was recorded on Big Mamou-101.

Mouton.
Aldus Mouton's Acadiana Two-Step is available on LL-8147, ©La Lou.

Newman.
Jimmy Newman's version of Les Huppés Taïauts
(Hippy Ti Yo) is on LL-140, ©La Lou.

Pitre.
Austin Pitre was vocalist and accordion player in his
band, The Evangeline Playboys. Recordings referenced
are: **SW-LP6041:** Valse des Opelousas, Grand Mamou
Blues, Jolies Joues Roses, Les Flammes d'Enfer, Pauv'
"Hobo," Rainbow Waltz, René's Special, Valse
d'Amour, ©Flat Town; **SW-LP6009:** Valse de
Châtaignier, ©Flat Town.

Prejean.
Leeman Prejean's Happy Playboys is another band that
I played with for a while in the mid 80's. He has made
recordings, but material I credited him with was ob-
tained live. His Valse d'Alléman is also on SW-101,
©Flat Town. (Also see "Pee Wee" Broussard.)

Quibodeaux.
Gervais Quibodeaux was a vocalist with Ambrose
Thibodeaux (See Thibodeaux.) He also plays accordion
and had his own band which I played in, too.

Reed.
Wallace "Cheese" Reed was a vocalist and very fine
violin player from near Eunice. Versions of songs I
have credited him with were obtained live. Valse de
Ville Platte and Tu Vas m' Faire Mourir are also on LL-
8135, ©La Lou.

Richard.
Belton Richard does vocal and accordion for his band,
The Musical Aces. His recording of Juste Un Rêve is on
SW-LP6010, ©Flat Town.

Johnny Richard was the vocalist on "Boy" Frugé's
recordings for La Louisiane.

Robin.
Moïse Robin played accordion with Leo Soileau for a
time, and recordings from this era have been included
on on **OT-108** and **OT-125.** His song Touche Pas Ça
Tu Vois was originally recorded on Jadar **J118-2.**
Otherwise, his versions of songs which I've mentioned
were obtained live, during a visit in Arnaudville.

Roger.
Aldus Roger is an outstanding accordion player and has
been written up in Ann Savoy's book. I played with his
band, the Lafayette Playboys for several years in the
mid 80's. His songs which I've mentioned can be found
on the following records: GB-1084: Valse de Duson,
©Tek. Kj-1053: Crowley Two-Step, ©Jamil. **LL-
LP122:** Chère Petite, Creole Stomp, Grand Texas,
KLFY Waltz, La Dernière Valse, Mamou Two-Step,
Valse de Port Arthur, Wafus Two-Step, ©La Lou. LL-

8131: Shamrock Two-Step, ©La Lou. **LL-LP107:**
Johnny Can't Dance; Lafayette Two-Step, ©La Lou.
LL-LP114: Danse de Mardi Gras, Diga Ding Ding
Dong, Hick's Wagon Wheel Special, J' m'Ennuie Pas
d' Toi, Lafayette Playboys' Waltz, Les Haricots Sont
Pas Salés, Lovesick Waltz, Une Aut' Chance, Valse
d'Ennui. Valse de Famille, Valse de la Louisiane, ©La
Lou. SW-10196: Attention, C'est Mon Coeur Qui Va
Casser, Marie; SW-LP6003: Valse à Alida; SW-
LP6007: O.S.T. Special, ©Flat Town. I obtained his
version of the Ossun Two-Step live, during the time we
played together, but it is also on CC-1001, ©Jamil.

Roy.
Dallas Roy's Valse de Prison is on **Cr-Cj-508.** Valse de
Samedi Soir is on **Cr-Cj-506.**

Royer.
Carrie "Mignonne" Royer Miller, married to my cousin,
was a talented violin player and I wanted to give her
credit for the song she taught me; she never made any
records. (Her picture, taken in 1939, is on the front
cover.)

Savoy.
Marc Savoy, from near Eunice, makes and plays
accordions. He has recorded with numerous musicians.
(See Reed, Roy, Rodney LeJeune.)

Segura.
The Segura Brothers' Les Maringouins Ont Tout Mangé
Ma Belle and New Iberia Polka have been reissued on
OT-108.

Semien.
John Semien's 'Tite Canaille is on **LLC-509,** ©La Lou.

Soileau.
Leo Soileau's songs mentioned in this book are
available on **OT-108:** J' Veux m' Marier, Valse
Pénitentiaire; **OT-114:** Ma Chère 'Tite Fille; **OT-125:**
Demain C'est Pas Dimanche, Embrasse-moi Encore,
Petite ou Grosse, Valse de Joséphine. Valse Criminelle
was originally recorded on Vi-21770.

Sonnier.
Joel Sonnier's Mother's Day Waltz and 'Tits Yeux
Bleus are on the Kajun label, ©Jamil.

"Shorty" Sonnier's version of songs mentioned in this
book were obtained live.

Tauzin.
Raymond Tauzin's Faire l'Amour dans l' Poulailler is
on SW-21016, ©Flat Town.

Theriot.
Dunice P. Theriot's version of Faire l'Amour dans les Rangs d' Coton is on SW-10220, ©Flat Town; his song Mermentau Waltz was originally recorded on his own label, ©Dunice P. Theriot; it is also available on BC-3000.

Thibodeaux.
Ambrose Thibodeaux's recordings mentioned in this book are on; **LL-112**: Chère Tout-Toute, La Valse Que J'Aime, Patassa Two-Step, Two-Step à Ambrose, Two-Step de Riché, ©La Lou; **LL-119**: Longue Pointe Two-Step, Pauv' "Hobo," Pointe Noire Two-Step, Valse de Tasseau, Valse des Chérokis, ©La Lou; **LL-143**: Chère Mam', Donnez-moi Mon Chapeau, ©La Lou.

Jimmy Thibodeaux played with Camey Doucet. His version of the Valse de Coeur Cassé is on SW-LP6028, ©Flat Town.

Touchet.
Archange "Coon" Touchet was a vocalist with The Louisiana Aces. His version of Valse des Grands Pins was on Rounder-6003.

Willis Touchet is a vocalist with the Touchet Brothers, a group from New Iberia. Their recordings of Old Fashion Two-Step (SW-10197) and La Vie J' croyais J' voulais (SW-10191) are ©Flat Town.

Venable.
Jimmy Venable's vocal of Trop Jeune Pour s' Marier is on **BEE-104**.

Walker.
Lawrence Walker's early Walker Brothers recordings, Breakdown la Louisiane and La Vie Malheureuse, are on **OT-108**. Other songs mentioned are on : AR-LP5013: Bosco Stomp; **LL-LP126**: 'Tits Yeux Noirs, Chère Alice, Mamou Two-Step, Reno Waltz, Tous les Deux Pour la Même, Valse d'Evangeline, Valse du Malchanceux, ©La Lou. SW-10133: Les Bons Temps, ©Flat Town; SW-Khoury label: Ton Papa et Ta Maman M'a Jeté Dehors; SW-LP6001: Valse de Minuit, ©Flat Town.

Young.
"Nonc'"Allie Young is an accordion player from Basile, Louisiana. He has played and recorded with a number of groups.

Index of Song Titles

Also available from Swallow Publications, Inc.

Rev. Jules O. Daigle (1900-1998) , an ordained Catholic priest since 1925, reared in Lafayette, Louisiana, spent thousands of hours compiling these two books, true examples of his deep love and dedication to the the Cajun culture and it s people. Rev. Daigle s Cajun Dictionary is recognized as a great accomplishment. His work was likened to that of Samuel Johnson compiling the first English dictionary in 1755. Rev. Daigle was the first to compose a seemingly complete dictionary of the Cajun language. Later, being the only priest old enough to have experienced the old, unaffected Cajun language, Rev. Daigle reverted to his life-long immersion in the Cajun language to compose a self-instructional guide for learning to speak the language which was so dear to him.

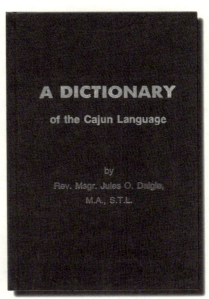

Tenth Printing
A DICTIONARY of the CAJUN LANGUAGE

By Rev. Jules O. Daigle.
The new revised edition **Dictionary of the Cajun Language** contains 640 pages including additional information gathered since the last printing. It comprises a section of English to Cajun and one of Cajun to English.
A must for every household of Cajun descent

6 x 9 inches   Hard cloth cover.   ISBN 0-9614245-3-2   **$32.00**

Fifth Printing
CAJUN SELF-TAUGHT

By Rev. Jules O. Daigle
Cajun Self-Taught is a 518 page
8 1/2 x 11 inch book, in large, easy to read type.
A companion to the Cajun Dictionary. This book is to help one read and speak Cajun correctly.

8.5 x 11 inches   Hard cloth cover.   ISBN 0-9614245-4-0

$36.00

**Book and Audio companion of a
3 compact disc set.**
(items shown all sold separately)

Book $36.00   **Set of 3 Compact Discs audio companion $22.00**   ISBN 0-9614245-6-7

Any of the above items can be purchased at your favorite book store or order directly from
Swallow Publications Inc., P.O. Drawer 10, Ville Platte, LA 70586. phone orders **(337) 363-2177.**
Order online at **www.SwallowPublications.com**